Maples
for
Gardens

Maples
for
Gardens

A COLOR
ENCYCLOPEDIA

C. J. van Gelderen
D. M. van Gelderen

Timber Press
Portland, Oregon

Half title page, *Acer pseudoplatanus* 'Leat's Cottage'
Frontispiece, *Acer palmatum* 'Ornatum'
Title page, *Acer palmatum* 'Heptalobum Rubrum'

Copyright © 1999 by Timber Press, Inc.
All rights reserved.

Reprinted 2000

Timber Press, Inc.
The Haseltine Building
133 S.W. Second Avenue, Suite 450
Portland, Oregon 97204, U.S.A.

Printed in Hong Kong
Designed by Susan Applegate

Library of Congress Cataloging-in-Publication Data

Gelderen, C. J. van (Cornelis Johannes), 1960–
    Maples for gardens: a color encyclopedia / C. J. van Gelderen and D. M.
van Gelderen.
        p.   cm.
    Includes bibliographical references (p.   ) and indexes.
    ISBN 0-88192-472-5
    1. Maple—Encyclopedias. 2. Maple—Pictorial works.
I. Gelderen, D. M. van. II. Title.
SB413.M365G45 1999
635.9'77378–dc21   98-44064
                                                                                CIP

Contents

Preface

To provide a photographic companion to the book *Maples of the World* we visited more than 30 arboretums, gardens, and nurseries in several countries in order to compile a representative survey of maples in cultivation. The largest collection in number of species and cultivars is that of the Esveld Aceretum, forming part of our nursery, Firma C. Esveld, in Boskoop, Netherlands. The Aceretum was founded in the early 1970s, anchored by a giant specimen of *Acer shirasawanum* 'Aureum' planted about 1870. The Aceretum now includes approximately 670 different kinds of maples and is the holder of the Dutch *Acer* Collection. In addition to the Aceretum we were pleased to be able to draw on a number of other notable collections, including, for example, the five great W's in England—Wakehurst Place Garden, Westonbirt Arboretum, Windsor Great Park, Winkworth Arboretum, and Wisley Garden—together having hundreds of different maples. Other notable maple collections open to the public are listed in Appendix 1, "Where to See Maples."

Our aim in this book is to encourage gardeners to plant one or more maples, the variety and beauty of which we hope are amply illustrated here.

Acknowledgments

We are indebted to Prof. Masato Yokoi, who provided lists of cultivar names correctly written in Japanese characters; Dr. Ellen van Weely, our authority on the correct romanization and spelling of Japanese cultivar names; Mr. Peter A. Gregory, retired curator of the Westonbirt Arboretum, who helped us on our visits to the arboretum and gave us much information; Mr. Hisao Nakajima, who provided information on many cultivars not in cultivation in Europe or America and who kindly shared his beautifully handmade portfolios of Japanese maples with us; Mr. Harry Olsen, Foliage Gardens, Bellevue, Washington, for help with photography and for providing information on dwarf cultivars; and Messrs J. R. P. van Hoey Smith and K. W. Verboom for additional help with photography.

The Magic of Maples

Maples are entrancing trees, with the ability to fascinate many more people than have already been enraptured. Maples are of interest throughout the year. In winter their bark and branches are on display. Maples may have splendid bark, such as the snakebark maples or the paperbark maple, *Acer griseum.* Many maples flower profusely in spring, such as the Norway maple, *A. platanoides,* with a wonderful display of clear yellow flowers. Later in spring maples unfold their leaves and a spectacular range of hues may be seen: green, purple, yellow, even pink and glistening red. By the end of spring and the beginning of summer the first flush of leaves has matured and we admire their various colors. Late summer is usually of less interest but depending on site and weather the display of the brilliant fall colors may be spectacular. Almost every maple shows wonderful color: red, orange-red, yellow, purple, dark wine-colored, almost black, or golden brown. Not only the leaves are beautiful in the fall; many maples present a good display of fruits in various colors. A number of Japanese maples, notably, have appealing red samaras, the winged fruits characteristic of maples.

Maples have long been cultivated, especially in Japan where the history of gardening with maples goes back hundreds of years. In Japan, maples are traditional in gardens and the trees are allowed to show colorful leaves in summer; other trees must have green foliage. Maples are thus important plants to the Japanese, with variously colored or otherwise distinctive forms highly appreciated. Many maples, especially the slower growing ones, may be used for bonsai, an art in Japan and China for hundreds of years and becoming ever more popular in Europe and America.

With such diversity in form and color, from plant to plant and throughout the seasons, maples have much to offer all gardeners, from prize landscape trees to richly varied shrubs to sculptural miniatures. Maples are truly one of the treasures of the plant world.

Maples in Nature

Maples inhabit the whole of the northern hemisphere and even touch the equator in Indonesia. They are widely distributed but are not the dominant forest trees where they occur. On the contrary, they are nowhere really abundant. Europe has a few indigenous species. The common species of northwestern and central Europe are *Acer campestre* (hedge maple), *A. platanoides* (Norway maple), and *A. pseudoplatanus* (sycamore maple). In France and southern and southwestern Europe there is *A. monspessulanum* (Montpellier maple). In southeastern Europe, *A. opalus* (Italian maple) is common and the close relatives of *A. pseudoplatanus*, that is, *A. heldreichii* and its subspecies *trautvetteri* (red-bud maple), are found. In southern Italy, in addition to some maples already mentioned, *A. cappadocicum* subsp. *lobelii* occurs, and on Crete, the more or less evergreen *A. sempervirens*.

Many maples occur in Turkey and the Caucasus, including *Acer monspessulanum* with a range of subspecies, and *A. hyrcanum* and *A. tataricum*, each with several subspecies. The evergreen *A. obtusifolium* is also present.

In Iran and adjacent countries are such rare maples as several subspecies of *Acer hyrcanum*, *A. pentapomicum*, and *A. pilosum* as well as the more common *A. tataricum*. Farther east, *A. caesium* and its allies inhabit Kashmir and Nepal together with *A. acuminatum* and several other maples such as *A. caudatum*. In Bhutan and Sikkim there are also some maples, often less hardy; *A. pectinatum* is common in Bhutan, *A. sikkimense* in Sikkim.

The vast country of China is perhaps the most important center of diversity in the genus. Many maples are widely distributed in the Himalayas, some going up to 3000 m (9800 feet). More than 30 species are native to the province of Sichuan, and the provinces of Hubei and Yunnan are also very rich in maples. Prominent Chinese maples include *Acer campbellii* subsp. *flabellatum*, *A. cappadocicum* subsp. *sinicum*, *A. caudatum*, *A. davidii*, *A. longipes*, *A. pectinatum* subspecies *forrestii* and *laxiflorum*, *A. pictum* (painted maple), *A. stachyophyllum*, and *A. sterculiaceum* subsp. *franchetii*. In northern China and Manchuria are *A. tataricum* subsp. *ginnala* (Amur maple) and some rarer species such as *A. mandshuricum* and *A. tegmentosum*. Quite a few Chinese species remain to be brought into cultivation more widely in the Western world.

Korea is also an important country for maples. *Acer pseudosieboldianum* and *A. tschonoskii* are indigenous there. Two maples occur on the small island to the east, Ullung Do: *A. okamotoanum* and *A. pseudosieboldianum* subsp. *takesimense*.

In more southerly parts of southeastern Asia, subtropical species are present, some also evergreen. In southern China, Myanmar (Burma), and Vietnam are *Acer cordatum*, *A. laevigatum*, *A. tonkinense*, and other, less well known maples.

Japan is famous for its diversity of maples. *Acer palmatum* is probably the most important maple in horticulture. It has given rise to a vast number of cultivars—many hundreds have been named. Other notable maples from Japan are *A. buergerianum* (trident maple), *A. capillipes*, *A. cissifolium*, *A. japonicum*, *A. maximowiczianum* (Nikko maple), *A. rufinerve*, *A. shirasawanum*, the interesting and somewhat unusual *A. nipponicum*, the rare *A. distylum* (linden-leaved maple), and *A. carpinifolium*, unique among maples in its hornbeamlike foliage.

A few evergreen maples occur in the Philippines and Indonesia. *Acer laurinum*, a mighty tree in its native habitat, is an example.

Finally, maples occur over much of North America, from the far north to Guatemala. Among the most well known species are *Acer saccharum* (sugar maple), with its subspecies scattered from the Atlantic far to the west and southwest. *Acer rubrum* (red maple) is famous for its brilliant fall color, especially in New England and eastern Canada, overlapping with *A. spicatum* (mountain maple) and *A. pensylvanicum*, the snakebark maple of North America. *Acer negundo* (box elder) and *A. saccharinum* (silver maple) are widely distributed. The two subspecies of *A. glabrum* occur in the Rocky Mountains and the ranges to the west. In the Pacific Northwest is *A. circinatum* (vine maple), evocative of the Japanese maples to which it is related. *Acer macrophyllum* has the largest leaves in the genus and inhabits Pacific Coast ranges from British Columbia to southern California.

Habit

Most maples are trees or treelike shrubs. Several species may reach to great heights, more than 25 m (82 feet). Many are multistemmed. Some have beautiful bark. The snakebark maples have white stripes on a green or purplish green background. Or bark may be gray, brown, or whitish, and some maples have brown-red or even wine-red color in their young branches. Sometimes the bark is smooth, as in *Acer cappadocicum* (Caucasian maple) and *A. pictum* (painted maple), or rough and fissured as in *A. truncatum* (Shantung maple). *Acer griseum* (paperbark maple) is famous for its orange-brown exfoliating bark; no other maple has that characteristic. Many maples are less conspicuous, but a maple in winter is always attractive with its statuesque branching.

Leaves

Most maples may be easily recognized by their leaves. The typical distinctively shaped maple leaf is palmately and sharply lobed, witness the most famous maple leaf, the symbol of Canada, a stylized leaf of *Acer saccharum*, sugar maple. Most of the species have three- or five- or seven-lobed deciduous leaves, but some have leaves with up to thirteen lobes. Only few of the hardier species have unlobed leaves, such as *A. carpinifolium*, hornbeam maple, and *A. davidii*. On the other hand, most subtropical species have unlobed and persistent leaves, often leathery.

The average leaf is about as wide as long, or somewhat longer, except in the unlobed species where the leaves are much longer than wide. Maple leaves are usually smooth underneath, but there are some exceptions such as *Acer rufinerve*, *A. sterculiaceum*, and *A. velutinum*. Different yet are maples with compound leaves such as *A. negundo*, box elder, and *A. griseum*, paperbark maple, which has trifoliolate leaves. One feature all maple leaves have in common is the leaf arrangement, which is opposite, not alternate.

The maple with the smallest leaves grows in Greece, *Acer hyrcanum* subsp. *reginae-amaliae*, with leathery leaves about 1 cm (3/8 inch) long. *Acer macrophyllum* has the largest leaves, to 35 cm (14 inches) wide, and inhabits Pacific Coast areas of the United States and Canada.

Flowers

Most maples have flowers with five sepals, five petals, eight stamens, and a two-chambered ovary. There are also a few species with four sepals, four petals, four stamens, and a three- or four-chambered ovary. The flowers are borne in inflorescences varying in size from only a few to many flowers. Some develop very conspicuous inflorescences, such as *Acer nipponicum*; others have only a small umbel, such as *A. palmatum* Corollas are usually yellow or cream, whitish or red.

Some species, such as *Acer negundo* (box elder), *A. sterculiaceum*, and *A. stachyophyllum*, are dioecious, which means that an individual plant is either male or female, bearing flowers that are functional for only one sex. Isolated female trees of such species in cultivation thus do not produce viable seeds. They may sometimes develop fruits but the fruits are empty; this is called parthenocarpy (see "Fruits and Seeds"). Pollination from a male tree is required to produce viable seed.

Fruits and Seeds

Maple fruits are distinctively shaped and arranged in the form of paired nutlets, each with a wing. Such a fruit is called a samara. The nutlets may be small and an entire samara not longer than 5 mm (³⁄₁₆ inch), or quite large with samaras 50 mm (2 inches) long.

Some maples produce fruits abundantly but may not set viable seed. The phenome-non of producing fruits without fertilization is called parthenocarpy. The tendency to parthenocarpy varies depending on the species. An example of a strong tendency to parthenocarpy is provided by *Acer griseum*, paperbark maple. One may harvest buckets full of fruits but usually they are all sterile. In addition to the phenomenon of dioecism, discussed with "Flowers," some maples may produce male and female flowers on different branches of the same tree, which is called monoecism. Usually there is sufficient pollination in monoecious maples to produce a crop of viable seeds.

Wood and Roots

All maples are woody. The wood is hard and finely grained and has been used for making tools, toys, furniture, and musical instruments. Among a diversity of uses of maples by Native North Americans, wood of *Acer glabrum* (Rocky Mountain maple) was used to make snowshoes and tepee pegs; *A. macrophyllum* (big-leaf maple), canoe paddles; and *A. saccharum* (sugar maple) and *A. saccharinum* (silver maple), arrows.

The root system is much branched, helping trees maintain their stability. Roots of most if not all maples develop a symbiotic relationship with particular fungi, forming structures called mycorrhizae. The fungi assist maples in the uptake of certain nutrients from the soil, such as phosphorus, potassium, and sulfur. Fertilizing a maple may reduce its mycorrhizal population.

Classification of Maples

The genus *Acer* entered formal botanical nomenclature when the Swedish botanist Carl Linnaeus first published his *Species Plantarum* in 1753. The word *Acer* is derived from a Greek word meaning "sharp" and was applied to the genus by the French botanist Joseph Pitton de Tournefort in 1700. Linnaeus recognized nine species, all of them European or American and in cultivation. No Asiatic species were initially described, the wealth of those species becoming known over the course of the next century or later.

Acer is the type genus of the family Aceraceae, the only other genus of which is *Dipteronia*, with two species of central and southern China characterized by having fruits with the wing all around the fruit instead of having the characteristic winged samara (often a double samara) of *Acer*. The family Aceraceae is one of approximately 300 families of dicotyledonous flowering plants and belongs to the order Sapindales, which includes 17 families thought to be more closely related to each other than to other families. Among the families of Sapindales are Anacardiaceae (*Cotinus*, smoke

bush, and *Toxicodendron*, poison oak and poison ivy), Burseraceae (*Commiphora*, myrrh and balm of Gilead), Hippocastanaceae (*Aesculus*, buckeyes and horsechestnuts), and Rutaceae (*Citrus*), a surprisingly diverse assemblage.

Taxonomy is the study of relationships and classification of taxa (singular, taxon). A taxon is a naturally occurring group of related plants (or animals) recognized at any rank in the taxonomic hierarchy. In plants the hierarchy is as follows, in descending order: division (e.g., Embryophyta, seed plants), subdivsion (e.g., Magnoliophyta, flowering plants) class (e.g., Magnoliopsida, dicotyledons), order, family, genus, species, subspecies, variety (sometimes a species may be divided into subspecies or varieties), form. The order Sapindales is a taxon; Aceraceae, Anacardiaceae, Burseraceae, etc., each family is a taxon; *Acer* is a taxon; *Acer saccharum* is a taxon; *Acer saccharum* subsp. *grandidentatum* is a taxon; and so on.

Populations of plants, just like those of animals, often show variability. Where to draw the line between one taxon and another is part of the science of taxonomy and as different methods are used different classifications may emerge over time. Assigning the correct names to the taxa recognized is also part of taxonomy, and the rules governing the choice of the correct name are provided by the *International Code of Botanical Nomenclature.*

The genus *Acer* is divided into 16 sections, 8 of which are subdivided into series, and includes 124 species. The following synopsis of the genus, accounting for the cultivated taxa included in the present book, follows the system used in *Maples of the World* (D. M. van Gelderen, P. C. de Jong, and H. J. Oterdoom, Timber Press, 1994). The sections and series are arranged, insofar as can be done in a linear sequence, into a "natural" sequence that groups related taxa together; species are listed alphabetically. In the following list the name of each maple taxon includes its "authority," that is, the name of the person who named the maple, and the date of publication of the maple name. When a "parenthetical authority" is included, it means, for example, that the taxon now recognized as *Acer caudatum* subsp. *ukurunduense* (Trautvetter & Meyer) Murray was first described as a separate species, *A. ukurunduense* Trautvetter & Meyer (in 1856), and was later (in 1966) classified as a subspecies of *A. caudatum* by Murray.

Taxonomy of the Genus *Acer*

Acer Linnaeus (1753)

Section *Parviflora* Koidzumi (1911)
  Series *Parviflora*
    A. nipponicum Hara (1938)
  Series *Distyla* (Ogata) Murray (1983)
    A. distylum Siebold & Zuccarini (1845)
  Series *Caudata* Pax (1886)
    A. caudatum Wallich (1830) subsp. *caudatum*
    A. caudatum subsp. *ukurunduense* (Trautvetter & Meyer) Murray (1966)
    A. spicatum Lamarck (1786)
Section *Palmata* Pax (1885)
  Series *Palmata*
    A. circinatum Pursh (1814)
    A. japonicum Thunberg ex Murray (1784)
    A. palmatum Thunberg ex Murray (1784) subsp. *palmatum*
    A. palmatum subsp. *amoenum* (Carrière) Hara (1954)
    A. palmatum subsp. *matsumurae* Koidzumi (1911)

    A. pauciflorum Fang (1932)
    A. pseudosieboldianum (Pax) Komarov (1904) subsp. *pseudosieboldianum*
    A. pseudosieboldianum subsp. *takesimense* (Nakai) de Jong (1994)
    A. pubipalmatum Fang (1932)
    A. shirasawanum Koidzumi (1911) var. *shirasawanum*
    A. shirasawanum var. *tenuifolium* Koidzumi (1911)
    A. sieboldianum Miquel (1865)
  Series *Sinensia* Pojarkova (1933)
    A. calcaratum Gagnepain (1948)
    A. campbellii Hooker fil. & Thomson ex Hiern (1875) subsp. *campbellii*
    A. campbellii subsp. *flabellatum* (Rehder) Murray (1977) var. *flabellatum*
    A. campbellii subsp. *flabellatum* var. *yunnanense* (Rehder) Fang (1939)
    A. campbellii subsp. *sinense* (Pax) de Jong (1994)
    A. campbellii subsp. *wilsonii* (Rehder) de Jong (1994)
    A. elegantulum Fang & Chiu (1979)
    A. erianthum Schwerin (1901)
    A. miaoshanicum Fang (1966)
    A. olivaceum Fang & Chiu (1979)
    A. oliverianum Pax (1889) subsp. *oliverianum*
    A. oliverianum subsp. *formosanum* (Koidzumi) Murray (1969)
    A. tonkinense subsp. *kwangsiense* (Fang & Fang fil.) Fang (1979)
    A. tutcheri Duthie (1908)
  Series *Penninervia* Metcalf (1932)
    A. cordatum Pax (1889)
    A. fabri Hance (1884)
    A. laevigatum Wallich (1830)
    A. lucidum Metcalf (1932)
Section *Macrantha* Pax (1885)
    A. capillipes Maximowicz (1867)
    A. caudatifolium Hayata (1911)
    A. crataegifolium Siebold & Zuccarini (1845)
    A. davidii Franchet (1885) subsp. *davidii*
    A. davidii subsp. *grosseri* (Pax) de Jong (1994)
    A. micranthum Siebold & Zuccarini (1845)
    A. morifolium Koidzumi (1914)
    A. pectinatum Wallich ex Nicholson (1881) subsp. *pectinatum*
    A. pectinatum subsp. *forrestii* (Diels) Murray (1977)
    A. pectinatum subsp. *laxiflorum* (Pax) Murray (1977)

A. pectinatum subsp. *maximowiczii* (Pax) Murray (1977)

A. pectinatum subsp. *taronense* (Handel-Mazzetti) Murray (1977)

A. pensylvanicum Linnaeus (1753)

A. rubescens Hayata (1911)

A. rufinerve Siebold & Zuccarini (1845)

A. sikkimense Miquel (1867) subsp. *sikkimense*

A. tegmentosum Maximowicz (1857)

A. tschonoskii Maximowicz (1886) subsp. *tschonoskii*

A. tschonoskii subsp. *koreanum* Murray (1977)

Section *Glabra* Pax (1885)

  Series *Glabra*

  A. glabrum Torrey (1828) subsp. *glabrum*

  A. glabrum subsp. *douglasii* (Hooker) Wesmael (1890)

  Series *Arguta* (Rehder) Rehder (1949)

  A. acuminatum Wallich ex D. Don (1825)

  A. argutum Maximowicz (1867)

  A. barbinerve Maximowicz (1867)

  A. stachyophyllum Hiern (1875) subsp. *stachyophyllum*

  A. stachyophyllum subsp. *betulifolium* (Maximowicz) de Jong (1994)

Section *Negundo* (Böhmer) Maximowicz (1880)

  Series *Negundo*

  A. negundo Linnaeus (1753) subsp. *negundo*

  A. negundo subsp. *californicum* (Torrey & Gray) Wesmael (1890)

  A. negundo subsp. *interius* (Britton) Á. & D. Löve (1954)

  Series *Cissifolia* (Koidzumi) Momotani (1962)

  A. cissifolium (Siebold & Zuccarini) Koch (1864)

  A. henryi Pax (1889)

Section *Indivisa* Pax (1885)

  A. carpinifolium Siebold & Zuccarini (1845)

Section *Acer*

  Series *Acer*

  A. caesium Wallich ex Brandis (1874) subsp. *caesium*

  A. caesium subsp. *giraldii* (Pax) Murray (1969)

  A. heldreichii Orphanides ex Boissier (1856) subsp. *heldreichii*

  A. heldreichii subsp. *trautvetteri* (Medvedev) Murray (1982)

  A. pseudoplatanus Linnaeus (1753)

A. velutinum Boissier (1846) var. *velutinum*

A. velutinum var. *glabrescens* (Boissier & Buhse) Murray (1969)

A. velutinum var. *vanvolxemii* (Masters) Rehder (1938)

Series *Monspessulana* Pojarkova (1933)

  A. hyrcanum Fischer & Meyer (1837) subsp. *hyrcanum*

  A. hyrcanum subsp. *intermedium* (Pančić) Bornmüller (1925)

  A. hyrcanum subsp. *keckianum* (Pax) Yaltirik (1967)

  A. hyrcanum subsp. *reginae-amaliae* (Orphanides ex Boissier) Murray (1970)

  A. hyrcanum subsp. *sphaerocarpum* Yaltirik (1967)

  A. hyrcanum subsp. *stevenii* (Pojarkova) Murray (1969)

  A. hyrcanum subsp. *tauricolum* (Boissier & Balansa) Yaltirik (1967)

  A. monspessulanum Linnaeus (1753) subsp. *monspessulanum*

  A. monspessulanum subsp. *turcomanicum* (Pojarkova) Murray (1969)

  A. obtusifolium Sibthorp & Smith (1809)

  A. opalus Miller (1768) subsp. *opalus*

  A. opalus subsp. *hispanicum* (Pourret) Murray (1969)

  A. opalus subsp. *obtusatum* (Willdenow) Gams (1925)

  A. sempervirens Linnaeus (1767)

Series *Saccharodendron* (Rafinesque) Murray (1970)

  A. saccharum Marshall (1785) subsp. *saccharum*

  A. saccharum subsp. *floridanum* (Chapman) Desmarais (1952)

  A. saccharum f. *glaucum* (Schmidt) Pax (1902)

  A. saccharum subsp. *grandidentatum* (Torrey & Gray) Desmarais (1952)

  A. saccharum subsp. *leucoderme* (Small) Desmarais (1952)

  A. saccharum subsp. *nigrum* (Michaux fil.) Desmarais (1952)

  A. saccharum var. *schneckii* Rehder (1913)

Section *Pentaphylla* Hu & Cheng (1948)

  Series *Pentaphylla*

  A. pentaphyllum Diels (1931)

  Series *Trifida* Pax (1886)

  A. buergerianum Miquel (1865) subsp. *buergerianum*

  A. buergerianum subsp. *ningpoense* (Hance) Murray (1982)

A. coriaceifolium Léveillé (1912)

A. oblongum Wallich ex de Candolle (1824)

A. paxii Franchet (1886)

Section *Trifoliata* Pax (1885)

Series *Grisea* Pojarkova (1933)

A. griseum (Franchet) Pax (1902)

A. maximowiczianum Miquel (1867)

A. triflorum Komarov (1901)

Series *Mandshurica* Pojarkova (1933)

A. mandshuricum Maximowicz (1867)

Section *Lithocarpa* Pax (1885)

Series *Lithocarpa*

A. diabolicum Blume ex Koch (1864)

A. sinopurpurascens Cheng (1931)

A. sterculiaceum Wallich (1830) subsp. *sterculiaceum*

A. sterculiaceum subsp. *franchetii* (Pax) Murray (1969)

A. sterculiaceum subsp. *thomsonii* (Miquel) Murray (1969)

Series *Macrophylla* Pojarkova ex Momotani (1962)

A. macrophyllum Pursh (1814)

Section *Platanoidea* Pax (1885)

A. campestre Linnaeus (1753) var. *campestre*

A. campestre var. *acuminatilobum* Papp (1954)

A. cappadocicum Gleditsch (1785) subsp. *cappadocicum*

A. cappadocicum subsp. *divergens* (Pax) Murray (1978)

A. cappadocicum subsp. *lobelii* (Tenore) Murray (1982)

A. cappadocicum subsp. *sinicum* (Rehder) Handel-Mazzetti (1933) var. *sinicum*

A. cappadocicum subsp. *sinicum* var. *tricaudatum* (Veitch ex Rehder) Rehder (1914)

A. longipes Franchet ex Rehder (1905) subsp. *longipes*

A. longipes subsp. *amplum* (Rehder) de Jong (1994)

A. longipes subsp. *catalpifolium* (Rehder) de Jong (1994)

A. miyabei Maximowicz (1888) subsp. *miyabei*

A. pictum Thunberg ex Murray (1784)

A. platanoides Linnaeus (1753)

A. tenellum Pax (1889)

A. truncatum Bunge (1833)

Section *Pubescentia* (Pojarkova) Ogata (1967)

A. pentapomicum Stewart ex Brandis (1874)

A. pilosum var. *stenolobum* (Rehder) Fang (1966)

Section *Ginnala* Nakai (1915)

A. tataricum Linnaeus (1753) subsp. *tataricum*

A. tataricum subsp. *aidzuense* (Franchet) de Jong (1994)

A. tataricum subsp. *ginnala* (Maximowicz) Wesmael (1890)

A. tataricum subsp. *semenovii* (Regel & Herder) Murray (1982)

Section *Rubra* Pax (1885)

A. pycnanthum Koch (1864)

A. rubrum Linnaeus (1753)

A. saccharinum Linnaeus (1753)

Section *Hyptiocarpa* Fang (1966)

A. laurinum Hasskarl (1843)

In addition to the species listed above, some hybrids have been given species names (see under "Hybrids").

The authority names for the sections and series listed above reveal those who have contributed to our understanding of maple classification. The German botanist Ferdinand Albin Pax (1858–1942), director of the botanic garden of the University of Breslau (now Wroclaw, Poland), was the "father" of the current system. He published his "Aceraceae" in *Das Pflanzenreich* (the plant kingdom) in 1902. He was also an important contributor to *Die natürlichen Pflanzenfamilien* (the natural plant families). The Japanese botanist Gen'ichi Koidzumi (1883–1953) adapted Pax's system, publishing his "Revisio Aceracearum Japonicarum" in 1911. Koidzumi tried to include a range of Japanese garden plants in his system, classifying them at the rank of form. These forms are now considered to be cultivars. Mrs. Antonia I. Pojarkova (1897–1980), a Russian botanist, dealt especially with the flora of Turkey and the Caucasus. In her later years she elaborated a classification based on the presumed phylogeny of *Acer*, altered and adapted by the Japanese botanists Y. Momotani and K. Ogata in the 1960s. Fang Wen-pei has been an important Chinese authority on maples, treating *Acer* in the *Flora Reipublicae Popularis Sinicae* in 1981. Finally, P. C. de Jong, a Dutch taxonomist and specialist in *Acer*, published his classification system in his thesis, "Flowering and Sex Expression in *Acer* L.," in 1976, which was used with minor revisions in *Maples of the World* in 1994.

Hybrids

Species of *Acer* usually do not hybridize readily in the wild. There are, however, some natural hybrids in southeastern Europe involving *A. monspessulanum*, *A. opalus*, and *A. pseudoplatanus* as parents, for example. Other hybrids have arisen mainly in gardens, either accidentally or by intentional crossing. A number of these have been described as species and their hybrid origin is indicated by the addition of a multiplication sign × before the species name. The multiplication sign is ignored in alphabetizing and the following *Acer* hybrids are in cultivation and are included in the present volume:

Acer ×*bornmuelleri* Borbás (1891), a naturally occurring hybrid, *A. monspessulanum* (section *Acer*, series *Monspessulana*) × *A. campestre* (section *Platanoidea*)

Acer ×*conspicuum* D. M. van Gelderen & Oterdoom (1994), a garden hybrid, *A. davidii* × *A. pensylvanicum*, both parents belonging to section *Macrantha*

Acer ×*coriaceum* Bosc ex Tausch (1829), a naturally occurring hybrid, *A. monspessulanum* × *A. opalus* subsp. *obtusatum*, both parents belonging to section *Acer*, series *Monspessulana*

Acer ×*durettii* Pax (1893), a garden hybrid, probably *A. opalus* × *A. monspessulanum*, both parents belonging to section *Acer*, series *Monspessulana*

Acer ×*freemanii* Murray (1969), a garden hybrid, *A. saccharinum* × *A. rubrum*, both parents belonging to section *Rubra*

Acer ×*hillieri* Lancaster (1979), a garden hybrid, *A. miyabei* × *A. cappadocicum* 'Aureum', both parents belonging to section *Platanoidea*

Acer ×*hybridum* Bosc (1821), perhaps a garden hybrid within section *Acer*, *A. opalus* × *A. monspessulanum*, both parents belonging to series *Monspessulana*, or *A. opalus* × *A. pseudoplatanus*, the latter belonging to series *Acer*

Acer ×*pseudoheldreichii* Fukarek & Celjo (1959), a naturally occurring hybrid, *A. heldreichii* × *A. pseudoplatanus*, both parents belonging to section *Acer*, series *Acer*; this hybrid is discussed in the description of *A. heldreichii* subsp. *heldreichii*

Acer ×*rotundilobum* Schwerin (1894), a garden hybrid, *A. monspessulanum* × *A. opalus* subsp. *obtusatum*, both parents belonging to section *Acer*, series *Monspessulana*.

Acer ×*zoeschense* Pax (1886), a garden hybrid, *A. campestre* × *A. cappadocicum* subsp. *lobelii*, both parents belonging to section *Platanoidea*

Hybridization also plays a role in the origin of some cultivars. For example, *Acer* ×*conspicuum* itself has a number of cultivars, such as *A.* ×*conspicuum* 'Elephant's Ear'. Some interspecific crosses have also been given cultivar names such as *Acer* 'White Tigress', in which in this case one of the parental species is not known. Cultivars are discussed in more detail below.

Cultivars

Most maples newly established in cultivation at present are cultivars with selected qualities that are often better for garden use than those of the original species. Cultivars are like taxa except that they are not "naturally occurring" but are rather selections made from wild populations or from cultivated "populations," such as plants raised from seedlings grown in gardens. Some cultivars are formed by hybridizing. To maintain the distinctive characteristics of the original selected individual, such plants should be propagated vegetatively—*cultivars* cannot be propagated by seed without losing their distinctive qualities; maple *species* in cultivation should only be propagated by means of seed when the seeds are harvested from well-identified, isolated, uniform specimens, without risk of cross-pollination. (See the chapter "Maples in the Garden," under the heading "Propagation.")

A few species of maples are the source of most cultivars. The following "five *p*'s" supply about 85 percent of the total number of cultivars: *Acer palmatum*, *A. pectinatum*, *A. pictum*, *A. platanoides*, and *A. pseudoplatanus*. *Acer palmatum* has by far the largest number of cultivars, more than 1000. Its cultivars may be divided into groups sharing many of the same characteristics; these groups are described just before the entries for *A. palmatum* in the alphabetical arrangement of maple photographs. Disappointingly, many old forms, which would now be considered cultivars, of the European species *A. campestre* (hedge maple), *A. platanoides* (Norway maple), and *A. pseudoplatanus* (sycamore maple) have been lost to cultivation. For example, a German dendrologist, Fritz Graf von Schwerin, president of the German Dendrology Society in the years 1890–1910, described a large number of variants of the European species. Although many would not now be so interesting, considering the number of cultivars since developed, it is a pity that so many of these maples have vanished from gardens and survive only in the literature.

Just as there are rules for naming taxa, the *International Code of Nomenclature for Cultivated Plants* governs the names of cultivars. The most important rule is that beginning 1 January 1959 and for all cultivars thereafter, such names must be written in a modern language, capitalized, and set off by single quotation marks, for example, *Acer davidii* 'Rosalie' and *A. palmatum* 'Burgundy Lace'. This prevents confusing cultivar names with names of taxa. Many previously named cultivars, however, bear names in Latin form. Following the *Code* such names should be written as, for example, *Acer negundo* 'Variegatum' and *A. platanoides* 'Globosum'. Although cultivars may be assignable to a particular subspecies or variety, for example, *A. buergerianum* subsp. *ningpoense* 'Kōshi miyasama', it is common to find such cultivars listed under the binomial, *A. buergerianum* 'Kōshi miyasama'. The Index of Maples by Scientific Name includes cross-references to facilitate finding such cultivars, and there is a separate Index of Maples by Common or Cultivar Name, in which all cultivar names are listed alphabetically, for further help.

Many cultivars of Japanese maples have names originally written in Japanese characters that have had to be transliterated into the Roman alphabet. Differences in pronunciation and the use of different transliteration schemes have resulted in various spellings for the same cultivar name in many instances. Professor Masato Yokoi, retired from Chiba University and now of the Japan Branch of the Royal Horticultural Society, was very helpful in transliterating names from the Japanese during preparation of *Maples of the World*. Nevertheless, the problems were not completely solved. Dr. Ellen van Weely, graduated in Japanese language and culture from the University of Leiden, has restudied the transliterations with special attention to the proper pronunciation of the words involved. Inevitably, some familiar names have had their spellings corrected.

Transliterations involving *o* and *u* sounds cause the most difficulties. By studying the Japanese characters it is possible to see whether an *o* or *u* is long or short, which is not only important for the correct pronunciation of the name but also for the meaning of the word. Consider *Acer palmatum* 'Yūgure', for example, in which *yū* with the long vowel means "evening" and *gure* means "cloud," hence "evening cloud." But *yu* with the short vowel means "hot water" and the meaning of 'Yugure' would change to "steam cloud." Another example is *A. palmatum* 'Shūzankō', in which *shū* means "autumn," *zan* "mountains," and *kō* "red," hence "red mountains in autumn." But 'Shuzanko' would translate as "child, master of the mountains," an absurdity.

Therefore, it is very important to distinguish long versus short vowels in the transcriptions. In accordance with the *International Code of Nomenclature for Cultivated Plants*, revised in 1995, the indication of a long *o* or *u* is made by placing a macron over the vowel, *ō* or *ū*. A practical problem presented by the Hepburn system is that such macrons are not always easily reproduced, on plant labels, for example. So we have provided alternative transliterations in which the long vowels *ō* and *ū* are replaced by *oh* and *uh*, for example, 'Yuhgure' and 'Shuhzankoh'. These alternatives, included as such under the appropriate cultivars and cross-referenced in the indexes, retain the correct meaning when macrons are not available, continuing to honor the language of the Japanese and, we hope, easing communication between Western and Japanese maple enthusiasts.

Another difficulty encountered with Japanese names is pronunciation in relation to word division. The Japanese language does not divide characters but a compound such as *Acer palmatum* 'Aomeshimenouchishidare' would be formidable, indeed. Often in the past, Japanese cultivar names have been divided without reference to the original Japanese characters, and transliterations so divided may be misleading or meaningless. For correct pronunciation, for example, the cultivar name could be divided as 'A o me shi me no u chi shi da re' but that is awkward and it would also split the word translated from the first Japanese character, *ao*, "green," into two, which would be misleading. With the added assistance of Mr. Hisao Nakajima, an expert on Japanese maples who was also of great help in providing information on the correct separation of names into individual words, we have restudied Japanese cultivar names in relation to the original characters to suggest meaningful divisions, in this case 'Ao meshime no uchi shidare'. Similarly, *A. palmatum* 'Matsu ga e' is divided to retain the Japanese pronunciation of "ga" separate from "e" whereas "gae" would present an ambiguous pronunciation problem. Such meaningful division is in the spirit of the rules of the *Code*, which, however, calls for insertion of hyphens around the particle *no*, meaning "for," "in," "of," or "to," but not other, similar particles. With correct word division such hyphenation seems superfluous and at the time of this writing we are urging refinements to the *Code* in an effort to ensure that names are pronounceable and correct, acceptable for both Japanese and Westerners.

Maples
in the
Garden

With such a variety to choose from, maples may be used in practically any garden, large or small. Most maples tolerate many kinds of soil and can flourish in both acid and alkaline conditions. With such adaptability it is unfortunate to see too often the same species or cultivar grown in so many gardens when there is such a rich palette of maples from which to choose.

Various maples are suitable for use as street trees, as trees for large parks and gardens, as multistemmed trees for smaller parks and gardens, as slow-growing shrubs for the small garden, and as specialties, usually rare or more difficult to grow, for connoisseurs and collectors.

Maples as street trees are widely used in Europe, North America, Japan, and China. In Europe these are mainly cultivars of *Acer pseudoplatanus* ('Bruchem', 'Negenia', and 'Rotterdam') and *A. platanoides* ('Deborah', 'Emerald Queen', and 'Summershade,' all with bright green foliage and a golden yellow fall color, or the purple-leaved 'Crimson King' or 'Royal Red'). *Acer rubrum* (the conical 'Bowhall', and 'October Glory' and

'Red Sunset') and *A. saccharum* are widely used in North America.

For large parks and gardens a wide range of maples may be planted. Some spectacular species are *Acer cappadocicum* (Caucasian maple), with its beautiful yellow fall color, *A. cissifolium*, with grayish green pinnate leaves, and *A. negundo* (box elder). Other trees are *A. heldreichii* subspecies *heldreichii* and *trautvetteri* (red-bud maple), from Greece and Turkey, with good displays of deeply cut leaves and the samaras usually reddish. Rarer trees include *A. caesium*, *A. cappadocicum* subsp. *lobelii*, *A. pictum* (painted maple), *A. sterculiaceum*, and *A. truncatum*. All develop into stately trees.

Smaller trees or multistemmed trees are also very useful in gardens and parks. Fall displays of foliage color and winter displays of bark can be very attractive. Good species for these purposes are *Acer carpinifolium* (hornbeam maple), *A. davidii*, *A. griseum* (paperbark maple), *A. japonicum*, *A. pensylvanicum* (a snakebark maple), *A. rufinerve*, and *A. spicatum* (mountain maple). Larger cultivars of *A. palmatum* are also suitable.

In the smaller garden the range of slower growing small trees and shrubs is very wide. Many cultivars of *Acer palmatum* are ideally suited for the purpose. Other beautiful maples are *A. capillipes*, *A. circinatum* (vine maple), *A. pectinatum* with its subspecies, *A. shirasawanum* (including the cultivar 'Aureum', full-moon maple), and *A. stachyophyllum*. *Acer monspessulanum* and *A. tataricum* subsp. *ginnala* (Amur maple) are also very worthwhile. Even in smaller gardens it is possible to grow some conspicuous maples. Consider *A. griseum* (paperbark maple), *A. crataegifolium* (hawthorn maple), and dwarf forms of *A. buergerianum* (trident maple), *A. palmatum*, and *A. triflorum*.

In a connoisseur's garden some very interesting maples should not be missed. Here we think of *Acer distylum* (linden-leaved maple), *A. mandshuricum*, *A. micranthum*, *A. nipponicum*, *A. sterculiaceum* subsp. *franchetii*, *A. tenellum*, or *A. tschonoskii*. In sheltered gardens one should try to establish gems such as *A. campbellii*, *A. fabri*, *A. pentaphyllum*, or *A. sempervirens* (Cretan maple).

Additional suggestions for use of maples may be found in Appendix 2, "Maples for Particular Purposes."

Establishment and Maintenance

Although most maples are quite adaptable, care must be taken at the time of planting to ensure the best success over the life of the plant. Very wet situations should be avoided, although *Acer rubrum* and *A. saccharum* subsp. *floridanum* are more tolerant of such conditions. Most species cope well with humidity, however. Soil for many maples may be alkaline or acid. Some choice species such as *A. distylum*, *A. micranthum*, and *A. nipponicum* prefer an acid soil with a pH of about 5.0. Soil should have a good, open structure; maples need oxygen at their roots. If the soil is a heavy clay, dig it regularly and improve its structure with compost. Mulch maples every year.

Pests and Diseases

With proper establishment and maintenance, maples are resistant to most diseases or other problems. The most common plant insect pests are aphids and they do not overlook maples, especially in early spring when the new growth is developing. If aphids become a serious problem, a spray the next winter can destroy up to 90 percent of aphid eggs and prevent a recurrence. Seek advice from local garden centers and nurseries on the most environmentally sound choice of effective spray. In hot, wet summers common mildew may occur, especially on *Acer campestre* (hedge maple) and its cultivars. The secondary growth of young plants of *A. palmatum* can also be affected.

Verticillium wilt disease is a widespread maple disease that may pose a serious problem, particularly in cultivars of *Acer palmatum*. The fungus occurs in the soil and can attack maples when the plant is weakened, for example, by stress. Young twigs wilt when the fungus enters through the roots into the vascular system of the plant, obstructing flow. Correcting the conditions in which the maple is growing often solves the problem. Soil should be of good structure, crumbly and not hard, allowing air to penetrate, creating conditions that are unfavorable to the fungus. Disinfecting the soil is possible but not practical in gardens because it is a complicated procedure. In any event, prevention is better than a cure.

If a maple succumbs to *Verticillium* wilt, another maple should not be planted in the same place unless the soil is changed because fungal spores remain in the soil. Remove dead wood because the orange canker fungus *Nectria cinnabarina* follows *Verticillium* infection and attacks still-living parts of the maple. *Pythium* fungus, the cause of a wilt disease in seedlings, is discussed under "Propagation."

Hardiness

The hardiness of maples depends on the characteristics of the localities in which they grow. One of the main determinants of hardiness is the stress produced by cold temperature in the winter. Maps for hardiness zones based on these cold temperatures are provided in Appendix 3. The map for North America is the familiar one based on U.S. Department of Agriculture hardiness zones. That for Europe has been modified for this volume, with somewhat different temperature ranges defining Zones 5–9, based on our experience and that of our European colleagues. Zone information for the maples illustrated in the present volume is given at the end of each description, for example, Zone 6 (Europe 7), meaning that as an approximation, the maple may be expected to be hardy in Zones 6–10 as shown on the North American map, and in Zones 7–10 as shown on the European map.

Cold hardiness itself is subject to some modification depending on other circumstances. Even an area in which the minimum winter temperature usually has not dipped below −30°F (−34°C), Zone 4, for example, may experience a period of unusually low temperature. Or a period of drying winds may be more challenging to a plant's hardiness than a colder period with snow cover. Differences in moisture-retention characteristics between particular kinds of soils may affect a plant's response to stress.

Local climate and weather are also subject to special local influences, such as the presence of a body of water. For example, the climate of the island of Mainau in Lake Constance, on the border of Austria, Germany, and Switzerland north of the Alps, is comparable to that of a warmer Mediterranean one. Microclimates produced by local changes in topography and exposure, or by the proximity of buildings and roads, must also be taken into account when evaluating the potential hardiness of a maple for a particular place. Fortunately, maples as a whole are quite "hardy" and with care in choosing it is almost always possible to find a maple with the desired characteristics for a particular situation.

Propagation

As mentioned in the chapter "Classification of Maples," under the heading "Cultivars," maple species may be grown from seed; hybrids and cultivars should be propagated vegetatively. Propagation by seed is often easy but not always so. Some of the commoner species often act weedy and unwanted seedlings must be removed! Well-identified seeds of well-documented wild origin may be trusted to breed true. Seeds of garden origin must be somewhat mistrusted unless precautions have been taken to prevent hybridization. Snakebark maples exhibit this problem unless seeds are harvested from isolated trees; hybrids can occur between species of their section, *Macrantha.* Hybrids between species of different taxonomic sections are rare. When no viable seed is available, or seed origin is suspect, species may also be propagated vegetatively.

Fruits (samaras, the winged fruits of maples) should be harvested in September or October, depending on weather. As discussed in the chapter "Maples in Nature," under the heading "Fruits and Seeds," the collector must also be aware of the possibility of sterile fruits produced through parthenocarpy. Open a good sample of fruits and check carefully before harvesting. In *Acer griseum,* paperbark maple, for example, a good result may be only 2–3 percent viable seed. Isolated individuals of dioecious species, such as *A. cissifolium* or *A. sterculiaceum,* may set fruits that are also empty. Harvested fruits should be stored in a cool, somewhat moist place, preferably not in plastic but in paper bags. It is possible to sow in the fall of the year in which the collection was made. Do not sow too deep, not deeper than the diameter of the nutlet. Cover seedbeds with sharp sand in order to retard growth of moss. Be aware that foraging mice may pose a threat to the seeds. Some species germinate very early, for example, *A. carpinifolium* (hornbeam maple), the first to germinate in the spring, often in early March. Others may need an additional year to germinate, such as *A. griseum* (paperbark maple) and *A. maximowiczianum* (Nikko maple). Young seedlings may be attacked by *Pythium* fungus, which causes a wilt disease that can kill seedlings within a few weeks. Check seedlings frequently and, if necessary, treat them with a fungicide. Seedlings may be lifted in November and potted or planted in the nursery. Provide shelter and some shade to the seedlings and protect them during dry spells, watering when necessary.

The simplest method of vegetative propagation is by layering. Bend a branch into a small ditch in the soil, fasten it there, and leave the branch alone for two summers. In fall or the following spring the connection with the "stool" or mother plant may be cut and the new, layered plant with its own roots may be carefully removed and replanted elsewhere.

Vegetative propagation by cuttings is done from softwood, before the wood has had a chance to harden. A cutting with two or three pairs of leaves and a pair of buds may be rooted by removing a thin slice of bark at the base and treating the cutting with rooting hormone. Problems of propagation by cuttings are discussed more thoroughly in *Maples of the World*. It is not a method we recommend for maples because cuttings must undergo new growth during summer before replanting and a number of maples propagated by cuttings seem especially susceptible to *Verticillium* wilt.

By far the best way to propagate maples vegetatively is by grafting. Usually best done by nursery professionals, grafting may be initiated at various times of the year using different methods, discussed in more detail in *Maples of the World*. Common to all is the proper selection of understock to which the scion is grafted; the understock, with its established roots, should be in the same taxonomic section as the scion. Scions chosen in summer should have undamaged leaves; those chosen in winter should be vigorous shoots taken in frost-free conditions, with good buds but no leaves. The scion is best secured to the understock using rubber rather than string ties. Temperature and humidity should be carefully controlled to prevent drying during the 4 to 6 weeks in summer or 8 to 10 weeks in winter required for the graft to form a good union before replanting.

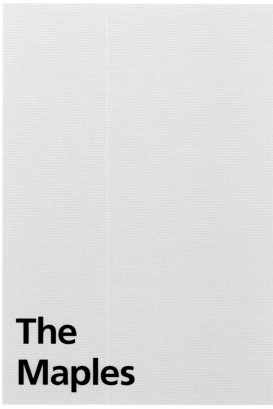

The Maples

About the Descriptions

For ready reference, descriptions and accompanying photographs are arranged in alphabetical order by scientific name and then, when given, cultivar name. A number of named maple species are known to be of hybrid origin, which is signified by the addition of a multiplication sign before the species name, for example, *Acer ×bornmuelleri*, resulting from the cross *A. monspessulanum × A. campestre.* The multiplication sign is ignored in alphabetizing. A number of cultivars are not illustrated but are discussed in comparison with those that are. Information on all maples mentioned in the book may be found by using the indexes, which provide references for all scientific and cultivar names, and cross-references from common names to scientific names and from synonymous scientific and cultivar names to correct names.

Descriptions include information in the following sequence: plant name, the section and series of the genus *Acer* to which the maple belongs, synonyms (only those names likely to be encountered on labels or in the nursery trade), habit, leaves, flowers, fruits, and distribution. This is followed by infor-

mation on who first described (or in the case of cultivars, raised or named or introduced) the plant. Because of the intricacies of nomenclature the first person to describe a plant may not always be the same as the correct "authority" for the plant name (see the discussion in the chapter "Classification of Maples"). If a plant has received special recognition from the Royal Boskoop Horticultural Society, Netherlands, or the Royal Horticultural Society, London, England, that is mentioned next. An indication of the plant's degree of cultivation, whether it is rare and limited mostly to the collections of those specializing in maples, or more common, is given. Comments on garden attributes and other useful information are provided. Comparisons with additional cultivars may be made. The description ends with hardiness zone information (see the maps in Appendix 3 and the discussion in the chapter "Maples in the Garden," under the heading "Hardiness"). In addition to information in the descriptions, maples are listed by various attributes in Appendix 2, "Maples for Particular Purposes." The photograph captions contain more information, as described below.

About the Photographs

The photographs for this book were selected from about 3000 made since 1993. We want to show maples as they appear in the open, without artificial light. A tripod and the same kind of film were used for almost all photographs. Ideal conditions for photography are obtained under a light but somewhat overcast sky to avoid undefined highlights and sharp shadows. When such conditions were not available we used a polarization filter to avoid unwanted reflections. Except for a very few photographs of rare maple species, the photographs in this book have not been published previously. Unless otherwise specified in the caption, photographs were made at the Esveld Aceretum, Boskoop, Netherlands. Additional locations at which maples may be observed are listed in Appendix 1, "Where to See Maples." Friends generously supplied some photographs we could not obtain for ourselves; we are indebted to Messrs J. R. P. van Hoey Smith, Harry Olsen, and K. W. Verboom.

Photographic Locations

Arboretum Belmonte, Generaal Foulkesweg 37, 6700 ED Wageningen, Netherlands

Arboretum des Grandes Bruyeres (Monsieur de la Rochefaucould), Forêt d'Orleans, Ingrannes, 45450 Fay-aux-Loges, France

Arboretum Kalmthout, Heuvel 2, 2920 Kalmthout, Belgium

Arboretum Thiensen, Thiensen 17, 25373 Ellerhoop, Germany

Stichting Arboretum Trompenburg, Honingerdijk 86, 3062 NX Rotterdam, Netherlands

M. M. Bömer, Vagevuurstraat 12, 4882 NK Zundert, Netherlands

Herr H. Boxleitner, Plauenerstrasse 37, 44139 Dortmund, Germany

R. Bulk, Rijneveld 115, 2771 XW Boskoop, Netherlands

Castle Gardens Arcen, Linghfortseweg 26, 5944 BE Arcen, Netherlands

Collingwood Grange, The Green, Benenden, Kent TN17 4DN, England

Esveld Aceretum, Rijneveld 72, 2771 XS Boskoop, Netherlands

Foliage Gardens (Mr. Harry Olsen), 2003 128th Street S.E., Bellevue, Washington 98005, U.S.A.

Fratelli Gilardelli, Viale delle Industrie 216, 20041 Agrate Brianza, Italy

Herkenrode Gardens, Bosveld 26, 3150 Wespelaar, Belgium

Sir Harold Hillier Gardens and Arboretum, Jermyns Lane, Ampfield, near Romsey, Hampshire SO51 0PA, England

Hof ter Saksen, public park, Beveren, Belgium

Hortus Haren, Kerklaan 34, 9751 NN Haren, Netherlands

Morris Arboretum of the University of Pennsylvania, 9414 Meadowbrook Avenue, Philadelphia, Pennsylvania 19118, U.S.A.

Princeton Nurseries, P.O. Box 191, Princeton, New Jersey 09540, U.S.A.

Research Station for Nursery Stock, Rijneveld 153, 2771 XV Boskoop, Netherlands

Romberg Park, Brünninghausen, Dortmund, Germany

Royal Botanic Gardens, Kew, Richmond, Surrey TW9 3AB, England

Savill Gardens, The Great Park, Windsor, Surrey SL4 2HT, England

Scott Arboretum of Swarthmore College, 500 College Avenue, Swarthmore, Pennsylvania 19081, U.S.A.

Sortimentstuin Zundert, Kleinzundertseweg 1–4, 4881 BG Zundert, Netherlands

Tharandt, Forstbotanischer Garten der Universität, 01737 Dresden, Germany

Valley Gardens, The Great Park, Windsor, Surrey SL4 2HT, England

Van den Bijl, M. Ringbandijk 1a, 4043 JH Opheusden, Netherlands

D. van der Maat, Voorofscheweg 120, Nursery Laag Boskoop, 2771 MG Boskoop, Netherlands

Ente Giardini di Villa Taranto, Intra Pallanza, Lago Maggiore, Italy

Von Gimborn Arboretum, Vossesteinsesteeg, Doorn; Rijksuniversiteit Utrecht, Harvardlaan 2, 3508 TD Utrecht, Netherlands

Washington Park Arboretum, University of Washington, 2300 Arboretum Drive East, Seattle, Washington 98195, U.S.A.

Westonbirt Arboretum, Westonbirt near Tetbury, Gloucestershire GL8 8QS, England

K. Wezelenburg & Sons, Hazerswoude, Netherlands (this nursery no longer exists)

Winkworth Arboretum, Hascombe Road, Godalming, Surrey GU8 4AD, England

Wisley Garden, near Ripley, Woking, Surrey GU23 6QB, England

Acer acuminatum. May, Herkenrode Gardens

Acer acuminatum

Section *Glabra*, series *Arguta*. Usually a multistemmed tree up to 10 m (33 feet) with green bark. Leaves with a long pointed apex, three- or five-lobed, outer lobes insignificant, color fresh green, turning yellow in fall. Flowers cream. Samaras 3–4 cm (1⅛–1½ inches) long, spreading at a right angle. Native to western part of the Himalayas in Nepal, Kashmir in India, and Pakistan. Described by Nathaniel Wallich and David Don in 1825. Note the elongated apex of the leaves. Quite rare in cultivation, it is suitable for large gardens. Zone 5 (Europe 6)

Acer argutum. October, Westonbirt Arboretum

Acer argutum

Section *Glabra*, series *Arguta*. Usually a multistemmed tree up to 6 m (20 feet) or a large shrub. Leaves 5–10 cm (2–4 inches) wide, sharply five-lobed, with reticulate veins; fall color yellow or orange. Flowers whitish. Samaras on slender stalks, horizontally spreading. A dioecious species, viable seeds are seldom available. Native to Japan, especially Honshū and Shikoku Islands. Described by Karl Johann Maximowicz in 1867. A collector's item, it is rather rare in cultivation and sometimes misidentified. Zone 4 (Europe 5)

Acer barbinerve. May

Acer barbinerve

Section *Glabra*, series *Arguta*. A multistemmed slender tree up to 6 to 7 m (20–23 feet), rarely a well-branched shrub, with green, smooth bark. Leaves five-lobed (outer lobes often underdeveloped) with rather long apexes, coarsely toothed, light green and dropping early in fall. Flowers creamy. Fruits usually few, samaras 4–6 cm (1½–2⅜ inches) long, arranged at an angle of 120 degrees. Native to Manchuria, valleys of the Ussuri River, and Shaanxi Province, China. Described by Karl Johann Maximowicz in 1867. Quite rare in collections, pointed-leaf maple is of interest primarily to collectors. Zone 4 (Europe 5)

Acer ×bornmuelleri. June

Acer ×bornmuelleri

A naturally occurring intersectional hybrid, *A. monspessulanum* (section *Acer*, series *Monspessulana*) × *A. campestre* (section *Platanoidea*). A small tree, densely branched, up to 8 m (26 feet), occasionally a shrub. Leaves 5 cm (2 inches) long and almost as wide, three- (or five-) lobed, texture thin, glossy green; fall color limited. Flowers in lax, terminal trusses, sterile. Due to its hybrid origin, fertile seed is not produced. Occurs in Bosnia-Herzegovina and adjacent regions. Described by Vincze tól Borbás in 1891. It is rare in cultivation and of interest primarily to collectors. Zone 4 (Europe 5)

Acer buergerianum subsp. *buergerianum.* May, Westonbirt Arboretum

Acer buergerianum

Section *Pentaphylla,* series *Trifida.* Described by Friedrich Anton Wilhelm Miquel in 1865. Two subspecies are cultivated, *buergerianum* and *ningpoense,* in addition to the cultivars. All of these are listed alphabetically. Also, a few other notable cultivars are listed at the end of the entries for *A. buergerianum.*

Acer buergerianum subsp. *buergerianum.* May, Herkenrode Gardens

Acer buergerianum subsp. buergerianum

Synonym, *A. trifidum* in the sense of J. D. Hooker and Arnott, not Thunberg. A tree up to 10 to 12 m (33–39 feet) in cultivation, in its habitat up to 20 m (66 feet); bark of the trunk sometimes strongly fissured. Depending on the climate also sometimes a large shrub. Leaves to 8 cm (3⅛ inches) long and 6 cm (2⅜ inches) wide, three-lobed, leathery, and in some forms persistent; juvenile leaves often very different from adult leaves. Flowers in small corymbs, almost white. Fruits often parthenocarpic and produced in quantity, samaras small. Native to eastern China and Japan. Although rarely seen in parks or gardens trident maple is rather common in specialists' collections. In Japan it is much more widely cultivated, even as a street tree, and it is also much used for bonsai. Zone 6 (Europe 7)

Acer buergerianum 'Goshiki kaede'. September

Acer buergerianum 'Goshiki kaede'

A medium-sized shrub up to 3 to 4 m (10–13 feet), rather densely branched. Many leaves white and pink variegated but not all; reverted twigs must be removed. Origin Japanese. Sought for bonsai, it is difficult to cultivate and thus rare. Similar cultivars include *A. buergerianum* 'Nusatori yama', a slowly growing shrub with purple leaves in spring, and 'Tō yō nishiki' (alternatively, 'Toh yoh nishiki', and not to be confused with a cultivar of *A. palmatum* of the same name), leaves variegated with pink flecks. Zone 7 (Europe 8)

with thin branches. Leaves 4–5 cm (1½–2 inches) long and almost as wide, distinctly three-lobed with an elongated apex, almost leathery, dark green, young foliage conspicuously purple-red. Origin Japanese. It needs shelter in winter and though it is rare it is a very attractive plant, suitable for bonsai. *Acer buergerianum* 'Nokoribi', leaves pink variegated although the variegation is rather unstable, is similar. Zone 7 (Europe 8)

Acer buergerianum 'Hime kaede'. June

Acer buergerianum 'Hime kaede'

A strongly growing shrub probably up to 10 m (33 feet), densely branched. Leaves three- (or five-) lobed, deeply cleft, with purple new growth. Origin Japanese and only more recently imported into Europe. It is rare but suitable for bonsai. Zone 6 (Europe 7)

Acer buergerianum Jōroku aka me'. November

Acer buergerianum 'Jōroku aka me'

Alternatively, *A. buergerianum* 'Johroku aka me'. A medium-sized, well-branched shrub probably up to 2 to 3 m (6½–10 feet)

Acer buergerianum 'Kifu nishiki'. July

Acer buergerianum 'Kifu nishiki'

A shrub up to 1 to 1.5 m (3¼–5 feet), densely branched. Leaves almost unlobed on adult branches, shiny dark green, occasionally white variegated. Flowers creamy white. Introduced by Masato Yokoi before 1989. The leaf variegation is quite unstable and may disappear; reverted twigs must be removed to maintain it. 'Kifu nishiki' is suitable for bonsai but rare. Zone 6 (Europe 7)

Acer buergerianum 'Mino yatsubusa'. October, Hillier Gardens and Arboretum

Acer buergerianum 'Mino yatsubusa'

A shrub barely more than 1 m (3¼ feet) high and about as wide, densely branched. Leaves 3–5 cm (1⅛–2 inches) long, differ-

ently shaped, three-lobed with long and narrow central lobes, shiny green above and glaucous underneath. An old Japanese cultivar, it is a very nice dwarf but unfortunately difficult to propagate. Zone 6 (Europe 7)

Acer buergerianum 'Mitsubatō kaede'. May, Savill Gardens

Acer buergerianum 'Mitsubatō kaede'. January

Acer buergerianum 'Mitsubatō kaede'

Alternatively, *A. buergerianum* 'Mitsubatoh kaede'. A small tree or large shrub up to 7 to 8 m (23–26 feet) or more, rather densely branched and with a strongly fissured trunk. Adult leaves 5–7 cm (2–2¾ inches) long, three-lobed, basal lobes short, olivegreen. Fruits in profusion but seeds usually not viable. Well known in Japan and introduced before 1970 but origin otherwise unknown. Widely available in Europe since

1975, it is suitable for medium-sized gardens and for bonsai. Not to be confused with *A. buergerianum* 'Marubatō kaede' (alternatively, 'Marubatoh kaede'), a different cultivar. Zone 6 (Europe 7)

Acer buergerianum 'Miyasama yatsubusa'. June

Acer buergerianum 'Miyasama yatsubusa'

A dense, well-branched shrub up to 2 m (6½ feet), often with stubby branches. Leaves distinctly three-lobed, somewhat leathery, glaucous underneath, young foliage purple. Origin Japanese and introduced before 1900. It is rare but suitable for small gardens and bonsai. Fast-growing plants should be avoided as they may be seedlings and not true to type. Zone 6 (Europe 7)

Acer buergerianum 'Naruto'. October

Acer buergerianum subsp. *ningpoense*. May, Savill Gardens

Acer buergerianum subsp. *ningpoense*

Synonym, *A. ningpoense*. A tree of moderate size but in favorable situations up to 15 m (50 feet). Leaves 4–6 cm (1½–2⅜ inches) long and wide, almost unlobed, texture thin. Flowers as in subspecies *buergerianum* but with longer stamens. Fruits with hard and round nutlets, profusely produced but usually not viable. Native to southeastern China, Zhejiang Province and adjacent regions. Originally described by Henry Fletcher Hance in 1873 as a variety of *A. trifidum*. Rarely found in Western gardens, it is often used as a street tree in southeastern China. Zone 7 (Europe 8)

Acer buergerianum 'Naruto'

A vase-shaped shrub up to 2.5 m (8 feet) or more, rather densely branched. Leaf shape peculiar, three-lobed with strongly incurved lobes, forming a T, leaf color gray-green. Origin Japanese, before 1900, now present in several collections in Europe and America. Suitable for small gardens and bonsai, it may only be confused with *A. buergerianum* 'Tanchō', which is slower growing as an old plant. Zone 6 (Europe 7)

Acer buergerianum subsp. *ningpoense* 'Kōshi miyasama'. June

Acer buergerianum 'Subintegrum'. May

Acer buergerianum subsp. *ningpoense* 'Kōshi miyasama'

Alternatively, *A. buergerianum* subsp. *ningpoense* 'Kohshi miyasama'. A rather large shrub or occasionally a small tree up to 6 to 7 m (20–23 feet). Leaves 4–5 cm (1½–2 inches) long and about as wide, distinctly three-lobed, somewhat leathery, partly evergreen. Flowers cream, rarely seen. Introduced by the Shibamichi Honten Nursery, Japan, before 1979. Rare in cultivation in Europe and America, more common in Japan, it can be used for bonsai and in smaller gardens. Zone 6 (Europe 7)

Acer buergerianum 'Subintegrum'

Synonym, *A. buergerianum* 'Integrifolium'. A tree of moderate size in cultivation, becoming large in China and Japan, up to 15 m (50 feet). Leaves 4–7 cm (1½–2¾ inches) long and 4–5 cm (1½–2 inches) wide, lobed but lobes often underdeveloped, glossy green, dropping late in the season. Flowers as in the species but with longer stamens. Fruits with hard and round nutlets, rarely viable. Originally described by Friedrich Anton Wilhelm Miquel in 1867 as a botanical form, this cultivar is very closely related to subspecies *ningpoense*. Good for medium-sized gardens and as a street tree in mild areas, it is rare in Europe and America although common in eastern Asia. Zone 6 (Europe 7)

Acer buergerianum 'Tanchō'

Alternatively, *A. buergerianum* 'Tanchoh'. A vase-shaped shrub up to about 2 m (6½ feet), rather densely branched. Leaves distinctly three-lobed, the lobes strongly incurved into the shape of a T, gray-green. An old Japanese cultivar, not to be confused with a cultivar of *A. palmatum* of the same name, it can be found in several Western collections. It cannot be distinguished from *A. buergerianum* 'Naruto' as a young plant but old plants of 'Tanchō' seem to remain smaller, according to Vertrees, *Japanese Maples*. Suitable as bonsai and good for small gardens. Zone 6 (Europe 7)

Acer buergerianum 'Tanchō'. July

Other Cultivars of *Acer buergerianum*

In addition to those illustrated or discussed, we mention the following:

'Akebono'. Leaves yellow-green when unfolding in spring, later greener.

'Eastwood Cloud', introduced by R. Gordon, Australia, has leaves almost white, turning to salmon; it is prone to sunburn.

'Hanachiru sato'. Leaves pink in spring and similar to *A. buergerianum* 'Wakō nishiki'.

'Inazuma nishiki'. Leaves speckled with yellow dots.

'Iwao nishiki'. Leaves large, with triangular lobes, leathery. *Iwao nishiki* means "rock maple." It is closely related to subspecies *ningpoense*.

'Kyūden' (alternatively, 'Kyuhden'). A miniature shrub, differing from most cultivars. Leaves two- or three-lobed. Not to be confused with a cultivar of *A. palmatum* with the same name.

'Miyadono'. A dwarf, leaves sometimes unlobed, similar to *A. buergerianum* 'Kyūden'.

'Shirley Debacq'. A fastigiate small tree with normal foliage found by A. Pousse, France, in 1995.

'Wakō nishiki' (alternatively, 'Wakoh nishiki'). Leaves entirely salmon-pink in spring, color similar to that of *A. pictum* 'Usugumo'. Not to be confused with *A. palmatum* 'Wakō nishiki'.

Acer caesium subsp. *caesium*. July

brown. Native to mountain forests in Sichuan and Yunnan Provinces of China, also in Kashmir in India and western Nepal, 2000–3000 m (6500–9800 feet). More frequently seen in botanical gardens, it is rare in other gardens and parks. Zone 6 (Europe 7)

Acer caesium subsp. *giraldii*. June, Arboretum des Grandes Bruyeres, courtesy of J. R. P. van Hoey Smith

Acer caesium

Section *Acer*, series *Acer*. Described by Nathaniel Wallich and Dietrich Brandis in 1874. Two subspecies are recognized, *caesium* and *giraldii*.

Acer caesium subsp. *caesium*

A rather large tree up to 15 m (50 feet), somewhat sparsely branched; young shoots often with a glaucous bloom. Leaves to 25 cm (10 inches) long and wide, five-lobed, of thin texture and typically crowded at the end of the shoot; fall color usually bright yellow. Flowers in upright corymbs, greenish white. Samaras 4–5 cm (1½–2 inches) long, wings rectangular, nutlets hard and

Acer caesium subsp. *giraldii*

Synonym, *A. giraldii*. A slow-growing tree up to 10 m (33 feet) or more, very sparsely branched; bark fissured and young shoots conspicuously white glaucous. Leaves to 25 cm (10 inches) long and wide, three- (or five-) lobed, not crowded as in subspecies *caesium.* Flowers greenish white but a maple very shy about flowering in cultivation. Fruits hard, reddish brown nutlets, almost never produced in cultivation. Native to Shaanxi and Yunnan Provinces of China. Originally described by Ferdinand Albin Pax as a separate species in 1902. Leafing out late, not before the end of May, the tree is difficult to propagate vegetatively and is rare in cultivation. Zone 6 (Europe 7)

Acer campbellii

Section *Palmata,* series *Sinensia.* Described by Joseph D. Hooker, Thomas Thomson, and William P. Hiern in 1875. Four subspecies are recognized, *campbellii, flabellatum* (with two varieties, *flabellatum* and *yunnanense*), *sinense,* and *wilsonii.*

Acer calcaratum. September, greenhouse, courtesy of J. R. P. van Hoey Smith

Acer calcaratum

Section *Palmata,* series *Sinensia.* Synonym, *A. craibianum.* A medium-sized tree probably up to 8 to 10 m (26–33 feet), much less in cultivation. Leaves 20–25 cm (8–10 inches) long and wide, three-lobed, margins coarsely lobed on juvenile growth and entire on adult branches. Flowers reported to be cream. Native to mountainous regions of Thailand, Myanmar (Burma), and Sikkim in northeastern India. Described by François Gagnepain in 1948. A charming but tender maple, it was cultivated for a decade in the Netherlands but was killed by frost and is probably no longer in cultivation. Zone 8 (Europe 9)

Acer campbellii subsp. *campbellii.* May, Valley Gardens

Acer campbellii subsp. *campbellii*

In its native habitat a tree up to 30 m (100 feet) but much smaller in cultivation, growing as a shrub in less favorable conditions. Leaves about 15 to 20 cm (6–8 inches) wide and fanlike, shallowly five- or seven-lobed; fall color a good yellow. Flowers terminal in slender panicles to 15 cm (6 inches) long, cream. Samaras 4–5 cm (1½–2 inches) long, spreading at an angle of about 150 degrees. Native to the Himalayas of western China, Nepal, and Sikkim in India, up to 3000 m (9800 feet), also in Vietnam and Myanmar (Upper Burma). Not uncommon in sheltered gardens in Britain, it is otherwise a rare plant in cultivation, needing mild conditions. The leaves are of great beauty and can turn brilliant in fall. Zone 7 (Europe 8)

Acer campbellii subsp. *flabellatum* var. *flabellatum*.
May

Acer campbellii subsp. *flabellatum* var. *flabellatum*

Synonyms, *A. flabellatum, A. heptalobum*.
A rather irregular tree or large shrub up to 6
to 8 m (20–26 feet) in cultivation and in its
native habitat up to 15 m (50 feet); bark
usually green. Leaves five- or seven-lobed,
narrower than in subspecies *campbellii* but
otherwise very similar. Flowers in slender
panicles, cream. Samaras 3 cm (1⅛ inches)
long, nutlets round and firm. Widespread in
Hubei, Sichuan, and northern Yunnan Provinces in southwestern China and in Laos,
usually in lightly forested mountainous
regions. Originally described as a separate
species by Alfred Rehder in 1905. Subspecies
flabellatum is easier to cultivate than subspecies *campbellii* and can also withstand
colder conditions better. Zone 7 (Europe 8)

Acer campbellii subsp. *flabellatum* var. *yunnanense*.
October, Westonbirt Arboretum

Acer campbellii subsp. *flabellatum* var. *yunnanense*.
May, Westonbirt Arboretum

Acer campbellii subsp. *flabellatum* var. *yunnanense*

Synonym, *A. flabellatum* var. *yunnanense*.
A shrub up to 13 m (43 feet) in its habitat,
much smaller in cultivation. Leaves five- or
seven-lobed, very similar in shape to those
of variety *flabellatum*, with sharply serrated
margins. Flowers cream. Originally described (as *A. flabellatum* var. *yunnanense*)
by Alfred Rehder in 1905. A rare plant in

cultivation and sometimes wrongly labeled, it is questionable whether varieties *yunnanense* and *flabellatum* should be maintained as separate entities. Zone 7 (Europe 8)

Acer campbellii subsp. *wilsonii*. May, Westonbirt Arboretum, courtesy of J. R. P. van Hoey Smith

Acer campbellii subsp. *sinense*. June, Fratelli Gilardelli

Acer campbellii subsp. *sinense*

Synonym, *A. sinense*. A small tree or more usually a dense shrub up to 8 to 9 m (26–30 feet); bark and twigs green. Leaves 9–10 cm (3½–2 inches) wide, distinctly smaller than in subspecies *campbellii*, leathery, usually five-lobed and lustrous green. Flowers cream. Samaras about 2 cm (¾ inch) long, nutlets small. Native to Hubei and Sichuan Provinces, China. Originally described as a separate species by Ferdinand Albin Pax in 1887. Although quite common in its native habitat this subspecies is rare in cultivation because of its tenderness. It can be confused with *A. oliverianum*, which is hardier and more commonly cultivated but has more leathery leaves. Zone 7 (Europe 8)

Acer campbellii subsp. *wilsonii*

Synonym, *A. wilsonii*. A small tree or merely an open shrub up to 4 to 5 m (13–16 feet) in cultivation but much larger in its habitat. Leaves 6–10 cm (2⅜–4 inches) wide, distinctly three-lobed, blackish green, base round. Flowers yellowish green. Samaras small, nutlets ovoid. Native to mountainous regions of Guangdong, Hubei, Sichuan, and Yunnan Provinces, China. Originally described as a separate species by Alfred Rehder in 1905. One of the rarest maples, even in specialist collections, in cultivation it almost always does poorly. Trees almost always have damaged, crinkled leaves. Zone 7 (Europe 8)

Acer campestre

Section *Platanoidea*. Described by Carl Linnaeus in 1753. Two varieties are recognized here, *acuminatilobum* and *campestre*, in addition to the cultivars, all listed alphabetically.

Acer campestre var. *acuminatilobum*

A shrub up to 8 to 10 m (26–33 feet) and as wide, vigorously growing. Leaves 10–12 cm (4–4¾ inches) wide, three- or five-lobed, more leathery and margins less rounded than those of variety *campestre*. Flowers greenish yellow. Found as a living plant by Joseph Papp in 1954, leaves like those of variety *acuminatilobum* were first found

Acer campestre var. *acuminatilobum*. May

as fossils in Hungary in the 1940s. Scions have been taken from the original plant; grafted specimens are rare in cultivation. It is debatable whether variety *acuminatilobum* should be recognized as a separate entity. Zone 4 (Europe 5)

Acer campestre. July

Acer campestre. May, Arboretum Belmonte

Acer campestre var. *campestre*

A tree or shrub up to 8 to 10 m (26–33 feet) and as wide, occasionally up to 20 m (66 feet) or more; bark variable, from almost smooth to corky. Leaves about 10 cm (4 inches) wide or smaller, three- or five-lobed, slightly pubescent and with rounded margins; fall color often very good. Flowers greenish yellow. Samaras horizontal, nutlets flat. Native throughout Europe into western Asia, also in northern Africa. Variable in leaf shape and proportion, many variants of *A. campestre* have been described. These are mostly now sunk into synonymy or treated as cultivars. In Europe *A. campestre* is frequently planted, including in hedgerows. It is also suitable as a street tree or for parks and large gardens. Sometimes mistaken for *A. monspessulanum*, *A. campestre* is easily recognized by the milky sap in its petioles. Zone 3 (Europe 4)

Acer campestre 'Carnival'. May, Westonbirt Arboretum

Acer campestre 'Carnival'

A slow-growing shrub up to 2 to 3 m (6½–10 feet), sometimes grafted on a standard. Leaves three-lobed, small, with white margins. Raised and introduced by A. van Nijnatten, Netherlands, in 1989. Found as a chance seedling, it is the only truly variegated cultivar of the species. It is prone to some sunburn and requires shelter against hot sun. Suitable for small gardens, this newer cultivar will probably become more readily available. Zone 5 (Europe 6)

Acer campestre 'Elsrijk'. June, van den Bijl

Acer campestre 'Elsrijk'

A straight-growing tree, suitable as a street tree, up to 12 m (39 feet) with a dense crown. Leaves somewhat larger than characteristic for the species, coloring well in fall. Raised and introduced by C. P. Broerse, Dutch garden architect, in 1953. Commonly planted in Europe along streets, it is also suitable for parks. *Acer campestre* 'Evelyn' (Queen Elizabeth, trademark name) and 'Zorgvlied' are similar to 'Elsrijk'. Zone 4 (Europe 5)

Acer campestre 'Green Weeping'

A tree with weeping branches when grafted on a standard, occasionally a large shrub. Found as a chance seedling, raised, and introduced by A. van Nijnatten, Netherlands, in 1981. Because of its relatively recent introduction it is not used as much as it might be. It should not be confused with the much older *A. campestre* 'Pendulum', probably lost to cultivation. 'Green Weeping' is suitable for medium-sized gardens or, because of its pendulous branches, as a tree for graveyards. Zone 4 (Europe 5)

Acer campestre 'Microphyllum'. July

Acer campestre 'Microphyllum'

A rather densely branched shrub up to 2 to 3 m (6½–10 feet) and about as wide. Leaves 2–3 cm (¾–1⅛ inches) wide, smaller than characteristic of the species, turning yellow in fall. Originally described as a botanical entity by Karl Koch in 1853, using a name proposed earlier by Philipp Maximilian Opiz. Seen only rarely, it has almost been forgotten in cultivation. It may a useful plant for hedges due to its dense growth. Zone 4 (Europe 5)

Acer campestre 'Nanum'

Synonyms, *A. campestre* 'Compactum', 'Globosum'. A rounded shrub to 4 to 5 m (13–16 feet) wide, heavily branched and very dense. Leaves smaller than characteristic of the species, olive-green when young and a splendid yellow in fall. Originally described as a botanical entity by John C. Loudon in 1839. Not common but present

Acer campestre 'Green Weeping'. June, van den Bijl

Acer campestre 'Nanum'. June

in several gardens and collections. Tolerant of drought, it is a good plant for use in tubs on balconies or terraces, also for bonsai. Low hedgerows can be made using this cultivar. Zone 4 (Europe 5)

Acer campestre 'Postelense'. May, Savill Gardens

Acer campestre 'Postelense'

A spreading shrub up to 2 to 3 m (6½–10 feet) and larger, sometimes grafted on *A. campestre* and grown as a tree. Leaves golden yellow in spring, turning greenish yellow in summer. Introduced by W. von Salisch, Postel, Silesia (now in Poland), described by R. Lauche in 1896. Not tolerant of much sun, the plant is not common but is present in several collections. When it leafs out the color makes the shrub look like a *Forsythia* in flower. Zone 5 (Europe 6)

Acer campestre 'Pulverulentum'. May

Acer campestre Queen Elizabeth. August, van den Bijl

Acer campestre Queen Elizabeth

(trademark name) *A. campestre* 'Evelyn'. A fast-growing tree with an almost columnar shape, making it a good tree for narrow roads. Leaves slightly larger than characteristic of the species. Found and introduced by the Studebaker and Lake County Nurseries, Ohio, before 1985; introduced into Europe by A. van Nijnatten, Netherlands. Comparatively new, it is not yet very common. Zone 4 (Europe 5)

Acer campestre 'Pulverulentum'

Usually a compact low shrub up to 2 to 2.5 m (6½–8 feet) and often wider than high, sometimes grown as a tree grafted on a standard of *A. campestre*. Leaves somewhat smaller than characteristic of the species, the blades white marbled. Found and named at the Muskau Arboretum, now in Poland, about 1859. Not common but present in several collections, it is a good shrub for smaller gardens. Its conspicuous foliage is prone to sunburn and needs some protection from the sun but it helps lighten up a shady area. Zone 5 (Europe 6)

Acer campestre 'Red Shine'

A large shrub or tree up to 10 m (33 feet). Leaves dark purple when leafing out, becoming dark green with age, finally moss green. Flowers yellow with a purplish hue. Raised and introduced by J. J. W. M. van den Oever, Netherlands, in 1980. The young purple foliage contrasts beautifully with the mature green leaves. Although prone to some mildew it is a good garden plant, also suitable for larger hedgerows. Zone 5 (Europe 6)

Acer campestre 'Red Shine'. May

Acer campestre 'Royal Ruby'. June

Acer campestre 'Royal Ruby'

Very similar to *A. campestre* 'Red Shine' but young leaves somewhat lighter purple. Flowers cream with purplish hue. Fruits almost never produced. Raised and introduced by A. van Nijnatten, Netherlands, in 1980. Although prone to mildew it is rather common in cultivation and is also good for hedgerows. Zone 5 (Europe 6)

Acer campestre 'Zorgvlied'

A medium-sized tree with the same habit and size as *A. campestre* 'Elsrijk'. Leaves slightly smaller than those of *A. campestre*, turning yellow in fall. Raised and introduced by C. P. Broerse, Netherlands, in 1953, from a seedling sister to that from which 'Elsrijk' was selected. 'Zorgvlied' is less frequently planted than 'Elsrijk' and has the reputation of being somewhat more prone to mildew. Zone 4 (Europe 5)

Acer campestre 'Zorgvlied'. June, van den Bijl

Acer capillipes. May, Herkenrode Gardens

Acer capillipes (hybrid?) 'Gimborn'. October, Von Gimborn Arboretum

Acer capillipes

Section *Macrantha*. A tree up to 10 m (33 feet), usually multistemmed, with a conspicuously striped bark and small rusty orange spots on the bark, densely branched. Leaves 6–10 cm (2⅜–4 inches) wide, usually three-lobed, sometimes five-lobed, margins distinctly serrate. Flowers cream; male and female racemes usually on different branches. Fruits small with short wings. Native to mountainous regions in Japan, mainly Honshū and Shikoku Islands. Described by Karl Johann Maximowicz in 1867. Given the Royal Horticultural Society's Award of Garden Merit in 1975. Present in almost every botanical collection, it is a valuable garden plant and deserves more attention. It is useful in larger gardens and parks, easy to grow from seed, and usually does not hybridize easily with related species. Zone 5 (Europe 6)

Acer capillipes (hybrid?) **'Gimborn'**

A single-stemmed tree up to 10 m (33 feet) with beautifully striped bark. Leaves 10–12 cm (4–4¾ inches) wide, larger than characteristic of *A. capillipes*, five-lobed, turning golden yellow in fall. Raised and introduced by the Von Gimborn Arboretum, Netherlands, in 1996, where it occurred as a chance seedling. The other parent is not known; 'Gimborn' may not be a hybrid. 'Gimborn' promises to be a tree valuable for several purposes where a smaller maple is required. Zone 6 (Europe 7)

Acer cappadocicum

Section *Platanoidea*. Described by Johann Gottlieb Gleditsch in 1785. Four subspecies are recognized, *cappadocicum, divergens, lobelii,* and *sinicum* (with two varieties, *sinicum* and *tricaudatum*), in addition to the cultivars, all listed alphabetically.

Acer cappadocicum 'Aureum'. May, Arboretum Belmonte

Acer cappadocicum 'Aureum'

Synonyms, *A. colchicum* f. *aureum, A. laetum* f. *aureum.* A tree up to 15 m (50 feet), occasionally more. Leaves somewhat smaller than those of the species, clear yellow, purplish to reddish when young but losing this color early in the summer. Raised and introduced by Hermann Albrecht Hesse, Hesse Nurseries, Germany, in 1914. Given the Royal Horticultural Society's Award of Garden Merit in 1969. Although rather common in collections it is less so in gardens because the tree may become too large. Zone 5 (Europe 6)

Acer cappadocicum subsp. *cappadocicum*

Synonyms, *A. colchicum, A. laetum.* A large tree up to 20 m (66 feet), occasionally even more, with smooth gray-brown bark; young branches and shoots smooth and green. Leaves 15–20 cm (6–8 inches) wide, five- or seven-lobed, green with a reddish hue when unfolding, later lustrous green. Leaf base cordate; petioles produce milky sap when broken. Flowers yellow in corymbs 6–8 cm (2⅜–3⅛ inches) long. Sama-

Acer cappadocicum 'Aureum'. June, Herkenrode Gardens

Acer cappadocicum subsp. *cappadocicum.* May, Westonbirt Arboretum

ras to 5 cm (2 inches) long but sometimes underdeveloped, nutlets flat. Native to northern Turkey, the Caucasus, and Iran in mixed forests. Caucasian maple is present in almost every sizable collection, is commonly planted in large gardens and parks, and is used as a street tree. It can be confused with *A. pictum.* Zone 5 (Europe 6)

lets flat. Native to eastern Turkey and the Caucasus on dry, sunny slopes. Originally described as a separate species by Karl Koch and Ferdinand Albin Pax in 1886. A rare plant in collections and often wrongly labeled. Plants grown from seeds collected in nature show much variation. Zone 5 (Europe 6)

Acer cappadocicum subsp. *divergens.* July, Von Gimborn Arboretum

Acer cappadocicum subsp. *divergens*

Synonym, *A. divergens.* A small tree or more often a large shrub up to 8 to 9 m (26–30 feet) and wider than high, usually densely branched. Leaves usually 2–4 cm (¾–1½ inches) wide, sometimes 5–7 cm (2–2¾ inches), three- or five-lobed, dark green with a reddish hue. Flowers yellowish on short corymbs. Samaras horizontal, nut-

Acer cappadocicum subsp. *lobelii.* October, Hillier Gardens and Arboretum

Acer cappadocicum subsp. *lobelii*

Synonym, *A. lobelii.* A tree of columnar shape up to 20 m (66 feet). Leaves 6–12 cm (2⅜–4¾ inches) wide, five-lobed, margins slightly wavy, base cordate. Flowers yellow-green in small corymbs, appearing with the leaves. Samaras horizontal, frequently underdeveloped, nutlets flattened. Native to mountain forests in southern Italy. Originally described as a separate species by Michele Tenore in 1819. This tree is present in most collections, less common in gardens. It is suitable as a street tree. A seedling of this subspecies with desirable characteristics has been selected and propagated vegetatively under the name *A. cappadocicum* 'Lobel'. Zone 5 (Europe 6)

Acer cappadocicum subsp. *lobelii.* July

Acer cappadocicum 'Rubrum'. July

Acer cappadocicum subsp. *sinicum* var. *sinicum.* June

Acer cappadocicum 'Rubrum'

Synonyms, *A. colchicum* f. *rubrum, A. laetum* f. *rubrum.* Leaves purple when young, later turning dark green. Raised and introduced by Booth Nurseries, Germany, in 1842. Given the Royal Horticultural Society's Award of Garden Merit in 1984. Very similar to *A. cappadocicum* and widely planted in parks and gardens, it is also suitable as a street tree. Zone 5 (Europe 6)

Acer cappadocicum subsp. *sinicum* var. *sinicum*

A tree up to 15 to 20 m (50–66 feet), sometimes wider than high, densely branched, with smooth gray-brown bark. Leaves dis-tinctly smaller than characteristic of *A. cappadocicum,* lobes tending to be caudate, young foliage often attractive purplish red. Flowers many in small corymbs, light yellow, quite decorative. Samaras 3–4 cm (1⅛–1½ inches) long and horizontal, nutlets flat. Native to mountainous regions, 2000–3000 m (6500–9800 feet), of Hubei, Sichuan, and Yunnan Provinces in China. First described (as *A. cultratum*) by Nathaniel Wallich in 1830. Usually present in sizable collections, it is rare in gardens and parks and is not suitable as a street tree. Its morphological characteristics are similar to those of smaller-leaved plants of *A. pictum.* Zone 5 (Europe 6)

Acer cappadocicum subsp. *sinicum* var. *tricaudatum.* June

Acer cappadocicum subsp. *sinicum* var. *tricaudatum*

Synonym, *A. laetum* var. *tricaudatum.* A large shrub or tree up to 15 m (50 feet) or more, wider than high; slender young shoots purplish. Leaves 10–15 cm (4–6 inches) wide, differing from those of its relatives by its three lobes, or with two insignificant outer lobes. Native to Hubei Province in China. Introduced by Veitch Nurseries, England, in 1901 and described by Alfred Rehder. Rare in collections and a tree that needs much space in the garden due to its spreading shape. Zone 5 (Europe 6)

Acer carpinifolium. May, Arboretum Belmonte   *Acer carpinifolium.* October, Arboretum Belmonte

Acer carpinifolium

Section *Indivisa.* A small tree but more often a large shrub up to 10 m (33 feet), rather densely branched, with dark gray bark. Leaves 8–12 cm (3⅛–4¾ inches) long and 4–5 cm (1½–2 inches) wide, shaped like those of a hornbeam, *Carpinus,* unlobed, doubly serrate, turning golden yellow or golden brown in fall. Flowers greenish, plants dioecious. Samaras curved like a bow, nutlets flat and small. Native to Japan where it is widely distributed. Described by Philipp Franz von Siebold and Joseph Gerhard Zuccarini in 1845. Hornbeam maple is a well-known, widely cultivated plant with no close relatives. Common in gardens and parks, even hedgerows could be made of it. It has good fall color. Zone 4 (Europe 5)

Acer carpinifolium 'Esveld Select'

A narrow, almost columnar shrub up to 3 m (10 feet), densely branched. Leaves 4–6 cm (1½–2⅜ inches) long and 3–4 cm (1⅛–1½ inches) wide, narrower and more serrate than those of the species, turning golden brown in fall. Flowers and fruits not seen, even on the original plant after 25 years. Raised and introduced by Firma C. Esveld, Netherlands, in 1978, where it was found in a seedbed of several hundred seedlings. Difficult to propagate, it is rare in cultivation but suitable for small gardens. Zone 4 (Europe 5)

Acer carpinifolium 'Esveld Select'. May

Acer caudatifolium. July, Hof ter Saksen

Acer caudatifolium

Section *Macrantha.* Synonyms, *A. kawaka-mii, A. morrisonense.* A slender tree up to 12 m (39 feet) in its habitat, much smaller in cultivation, with densely packed, thin branches; bark white striped. Leaves 8–15 cm (3⅛–6 inches) long and 4–5 cm (1½–2 inches) wide, ovate, almost unlobed, papery with a long apex, dull green. Flowers somewhat purplish. Samaras small, nutlets about 0.5 cm (³⁄₁₆ inch) long. Native to mountain forests, 2000–3000 m (6500–9800 feet), in Taiwan. First described (as *A. insulare*) by Tomitarō Makino in 1910. Given the Royal Horticultural Society's Award of Merit in 1975 and Award of Garden Merit in 1984. Rare in cultivation, in part because of its tenderness. Zone 7 (Europe 8)

Acer caudatum

Section *Parviflora*, series *Caudata.* Described by Nathaniel Wallich in 1830. Two subspecies are cultivated, *caudatum* and *ukurunduense*.

Acer caudatum subsp. *caudatum.* May, Valley Gardens

Acer caudatum subsp. *caudatum*

Synonym, *A. papilio.* A small tree, often multistemmed, or a large shrub up to 6 to 7 m (20–23 feet); bark dark and smooth, sometimes fissured. Leaves 7–12 cm (2¾–4¾ inches) wide, five-lobed, lobes almost triangular, margins coarsely serrate. Flowers in erect panicles, almost white, plants dioecious. Fruits in racemes about 10 cm (4 inches) long, samaras 3 cm (1½ inches) long, nutlets round. Native to the eastern Himalayas, Myanmar (Upper Burma), Manchuria in China, and northern Japan, where it is abundant in mountainous forests. Widespread and quite common in much of Asia, it is rarely cultivated. There seems to be some sort of barrier that hinders the tree in cultivation. Zone 6 (Europe 7)

Acer caudatum subsp. *ukurunduense*. May, Valley Gardens

Acer caudatum subsp. *ukurunduense*. May, Valley Gardens

Acer caudatum subsp. *ukurunduense*

Synonym, *A. ukurunduense*. A rather narrow tree or treelike shrub up to 7 to 8 m (23–26 feet); bark conspicuously fissured, blackish brown. Leaves 8–12 cm (3⅛–4¾ inches) wide, five-lobed, with coarse serrations and densely tomentose underneath. Flowers in erect panicles, whitish, plants dioecious. Fruits in corymbs, samaras 3–4 cm (1⅛–1½ inches) long. Native from Manchuria to Hubei Province in China, also in Japan on Honshū Island. Originally described as a separate species by Ernst Rudolph von Trautvetter and Carl Anton von Meyer in 1856. It is more frequently cultivated than variety *caudatum* but is still rare. Young shoots and twigs are often a very nice red, later turning gray. Zone 4 (Europe 5)

Acer circinatum

Section *Palmata*, series *Palmata*. A shrub up to 4 to 5 m (13–16 feet) or more, sometimes forming impenetrable thickets; young twigs purplish. Leaves 8–15 cm (3⅛–6 inches) wide, almost round, seven- or nine-lobed, lobes very regular, color often dark gray-green; fall color spectacular. Flowers in small corymbs, purple. Samaras red, horizontal, nutlets flat. Native to British Columbia, Washington, Oregon, and northern California. Described by Friedrich Pursh in 1814. Given the Royal Horticultural Society's Award of Garden Merit in 1933. Vine maple is easily propagated from seed and widely cultivated, especially in the United States. Suitable for woodland gardens, vine maple is famous for its fall color. Zone 4 (Europe 5)

Acer circinatum. October, Savill Gardens

Acer circinatum 'Monroe'

A firm, rounded shrub up to 3 to 4 m (10–13 feet), often wider than high, with stiff, purplish branches. Leaves 6–10 cm (2³⁄₈–4 inches) wide, seven-lobed, deeply incised to the base, turning yellow in fall. Flowers in small umbels, red. Warner Monroe of Portland, Oregon, layered the plant where he found it along the McKenzie River in the Cascade Range of Oregon and brought it into cultivation in 1965; it was named by Brian O. Mulligan, Seattle, Washington. Later propagated by grafting onto *A. palmatum*, it is a rather rare plant. Zone 5 (Europe 6)

Acer circinatum 'Monroe'. May, Herkenrode Gardens

Acer circinatum 'Si yama'. July, courtesy of H. Olsen

Acer circinatum 'Si yama'. August, courtesy of H. Olsen

Acer circinatum 'Si yama'

A small shrub, densely branched, probably a witches'-broom. Leaves about 4 to 5 cm (1½–2 inches) wide, smaller than characteristic of the species. It appears to be valuable for bonsai. Zone 5 (Europe 6)

Acer circinatum 'Victoria'. October, Von Gimborn Arboretum

Acer cissifolium. June, Fratelli Gilardelli

Acer circinatum 'Victoria'

A shrubby plant, similar to the species. Samaras blood-red. Originating as a chance seedling selected from the Von Gimborn Arboretum, named by P. C. de Jong, former director of the arboretum, and introduced by Firma C. Esveld, Netherlands, in 1994. Zone 5 (Europe 6)

Acer cissifolium

Section *Negundo*, series *Cissifolia*. A tree up to 15 m (50 feet) or a large multistemmed shrub; branches gray and smooth, bark dotted with red. Leaves trifoliolate, coarsely serrate at the margins, gray-green or sometimes olive-green. Flowers in dense pendulous panicles, plants dioecious. Fruits in long trusses. Native to forests in Japan from Hokkaidō to Kyūshū Islands. Described by Philipp Franz von Siebold and Joseph Gerhard Zuccarini in 1845. It is common in cultivation. Female trees are available in the nursery trade, propagated by layering. These produce quantities of sterile fruits. *Acer cissifolium* 'Gotenba nishiki' is the only cultivar of the species known to us. Its leaves are dotted with yellow. Zone 5 (Europe 6)

Acer cissifolium. May, Westonbirt Arboretum

Acer cissifolium. October, Arboretum Belmonte

Acer ×conspicuum

Acer ×conspicuum is a garden hybrid, *A. davidii* × *A. pensylvanicum*, both parents belonging to section *Macrantha*. Described by D. M. van Gelderen and H. J. Oterdoom in 1994.

Acer ×conspicuum 'Phoenix'. October

Acer ×conspicuum 'Elephant's Ear'. October, Bulk

Esveld, Netherlands, in 1986. It is suitable for medium-sized gardens and is perhaps the most brilliant of all maples with coral-red branches. Zone 6 (Europe 7)

Acer ×conspicuum 'Elephant's Ear'

A sparsely branched shrub probably up to 8 to 10 m (26–33 feet); bark striped. Leaves 30 cm (12 inches) long when juvenile, smaller on adult branches, almost unlobed or three-lobed. Raised and introduced by R. Bulk Nurseries, Netherlands, in 1990. Difficult to propagate because of the untidy scions needed for grafting, this newer cultivar is not yet readily available. It is suitable for larger gardens. Zone 6 (Europe 7)

Acer ×conspicuum 'Phoenix'

A sparsely branched shrub up to 5 to 6 m (16–20 feet) with brilliant crimson-red branches with white stripes; branches yellowish in summer. Leaves 12–18 cm (4¾–7 inches) long and almost as wide, three-lobed (the lobes often underdeveloped), green, with good yellow fall color. Found as a chance seedling from a batch of 'Silver Vein', raised and introduced by Firma C.

Acer ×conspicuum 'Phoenix'. February

Acer ×*conspicuum* 'Silver Cardinal'. October, Valley Gardens

Acer ×*conspicuum* 'Silver Vein'. May, Herkenrode Gardens

Acer ×*conspicuum* 'Silver Cardinal'

Synonym, *A. rubescens* 'Silver Cardinal'. A shrub up to 4 to 5 m (13–16 feet) with striped bark. Leaves 8–12 cm (3⅛–4¾ inches) long and 5–7 cm (2–2¾ inches) wide, almost unlobed, wrinkled, in part heavily white and pink variegated, many leaves turning green in late summer; fall color yellow-pink. Raised and introduced by the Crown Estate Commissioners, United Kingdom, in 1985. Given the Royal Horticultural Society's Award of Merit in 1985. A rare plant, it is suitable for smaller gardens. It tends to revert to green but after cutting back hard the variegated foliage appears again. Zone 7 (Europe 8)

Acer ×*conspicuum* 'Silver Vein'

Synonym, *Acer* 'Silver Vein'. A tree up to 12 m (39 feet), rarely a shrub, rather sparsely branched; bark conspicuously white striped. Leaves 15–25 cm (6–10 inches) wide, shallowly three- or five-lobed; fall color golden yellow. Flowers in hanging panicles, yellow. Samaras small, nutlets flat. Raised and introduced by Hillier's Nurseries, England, in 1975. One of the best snakebark maples, the stripes remaining visible for many years, this cultivar is still rather uncommon. It is suitable for medium-sized gardens. Zone 6 (Europe 7)

Acer ×*conspicuum* 'Silver Vein'. November, Von Gimborn Arboretum

Acer cordatum. August, Bömer

Acer cordatum

Section *Palmata*, series *Penninervia*. In its habitat a tree or multistemmed shrub up to 10 to 13 m (33–43 feet), much smaller in cultivation, often only 1–2 m (3¼–6½ feet) high. Leaves 6–8 cm (2⅜–3⅛ inches) long and 3–4 cm (1⅛–1½ inches) wide, unlobed, leathery and persistent, glaucous underneath. Flowers very small in reddish corymbs. Samaras 2.5 cm (1 inch) long, spreading at a wide angle. Native to Fujian, Hubei, and Zhejiang Provinces in China. Described by Ferdinand Albin Pax in 1889. This tender maple is extremely rare in cultivation. Hardy in only the most sheltered gardens, it must be treated as a tub plant in most parts of Europe and America. Zone 8 (Europe 9)

Acer ×coriaceum. October, Hillier Gardens and Arboretum

Acer coriaceifolium. October, Bömer

Acer coriaceifolium

Section *Pentaphylla*, series *Trifida*. Synonym, *A. cinnamomifolium*. A tree up to 15 m (50 feet) in its habitat, usually shrubby in cultivation. Leaves 7–12 cm (2¾–4 inches) long and 3–4 cm (1⅛–1½ inches) wide, oblong, unlobed, persistent. Flowers small, cream. Samaras 3–5 cm (1⅛–2 inches) long, obtuse. Native to subtropical areas in Guangxi Autonomous Region and Yunnan Province in China, also in Taiwan. Described by Augustin Abel Hector Léveillé in 1912. Not hardy enough for outdoor cultivation in most areas, it is rare in cultivation and usually must be treated as a tub plant. Zone 8 (Europe 9)

Acer ×coriaceum

A naturally occurring hybrid, *A. monspessulanum* × *A. opalus* subsp. *obtusatum*, both parents belonging to section *Acer*, series *Monspessulana*. A small tree or large shrub up to 8 to 10 m (26–33 feet), rather densely branched; bark dark brown. Leaves 6–10 cm (2⅜–4 inches) long and 4–5 cm (1½–2 inches) wide, broadly ovate, shallowly three-lobed, leathery but not persistent; fall color appearing late in the season, sometimes as late as December. Flowers yellow-green, in corymbs. Fruits rarely produced, samaras 2.5 cm (1 inch) long, diverging less than 60 degrees, usually sterile. Native to Croatia and Bosnia-Herzegovina but probably no longer present in the wild. Described by Louis Augustin Guillaume Bosc and Ignaz Friedrich Tausch in 1829. An unjustly neglected plant that should be planted more often, it is suitable as a medium-sized tree in smaller parks. Zone 5 (Europe 6)

Acer crataegifolium. May, Westonbirt Arboretum

Acer crataegifolium

Section *Macrantha*. A multistemmed tree or densely branched shrub up to 7 to 8 m (23–26 feet) but often less; branches purple with inconspicuous stripes. Leaves 4–7 cm (1½–2¾ inches) long, three-lobed or almost unlobed and leaf margins wavy, dark green to bluish green, bases cordate. Flowers in small panicles, creamy. Samaras 1 cm (⅜ inch) long, nutlets not more than 4 mm (³⁄₁₆ inch) wide. Native to moist regions in central and southern Japan. Described by Philipp Franz von Siebold and Joseph Gerhard Zuccarini in 1845. A somewhat difficult plant to cultivate, this maple is present in many sizable collections and some arboretums but is otherwise rare. It is suitable for smaller gardens. Its leaves bear some similarity to those of hawthorn, *Crataegus*. Variety *macrophyllum* (described by Hiroshi Hara in 1934) differs in its large leaves, to 15 cm (6 inches) long. Zone 6 (Europe 7)

Acer crataegifolium 'Me uri no ōfu'. July

Acer crataegifolium 'Me uri no ōfu'

Alternatively, *A. crataegifolium* 'Me uri no ohfu'. A slow-growing shrublet perhaps up to 2 m (6½ feet) after many years; branchlets and twigs thin and weak. Leaves almost unlobed, dark green with large pink blotches. Introduced by Ishii Yuga, Japan. Outside of Japan it is very rare in cultivation and a collector's item. It is similar to *A. crataegifolium* 'Mikage nishiki', also to 'Veitchii', which seems to be stronger. Zone 6 (Europe 7)

Acer crataegifolium 'Veitchii'

A shrub up to 3 to 4 m (10–13 feet) after many years, densely branched. Leaves 5–7 cm (2–2¾ inches) long, almost unlobed, dark green, white and pink variegated. Described by George Nicholson in 1881. Sometimes present in collections but often difficult to obtain, it has a tendency to revert to unvariegated foliage and such branchlets must be removed. It is also suitable for bonsai. *Acer crataegifolium* 'Eiga nishiki', also a slow-growing plant, is similar with leaves with creamy white margins and dots. Zone 6 (Europe 7)

Acer crataegifolium 'Veitchii'. June

Acer davidii

Section *Macrantha.* Two subspecies are recognized, *davidii* and *grosseri,* in addition to the cultivars, all listed alphabetically.

Acer davidii 'Canton'. July

Acer davidii 'Canton'

Synonym, *A. davidii* 'Cantonspark'. A multistemmed medium-sized tree; bark purplish green with white stripes. Leaves smaller than the average for the species, oval, unlobed, dark green. Raised at the Cantonspark, Baarn, Netherlands, about 1980. An uncommon cultivar, it is more or less fastigiate and suitable for smaller gardens. Zone 6 (Europe 7)

Acer davidii subsp. *davidii*. June, Arboretum Belmonte

Acer davidii subsp. *davidii*. October, Wisley Garden

Acer davidii subsp. davidii

Usually a multistemmed tree up to 10 m (33 feet) or more, rather sparsely branched, growing vigorously when young; bark white striped. Leaves 7–15 cm (2¾–6 inches) long and 3–6 cm (1⅛–2⅜ inches) wide, oval to oblong, unlobed, dark green; juvenile leaves on long, vigorous shoots usually coarsely three-lobed and somewhat larger than adult

oliage. Flowers in long racemose corymbs,
ight yellow, plants monoecious with male
and female flowers usually on different
branches. Fruits numerous, samaras 3 cm
(1⅛ inches) long or shorter, nutlets flat-
ened. Native to mountainous regions up
to 3000 m (9800 feet) in central and western
China, including Hubei, Sichuan, and Yunnan Provinces, in moist situations. Described by Adrien René Franchet in 1885.
Given the Royal Horticultural Society's
Award of Garden Merit in 1984. Easy to
grow, Father David's maple is one of the best
and, together with *A. rufinerve,* one of the
most commonly cultivated snakebark maples. Deserving a place in medium-sized gardens, not all specimens are equally beautiful
and some care is needed in selection (see the
cultivars listed below). Zone 6 (Europe 7)

Acer davidii 'Ernest Wilson'. October, Wisley Garden

Acer davidii 'Ernest Wilson'

A multistemmed medium-sized tree; bark
conspicuously striped. Leaves 7–12 cm
(2¾–4¾ inches) long and 3–6 cm (1⅛–2⅜
inches) wide, oval to oblong, unlobed,
green. Named by J. Keenan in 1957, the
original tree has been grown at the Royal
Botanic Garden, Edinburgh, since 1907. A
good specimen started from seed collected
by Charles Maries in Hubei Province,
China, is present in the Westonbirt Arboretum, England. Rather common in cultivation but there are seedlings in the nursery
trade under this name that, of course, are
not all identical. It is suitable for medium-
sized gardens. Zone 6 (Europe 7)

Acer davidii 'George Forrest'. July

Acer davidii 'George Forrest'

Often a multistemmed medium-sized tree;
good, striped bark, young shoots purplish.
Leaves 10–20 cm (4–8 inches) long and 6–9
cm (2⅜–3½ inches) wide, larger than those
of 'Ernest Wilson', oval to oblong, unlobed,
reddish when unfolding, green later. Named
by J. Keenan in 1957, grown at the Royal
Botanic Garden, Edinburgh, from a batch
of seeds collected by George Forrest. Given
the Royal Horticultural Society's Award of
Garden Merit in 1983. Not to be confused
with *A. pectinatum* subsp. *forrestii,* 'George
Forrest' is not frequently seen although
there were seedlings of this cultivar available in the nursery trade in previous years.
Zone 6 (Europe 7)

Acer davidii subsp. *grosseri*. September, Arboretum Belmonte

Acer davidii subsp. *grosseri*. July, Arboretum Belmonte

Acer davidii subsp. *grosseri*

Synonyms, *A. grosseri*, *A. grosseri* var. *hersii*, *A. hersii*. A multistemmed shrubby tree up to 12 m (39 feet) or occasionally more; good, striped bark, the white stripes remaining visible for many years. Leaves 7–10 cm (2¾–4 inches) wide, almost triangular, three-lobed, doubly serrate, glabrous but juvenile leaves may be slightly pubescent. Flowers in pendulous racemes, light yellow, plants monoecious, male and female flowers appearing on different branches. Samaras about 2 cm (¾ inch) long, nutlets small. Native to Hunan, Shaanxi, and Sichuan Provinces in northern and central China. Originally described as a separate species by Ferdinand Albin Pax in 1902. Given the Royal Horticultural Society's Award of Garden Merit (as *A. grosseri* var. *hersii*) in 1993. Common in cultivation but often labeled with one of the synonymous names. A good plant for larger gardens and parks, usually with beautiful yellow and orange-red fall color, but beware of hybrid seedlings. Zone 6 (Europe 7)

Acer davidii 'Hagelunie'. March

Acer davidii 'Hagelunie'

A sparsely branched shrubby tree up to 10 m (33 feet); bark purple to dark green with conspicuous white stripes. Juvenile leaves coarsely serrate. Raised and introduced by Firma C. Esveld, Netherlands, in 1992, and named for Hagelunie, a company insuring horticultural enterprises against damage by hail. It was distributed as a corporate gift and thus is present in Dutch gardens on a limited scale. Zone 6 (Europe 7)

Acer davidii 'Karmen'. April

Acer davidii 'Karmen'. April

Acer davidii 'Karmen'

An openly branched treelike shrub up to 10 to 12 m (33–39 feet); bark conspicuously white striped. Leaves 8–20 cm (3⅛–8 inches) long and 4–6 cm (1½–2⅛ inches) wide, narrowly oblong, unlobed or sometimes with small lobes when young, chocolate-brown, later turning reddish green; fall color yellow to orange. Flowers in drooping corymbs to 15 cm (6 inches) long, light yellow. The original plant was discovered in a garden by P. C. de Jong about 1975; introduced by Firma C. Esveld, Netherlands, in 1985, and named for Karmen Rosalie van Gelderen, daughter and granddaughter of the authors of the present book. It is a beautiful plant suitable for parks and larger gardens. Zone 6 (Europe 7)

Acer davidii 'Madeline Spitta'

A densely branched shrubby tree up to 10 m (33 feet) or maybe more; bark green with white stripes. Leaves oblong to oval, sometimes with small lobes, shiny green. Flowers in extremely long, pendulous corymbs, light yellow or greenish. Samaras to 3 cm (1⅛ inches) long, nutlets small. Introduced by Wilfred Fox, founder of the Winkworth Arboretum, England, in 1950 and named for Mrs. Spitta, who was involved in planning the arboretum. It is a beautiful plant that has been unjustly neglected. Zone 6 (Europe 7)

Acer davidii 'Madeline Spitta'. June

Acer davidii 'Purple Bark'. January *Acer davidii* 'Purple Bark'. August

Acer davidii 'Rosalie'. March

Acer davidii 'Purple Bark'

Synonym, *A. grosseri* 'Purple Bark'. A shrub up to 6 to 8 m (20–26 feet); bark purple in winter, with white stripes. Leaves three-lobed as in subspecies *grosseri*. Flowers in small but numerous corymbs, pendulous, yellow-green. Raised and introduced by J. van Alphen, Netherlands, in 1988. Rare, this shrub is very attractive in winter with its conspicuous purple bark; its compact habit makes it suitable for medium-sized gardens. Zone 6 (Europe 7)

Acer davidii 'Rosalie'

A well-branched shrubby tree up to 10 m (33 feet); bark purplish in winter, bright green in summer, beautifully white striped, the stripes remaining on the branches for many years. Leaves 6–15 cm (2⅜–6 inches) long and 3–5 cm (1⅛–2 inches) wide, smaller than in most cultivars of the species, oblong; fall color usually golden yellow. Flowers in corymbs about 7 to 10 cm (2¾–4 inches) long, greenish yellow. Few fruits usually produced. Raised and introduced by Firma C. Esveld, Netherlands, in 1985 and named for Karmen Rosalie van Gelderen, daughter and granddaughter of the authors of the present book. It is one of the nicest snakebark maples for medium-sized gardens. Zone 6 (Europe 7)

Acer davidii 'Serpentine'. July

Acer diabolicum. May, Westonbirt Arboretum

Acer davidii 'Serpentine'

A densely branched shrub distinctly smaller than most cultivars of *A. davidii*; bark purplish green, branches nicely striped. Leaves to 10 cm (4 inches) long, small for *A. davidii*, oblong to oval; fall color yellow to orange. Flowers in small, dense corymbs, yellow. Fruits abundant, samaras to 2 cm (¾ inch) long, nutlets small. Discovered as a chance seedling in a nursery in Boskoop, Netherlands, raised, and introduced by W. J. Hooftman in 1976. Awarded a Silver Medal at the Flora Nova exhibition in Boskoop in 1976 and given the Royal Horticultural Society's Award of Garden Merit in 1993. Readily available in the nursery trade, it is a good plant for smaller gardens. It resembles what might be an intermediate hybrid between *A. davidii* and *A. crataegifolium* but the latter was not present in the nursery and seedlings of 'Serpentine' develop true to the cultivar or nearly so. Zone 6 (Europe 7)

Acer diabolicum. July

Acer diabolicum

Section *Lithocarpa*, series *Lithocarpa*. A tree with stout branches, in favorable conditions up to 15 m (50 feet) or more but usually much smaller; bark gray-brown and rather smooth. Leaves 10–20 cm (4–8 inches) wide, five-lobed, lobes broadly ovate with a few large teeth, cordate at the base and rather stiff when mature. Flowers yellow, males with dark red stamens, plants dioecious. Samaras 4 cm (1½ inches) long, nutlets round and hard with two hornlike persistent styles attached. Native to mountain forests in open sunny areas in Japan, but not on Hokkaidō or northern Honshū Islands. Described by Carl Ludwig Blume and Karl Koch in 1864, introduced into Britain by Charles Maries in 1880. Devil's maple or horned maple, as it is called, is present in many sizable collections but otherwise is rarely cultivated and difficult to obtain in the nursery trade. It is suitable for larger gardens. The form *purpurascens*, with purplish young foliage, is not recognized as taxonomically distinct. *Acer diabolicum* 'Nagashima' is the only cultivar of the species known to us; its leaves are dotted with yellow. Zone 5 (Europe 6)

Acer distylum. August

Acer distylum

Section *Parviflora*, series *Distyla*. A treelike shrub up to 10 m (33 feet) in favorable conditions, often much smaller, well branched; bark somewhat corky. Leaves to 15 cm (6 inches) long and 5–8 cm (2–3⅛ inches) wide, ovate, not lobed, deeply cordate at the base and apex acuminate, resembling those of a linden, *Tilia*; leaves pinkish when juvenile, gray-green when mature; fall color yellow. Flowers in erect spikes, greenish white. Fruits sometimes nodding because of the weight of the nutlets. Native to northern part of Honshū Island in Japan. Described by Philipp Franz von Siebold and Joseph Gerhard Zuccarini in 1845, introduced by Charles Maries in 1879 for the nursery, Messrs J. H. Veitch & Sons, England. One of the most unusual maples, linden-leaved maple can be propagated

from seed but usually with limited success. A rare small tree, it is a collector's item. There is one cultivar in Japan, 'Angyō no sato' (alternatively, 'Angyoh no sato'), yet to be introduced into Europe or America. Its leaves are dotted with yellow. Zone 6 (Europe 7)

Acer ×durettii. July

Acer ×durettii

A garden hybrid, probably *A. opalus* × *A. monspessulanum*, both parents belonging to section *Acer*, series *Monspessulana*. A small or medium-sized tree up to 10 to 12 m (33–39 feet); bark smooth, brown-gray. Leaves 6–10 cm (2⅜–4 inches) long and 5–12 cm (2–4¾ inches) wide, somewhat leathery, three- or five-lobed, lobes large and triangular. Flowers in stalked racemes, greenish. Described by Ferdinand Albin Pax in 1893. The only mature specimen known to us grows in the Arboretum des Barres, France. Zone 5 (Europe 6)

Acer elegantulum

Section *Palmata*, series *Sinensia*. In its habitat a tree up to 15 m (50 feet), in cultivation much smaller, probably not more than 5 m (16 feet), rather densely branched, similar to *A. campbellii* and its other relatives. Leaves 7–10 cm (2¾–4 inches) wide, thin and somewhat papery, five-lobed, basal lobes much smaller than the others, leaf color light purple when unfolding, becoming green when fully mature. Flowers green. Samaras 2–3 cm (¾–1⅛ inches) long, brownish yel-

Acer elegantulum. May, Westonbirt Arboretum

low, nutlets swollen. Native to Jiangxi and Zhejiang Provinces in China. Described by Fang Wen-pei and Chiu Pao-ling in 1979 and introduced into Europe about 1990 through seeds supplied courtesy of Wang Dajun, former curator of the Long Wu Lu Botanic Gardens, Shanghai. Rare in cultivation, it is rather tender. Zone 7 (Europe 8)

Acer fabri. May, greenhouse

Acer erianthum. June

Acer erianthum

Section *Palmata*, series *Sinensia*. Usually a shrub, occasionally a tree up to 8 to 9 m (26–30 feet); young branches olive-green with small whitish dots. Leaves 8–12 cm (3⅛–4¾ inches) wide, texture thin and papery, seven-lobed, lobes triangular; leaf underside with white tufts of hair. Flowers in slender tomentose panicles, yellowish. Samaras to 3 cm (1⅛ inches) long, in cultivation often deformed, nutlets firm, glabrous. Native to mountainous regions, 1500–2500 m (4900–8200 feet), of Guangxi Autonomous Region and Hubei and Sichuan Provinces in China. Described by Fritz Graf von Schwerin in 1901 and introduced to Britain in 1907 by Charles Maries. It is of botanical interest but is not a very successful plant in cultivation. Its leaves tend to shrivel in the sun and there is almost no fall color. Zone 6 (Europe 7)

Acer fabri

Section *Palmata*, series *Penninervia*. Synonym, *A. fargesii*. In its habitat a tree up to 20 m (66 feet) but much smaller in cultivation; branches and shoots reddish, turning green. Leaves to 15 cm (6 inches) long and 3–4 cm (1⅛–1½ inches) wide oblong, unlobed, margins finely serrated or entire, shiny dark green, persistent. Flowers white and purple. Samaras to 3 cm (1⅛ inches) long, nutlets rounded. Native to Guangxi Autonomous Region and Guangdong, Hainan, Hubei, and Sichuan Provinces in China. Described by Henry Fletcher Hance in 1884. Able to be cultivated only in the mildest localities, it is grown mainly as a greenhouse plant and then as a collector's item. It can be confused with *A. laevigatum* but that species has leaves with entire margins, not serrate and undulate as usual in *A. fabri*. Zone 7 (Europe 8)

Acer ×freemanii 'Autumn Blaze'. June, Fratelli Gilardelli

Acer glabrum

Section *Glabra,* series *Glabra.* Described by John Torrey in 1828. Two subspecies are cultivated, *douglasii* and *glabrum.*

Acer glabrum subsp. *douglasii.* August, courtesy of J. R. P. van Hoey Smith

Acer ×freemanii 'Autumn Blaze'

Acer ×freemanii a garden hybrid, *A. saccharinum* × *A. rubrum,* both parents belonging to section *Rubra,* hybridized by Oliver M. Freeman in 1933 and named by A. E. Murray in 1969. 'Autumn Blaze' a tree up to 20 to 25 m (66–82 feet), usually with a dense crown. Leaves intermediate between those of parents, 10–20 cm (4–8 inches) wide, deeply dissected, color fresh green; fall color good. Flowers yellow. Fruits sterile, samaras 3–5 cm (1⅛–2 inches) long. Named by Jeffers, Ohio. Common as a street tree, it is also good for large parks. It is too large for the average garden. *Acer ×freemanii* 'Celzam' (synonym, Celebration, trademark name) is almost identical to *A. saccharinum,* which is one of the parents of *A. ×freemanii,* and *A. ×freemanii* 'Elegant' (synonym, *A. saccharinum* 'Elegant') is very similar to *A. saccharinum* 'Laciniatum Wieri'. Zone 5 (Europe 6)

Acer glabrum subsp. *douglasii*

Synonym, *A. douglasii.* A shrub or treelike shrub up to 6 m (20 feet); young shoots attractively reddish, later turning brown. Leaves 5–10 cm (2–4 inches) wide, three- or five-lobed (the lobes often underdeveloped) or almost subtrifoliolate, dark green; fall color yellow. Flowers in terminal corymbs, yellow-green, plants usually dioecious. Samaras larger than those of subspecies *glabrum,* nutlets small. Native to mountainous areas of western North America, from Alaska to southern Oregon, east to Alberta, Canada. Originally described as a separate species by William Jackson Hooker in 1847. It is more commonly cultivated in western America than in eastern America or Europe, where it does poorly. Zone 4 (Europe 5)

Acer glabrum subsp. *glabrum*. June

Acer glabrum subsp. *glabrum*

A large shrub or occasionally a tree up to 8 to 10 m (26–33 feet); young shoots and stems purplish red, later turning gray. Leaves three- or five-lobed, outer lobes sometimes underdeveloped, or subtrifoliolate, color light green, leaves dropping early in fall. Flowers in terminal corymbs, yellow. Samaras erect, 3–5 cm (1⅛–2 inches) long. Native to the Rocky Mountains in North America and the Black Hills, South Dakota. More commonly cultivated in America, less so in Europe, Rocky Mountain maple fares better in a continental rather than a maritime climate. Zone 4 (Europe 5)

Acer griseum

Section *Trifoliata*, series *Grisea*. A slender tree, sometimes multistemmed, up to 15 m (50 feet); bark an attractive papery orange-brown, peeling off. Leaves trifoliolate, leaflets 3–8 cm (1⅛–3⅛ inches) long, incised or lobulate, dark green above, light gray-green underneath; fall color beautiful orange, red, and yellow. Flowers yellow, plants usually monoecious. Samaras to 5 cm (2 inches) long, nutlets woody and usually empty, the parthenocarpic tendency strong. Native to China, including the provinces of Anhui, Guizhou, Hubei, Shaanxi, and Sichuan, but trees scattered and by no means common. Originally described (as *A. nikoense* var. *griseum*) by Adrien René Franchet in 1894 and introduced by Ernest Henry Wilson in 1901. Given the Royal Horticultural Society's Award of Merit in 1922 and Award of Garden Merit in 1984. One of the nicest of all maples and now generally available,

Acer griseum. June, Villa Taranto

Acer griseum. November

paperbark maple deserves still more attention as it is very easy to handle in any garden. Zone 4 (Europe 5)

Acer griseum. June, Villa Taranto

Acer heldreichii

Section *Acer,* series *Acer.* Described by Theodoros Georgios Orphanides and Pierre Edmond Boissier in 1856. Two subspecies are recognized, *heldreichii* and *trautvetteri.*

Acer heldreichii subsp. *heldreichii.* July

Acer heldreichii subsp. heldreichii

A large tree up to 15 to 20 m (50–66 feet) with a smooth trunk with few fissures; branches dark gray, buds almost black. Leaves 15 cm (6 inches) wide, three- or five-lobed, deeply incised, almost to the base, shiny dark green, somewhat papery; petioles usually red. Flowers in large terminal corymbs, yellow. Samaras to 5 cm (2 inches) long, obtusely angled, nutlets 0.7 cm (¼ inch) wide. Native to northern Greece, Albania, Serbia, Bosnia-Herzegovina, and Bulgaria, mainly in low mountains, and also forming forests. This Balkan maple is present in most collections but rarely grown to its full ornamental value. Subspecies *heldreichii* is easily confused with subspecies *trautvetteri. Acer heldreichii* also hybridizes easily with *A. pseudoplatanus,* another member of section *Acer,* series *Acer,* with which it overlaps in distribution. Such hybrids are called *A. ×pseudoheldreichii,* described by P. Fukarek and A. Celjo in 1959. Zone 6 (Europe 7)

Acer heldreichii subsp. *trautvetteri*

Synonym, *A. trautvetteri*. A tree up to 20 m (66 feet), occasionally more, with a smooth trunk but sometimes slightly fissured branches; shoots brown-gray. Leaves 8–15 cm (3⅛–6 inches) wide, five-lobed, divided almost to the base, dark green, margins toothed, petioles usually fiery red. Flowers in large erect terminal corymbs, yellow. Samaras 6–7 cm (2⅜–2¾ inches) long, at an obtuse angle, nutlets hard. Native to northern Turkey and the Caucasus. Discovered by Gustav Ferdinand Richard Johannes Radde in 1864, introduced in 1866, and eventually described as a separate species by Jakov S. Medvedev in 1880. Present in most sizable collections, red-bud maple is otherwise rare in cultivation. Zone 5 (Europe 6)

Acer heldreichii subsp. *trautvetteri*. May, Westonbirt Arboretum

Acer henryi

Section *Negundo*, series *Cissifolia*. Synonym, *A. cissifolium* subsp. *henryi*. A tree up to 10 m (33 feet) and as wide, more frequently a large shrub, with brownish green shoots, turning darker when mature; shoots slightly tomentose. Leaves trifoliolate, leaflets 5–10 cm (2–4 inches) long, margins serrate or entire, bluish green to olive-green, petioles to 10 cm (4 inches) long; juvenile leaves coarsely serrate, similar to those of *A. cissifolium*. Flowers in slender spikes, almost white, plants dioecious. Samaras in drooping racemes, 2 cm (¾ inch) long, nutlets flat, usually sterile. Native to central China, mainly Hubei and Sichuan Provinces. Described by Ferdinand Albin Pax in 1889. Rare in cultivation, some plants labeled as such are actually *A. cissifolium*, which is much more common. It has also been confused with *A. sutchuenense*, which is not in cultivation in the Western world. The true species is a collector's item. Zone 6 (Europe 7)

Acer henryi. September, Hof ter Saksen

Acer ×hillieri 'Summergold'

Acer ×hillieri a garden hybrid, *A. miyabei* × *A. cappadocicum* 'Aureum', both parents belonging to section *Platanoidea*. Described by Roy Lancaster in 1979. 'Summergold' a tree up to 8 to 10 m (26–33 feet) with a crown wider than high. Leaves 10–20 cm (4–8 inches) wide, seven-lobed, deeply cordate, glabrous above, slightly pubescent underneath; summer color golden yellow.

Acer ×hillieri 'Summergold'. May, Valley Gardens

Flowers in small corymbs, creamy yellow. Samaras spreading at a wide angle, nutlets pubescent. Introduced by R. A. and W. L. Banks, Hergest Croft Gardens, England, and named by Roy Lancaster in 1979. A tree with green foliage was found at the Sir Harold Hillier Gardens and Arboretum, England. It had been raised from a packet of seeds sent from the Royal Botanic Gardens, Kew, that proved to be of hybrid origin. The yellow-leaved tree came from the same batch. Useful for larger gardens, this tree deserves more attention. *Acer ×hillieri* 'West Hill', a medium-sized tree with dull green leaves, is the green counterpart to 'Summergold'. Zone 6 (Europe 7)

Acer hyrcanum

Section *Acer*, series *Monspessulana*. Described by Friedrich Ernst Ludwig von Fischer and Carl Anton von Meyer in 1837. Seven subspecies are currently recognized, *hyrcanum*, *intermedium*, *keckianum*, *reginae-amaliae*, *sphaerocarpum*, *stevenii*, and *tauricolum*, but the knowledge of the subspecies is full of gaps. Few plants are in cultivation and when more material becomes available it is possible that some names will be sunk into synonymy.

Acer ×hybridum. July

Acer hyrcanum subsp. *hyrcanum.* May, Westonbirt Arboretum

Acer ×hybridum

Perhaps a garden hybrid within section *Acer*, *A. opalus × A. monspessulanum*, both parents belonging to series *Monspessulana*, or *A. opalus × A. pseudoplatanus*, the latter belonging to series *Acer*. A tree up to 15 m (50 feet) with a bold, rounded crown; branches and shoots dark brownish. Leaves 4–10 cm (1½–4 inches) wide, three-lobed, unevenly toothed with rounded lobes, somewhat leathery, dark green, glaucous underneath. Flowers in pendulous racemes, cream. Samaras connivent, nutlets round, usually sterile. Described by Louis Augustin Guillaume Bosc in 1821. This maple may not be a hybrid but rather an odd expression of *A. opalus* or *A. pseudoplatanus*. An old tree is present in Arboretum des Barres, France. Zone 4 (Europe 5)

Acer hyrcanum subsp. hyrcanum

A tree, sometimes a large multistemmed shrub up to 12 m (39 feet), occasionally more, densely branched. Leaves 3–10 cm (1⅛–4 inches) wide, five-lobed, very variable, dark green above and glaucous underneath. Flowers in short corymbs, yellow. Samaras erect to connivent, 3 cm (1⅛ inches) long, nutlets rounded. Native to forests in mountainous regions in the Balkans in Europe, also in Turkey and western Iran. Not a great beauty, this Balkan maple is mainly a collector's item and is seldom seen in cultivation outside botanical gardens. There is a large specimen in the Westonbirt Arboretum, England. Zone 5 (Europe 6)

Acer hyrcanum subsp. *intermedium.* July

Acer hyrcanum subsp. *keckianum.* June

Acer hyrcanum subsp. *intermedium*

Synonym, *A. hyrcanum* var. *cordisectum.* A densely branched shrub up to 5 to 6 m (16–20 feet); branches brown. Leaves 3–8 cm (1⅛–3⅛ inches) wide, usually larger than those of subspecies *hyrcanum*; five-lobed; fall color usually brownish yellow. Native to lower mountainous areas in the central Balkans. Originally described as a separate species by Josef Pančić in 1871. The main difference from subspecies *hyrcanum* is the color of the underside of the leaf, which is bluish in subspecies *intermedium*. It is a rare plant in cultivation, of interest only to collectors. Zone 5 (Europe 6)

Acer hyrcanum subsp. *keckianum*

Synonym, *A. hyrcanum* f. *tomentellum.* A shrubby plant up to 4 to 5 m (13–16 feet) with firm and stout branches. Leaves 6–8 cm (2⅜–3⅛ inches) wide, large for the species, shallowly five-lobed. Originally described by Ferdinand Albin Pax in 1893. It is unusual and rare in cultivation. Zone 6 (Europe 7)

Acer hyrcanum subsp. *reginae-amaliae*

Synonym, *A. reginae-amaliae.* A densely branched shrub up to 3 to 4 m (10–13 feet) with many thin shoots. Leaves about 1 cm (⅜ inch) long, very small, the smallest in the genus, five-lobed with slightly serrate margins. Native to dry and stony areas in Greece and western Turkey. Originally described as a separate species by Theodoros Georgios Orphanides and Pierre Edmond Boissier in 1853. Rare in collections and almost never available in the nursery trade, it is a collector's item. Zone 6 (Europe 7)

Acer hyrcanum subsp. *reginae-amaliae.* July

Acer hyrcanum subsp. *sphaerocarpum*. June, Kasnak, Turkey, courtesy of J. R. P. van Hoey Smith

Acer hyrcanum subsp. *sphaerocarpum*

A densely branched shrub probably up to 4 to 6 m (13–20 feet). Leaves to 5 cm (2 inches) wide, three-lobed, margins entire. Samaras small. Native to southern Turkey. Described by Faik Yaltirik in 1967. Zone 6 (Europe 7)

Acer hyrcanum subsp. *stevenii*. July

Acer hyrcanum subsp. *stevenii*

Synonym, *A. stevenii*. A shrubby tree not more than 5 m (16 feet) high. Leaves five-lobed, the central lobe prominent, color dark bluish green above, paler underneath. Native to a small woodland area in the Ai Petri Mountains, Crimea, Ukraine. Originally described as a separate species by An-

tonia I. Pojarkova in 1933. Rare in nature, also in cultivation, it is of interest primarily to collectors. Zone 6 (Europe 7)

Acer hyrcanum subsp. *tauricolum*. June, Kasnak, Turkey, courtesy of J. R. P. van Hoey Smith

Acer hyrcanum subsp. *tauricolum*

Synonym, *A. tauricolum*. A small tree or a large shrub up to 6 m (20 feet), densely branched. Leaves 5–10 cm (2–4 inches) wide, five-lobed, deeply incised, shiny dark green, somewhat leathery. Native to the Anti-Taurus Mountains of Turkey, western Syria, and Lebanon. Originally described as a separate species by Pierre Edmond Boissier and Benjamin Balansa in 1856. Rarely cultivated, it is a collector's item. Zone 6 (Europe 7)

Acer japonicum

Section *Palmata*, series *Palmata*. A shrubby tree in cultivation, up to 10 to 12 m (33–39 feet) in favorable locations; branches dark gray-brown, smooth, not sticky. Leaves 8–15 cm (3⅛–6 inches) wide, roundish, seven- or nine- (or eleven-) lobed, lobes incised to half the diameter of the leaf, margins serrate. Flowers attractive in long, drooping corymbs, purplish red, appearing before the leaves. Samaras about 3 cm (1⅛ inches) long, always hanging under the leaves, never erect. Native to mountain forests in Japan, including all of Honshū Island and large parts of Hokkaidō Island. Described by Carl Peter Thunberg and Johan

Acer japonicum. October, Valley Gardens

Andreas Murray in 1784. Cultivars of this Japanese maple are present in almost every maple collection. The cultivars are difficult to identify because of their close resemblance to seedlings of the species. The fall color of *A. japonicum* is splendid, turning all shades of red, orange, and yellow. Zone 6 (Europe 7)

Acer japonicum 'Aconitifolium'

Synonyms, *A. japonicum* 'Filicifolium', 'Laciniatum', 'Parsonsii', 'Veitchii'. A sparsely branched shrubby tree up to 10 m (33 feet) or more, tall and wide in favorable conditions. Leaves 10–20 cm (4–8 inches) wide, palmate, seven- to eleven-lobed, deeply incised to the base, each lobe serrulate. Flowers even redder than those of the species. Fruits not profusely set as in the species. Originally described as a botanical form by Thomas Meehan in 1888. Given the Royal Horticultural Society's Award of Garden Merit in 1984. Suitable for larger rather than smaller gardens, this frequently planted cultivar has splendid fall color. *Acer japonicum* 'Kujaku nishiki', with some white spots on the leaves, is similar. Zone 5 (Europe 6)

Acer japonicum 'Aconitifolium'. May, Herkenrode Gardens

Acer japonicum 'Aconitifolium'. October, Valley Gardens

Acer japonicum 'Attaryi'. October

Acer japonicum 'Dissectum'. May

Acer japonicum 'Attaryi'

An openly branched treelike shrub up to 10 m (33 feet) or more; branches dark brown-gray. Leaves 15–30 cm (6–12 inches) wide, larger than those of 'Aconitifolium', almost round, seven- or nine-lobed, deeply cleft almost to the leaf base. Flowers pendulous, purplish red. Introduced by J. D. Vertrees, Oregon, before 1965. Originally grown by Vertrees under the name 'Aconitifolium' but later found to be identical to 'Attaryi', which until then had mistakenly been identified as a cultivar of *A. sieboldianum*. 'Attaryi' is probably more commonly cultivated in the United States than in Europe, where it is found only in major collections. Zone 5 (Europe 6)

Acer japonicum 'Dissectum'

A spreading shrub not more than 2 m (6½ feet) high but perhaps to 8 to 10 m (26–33 feet) wide. Leaves seven- or nine-lobed, deeply incised as in 'Aconitifolium', color fresh green. Flowers in small hanging corymbs, purplish. Found in the Botanical Garden Kolding, Denmark, before 1959. Needing a lot of space, this cultivar is similar to the better known 'Green Cascade' in its fall color but its leaves are somewhat larger. Zone 5 (Europe 6)

Acer japonicum 'Green Cascade'

A spreading shrub not much more than 1 m (3¼ feet) high but much wider. Leaves similar in shape to 'Aconitifolium' but smaller, seven- or nine-lobed, deeply incised almost to the leaf base, color fresh dark green.

Acer japonicum 'Green Cascade'. June

Flowers in small pendulous corymbs, purple-red. Raised and introduced by Arthur Wright, Oregon, in 1955. This cultivar is like *A. japonicum* 'Dissectum' but is even more spreading if not staked to form a small tree with pendulous branches. Fall color is very good: red, orange, and yellow. *Acer japonicum* 'Fairy Lights', an Australian introduction, has even more finely dissected leaves. Zone 5 (Europe 6)

Acer japonicum 'Green Cascade'. October

Acer japonicum 'Meigetsu'. July

Acer japonicum 'Meigetsu'

A sparsely branched treelike shrub up to 10 m (33 feet); branches brown-gray. Leaves 8–15 cm (3⅛–6 inches) wide, seven- or nine-lobed, lobes serrulate. It is a handsome plant suitable for medium-sized gardens. 'Meigetsu' the cultivar of *A. japonicum* is not to be confused with *meigetsu,* the Japanese word for the species *A. japonicum. Acer japonicum* 'Aka omote', the young leaves of which are bronze when unfolding, is similar to 'Meigetsu'. Zone 5 (Europe 6)

Acer japonicum 'Mikasa yama'

A shrub up to 5 to 6 m (16–20 feet). Leaves 7–15 cm (2¾–6 inches) wide, seven- or nine-lobed, fresh green, margins serrate. Origin Japanese. 'Mikasa yama' is a somewhat smaller-leaved cultivar, and rare. Zone 5 (Europe 6)

Acer japonicum 'Mikasa yama'. May, Valley Gardens

Acer japonicum 'Ō isami'. May, Herkenrode Gardens

Acer japonicum 'Ōtaki'. October, Valley Gardens

Acer japonicum 'Ō isami'

Alternatively, *A. japonicum* 'Oh isami'. A sparsely branched, open, shrubby tree up to 10 m (33 feet) and almost as wide; branches gray-brown. Leaves nine- or eleven-lobed, almost round, incised to half the blade, dark green, olive-green when young. Flowers in hanging corymbs, purplish red. Described by Gen'ichi Koidzumi in 1911. It is frequently present in major maple collections and differs from the species in its habit and the color of the young foliage. Zone 5 (Europe 6)

Acer japonicum 'Ōtaki'

Alternatively, *A. japonicum* 'Ohtaki'. A sturdy, usually not treelike shrub up to 5 m (16 feet) and 3–4 m (10–13 feet) wide. Leaves 8–12 cm (3⅛–4¾ inches) wide, almost round, nine- or eleven-lobed, divided to half the blade, margins serrulate, dark green. Flowers in small corymbs, purplish. Origin Japanese. It is a good plant for large gardens. Rare in cultivation, it is occasionally available in the nursery trade and should be planted more often. Fall color is usually spectacular. Zone 5 (Europe 6)

Acer japonicum 'Taki no gawa'

A sparsely branched treelike shrub or tree up to 10 to 15 m (33–50 feet) with brown-gray branches. Leaves seven- or nine- (or eleven-) lobed, divided to half the blade, green; fall color splendid. Flowers in drooping corymbs, purplish red. Origin Japanese. Not to be confused with *A. palmatum* 'Taki no gawa'. *Acer japonicum* 'Taki no gawa' needs a lot of space for good results. It is similar if not identical to *A. japonicum* 'Meigetsu'. Zone 5 (Europe 6)

Acer japonicum 'Vitifolium'

A shrubby tree up to 10 to 15 m (33–50 feet); bark smooth, gray-brown. Leaves seven- or nine- (or eleven-) lobed, somewhat more deeply divided than those of the species, just over half the blade; fall color orange-yellow. Flowers in drooping corymbs, purplish. Introduced by N. E. Brown,

Acer japonicum 'Taki no gawa'. July

Acer japonicum 'Vitifolium'. October, Westonbirt Arboretum

3ritain, in 1876. Given the Royal Horticul-
:ural Society's First Class Certificate in
1974 and Award of Garden Merit in 1984.
One of the most impressive and common
apanese maples, differences from the spe-
:ies are minor and, according to Krüss-
nann, *Manual of Cultivated Broad-leaved
Trees & Shrubs*, many trees labeled 'Viti-
'olium' are in fact simply *A. japonicum*. It
nas brilliant fall color: red, orange, and yel-
.ow. 'Vitifolium' is difficult if not often impossible to distinguish from *A. japonicum*
'Meigetsu' or 'Taki no gawa'. *Acer japon-
!cum* 'Tsukikage' (meaning "moonlight")
nas dull yellow-green leaves the shape of
:hose of 'Vitifolium'. Zone 5 (Europe 6)

Acer japonicum 'Vitifolium'. May, Valley Gardens

Acer laevigatum

Section *Palmata*, series *Penninervia*. A small
tree in cultivation, much larger in its habitat where it reaches 12–15 m (39–50 feet);
branches smooth, olive-green. Leaves 8–15
cm (3⅛–6 inches) long and 3–5 cm (1⅛–2
inches) wide, leathery and persistent but
dropping leaves in bad conditions such as
frost at –5°C (23°F), unlobed, margins entire
or slightly serrulate, especially on juvenile
leaves. Flowers terminal, yellow. Samaras
4–7 cm (1½–2¾ inches) long, purplish.
Native to mountainous regions in Nepal
through southeastern China to Hong Kong,

Acer laevigatum. May, greenhouse

usually solitary. Described by Nathaniel Wallich in 1830. It is one of the better-known species of series *Penninervia* yet rare even in maple collections because it is too tender for most locations. It may be confused with *A. fabri,* differing from that maple mainly in its serrulate margins. Zone 7 (Europe 8)

Acer longipes

Section *Platanoidea.* Described by Adrien René Franchet and Alfred Rehder in 1905. Three subspecies are cultivated, *amplum, catalpifolium,* and *longipes.*

Acer laurinum. September, Hortus Haren, courtesy of J. R. P. van Hoey Smith

Acer longipes subsp. *amplum.* May, Herkenrode Gardens

Acer laurinum

Section *Hyptiocarpa.* Synonym, *A. javanicum.* A small shrubby tree in cultivation, in its habitat a tree up to 30 m (100 feet). Leaves 9–15 cm (3½–6 inches) long and 5–8 cm (2–3⅛ inches) wide, unlobed, evergreen and dark green. Flowers yellow, plants dioecious. Fruits erect, samaras 3–7 cm (1⅛–2¾ inches) long. Native to mountainous regions, 1000–1500 m (3300–4900 feet), in Indonesia, Malaysia, Myanmar (Upper Burma), Hainan Province in China, and the Philippines. Originally described (as *A. javanicum*) by Franz Wilhelm Junghuhn in 1842. A plant cultivated in the Netherlands for several years was killed in the winter of 1991. Another specimen from a tropical greenhouse was transplanted but did not survive the operation. The species is probably extinct in cultivation. Zone 8 (Europe 9)

Acer longipes subsp. *amplum*

Synonyms, *A. amplum, A. cappadocicum* subsp. *amplum.* A tree up to 10 to 12 m (33–39 feet), in cultivation usually smaller; bark smooth, gray. Leaves 6–15 cm (2⅜–6 inches) long and 4–8 cm (1½–3⅛ inches) wide but variable in size, five-lobed, glossy green, similar to those of *A. cappadocicum*; petioles producing milky sap when broken. Flowers in loose, drooping corymbs to 20 cm (8 inches) long, yellow. Fruits few per corymb, wings often underdeveloped. Native to Guangxi Autonomous Region and Hubei, western Sichuan, and Zhejiang Provinces in China. Originally described as a separate species by Alfred Rehder in 1911. Closely related to *A. cappadocicum* and *A. pictum,* it is represented in several maple collections but otherwise rarely planted, which it should be more often. Zone 6 (Europe 7)

Acer longipes subsp. *amplum* 'Gold Coin'. May

Acer longipes subsp. *amplum* 'Gold Coin'

Synonym, *A. amplum* 'Gold Coin'. A shrub up to 4 m (13 feet) after 20 years and rather irregularly branched; bark gray. Leaves 5–12 cm (2–4¾ inches) wide, five-lobed, golden yellow in spring, turning somewhat duller yellow in summer; petioles producing milky sap when broken. Found in a batch of seedlings collected in the Zuiderpark, The Hague, and raised and introduced by Firma C. Esveld, Netherlands, in 1985. The foliage does not tolerate much wind so the plant needs a sheltered place. Unfortunately, it is difficult to propagate. Zone 6 (Europe 7)

Acer longipes subsp. *catalpifolium*

Synonym, *A. catalpifolium*. A tree in its habitat up to 20 m (66 feet), in cultivation not yet determined but certainly much smaller. Leaves to 25 cm (10 inches) wide, rounded, lobes often underdeveloped, color dark green; fall color not known. Flowers yellow-green. Fruits rather large. Native to Guangdong and Sichuan Provinces in China up to 1000 m (3300 feet) in low mountains. Originally described as a separate species by Alfred Rehder in 1911. Zone 6 (Europe 7)

Acer longipes subsp. *catalpifolium*. July

Acer longipes subsp. *longipes*. May, Valley Gardens

Acer longipes subsp. *longipes*

Synonym, *A. fulvescens.* A tree up to 15 m (50 feet), usually wider than high; bark gray, smooth but rougher when older. Leaves 8–15 cm (3⅛–6 inches) wide with an elongated apex, three-lobed, young leaves with a yellowish down but darker when mature; broken petioles producing milky sap. Flowers in long, drooping racemes, yellow. Nutlets flat. Native to mountainous forests, 1500–2500 m (4900–6500 feet), in Sichuan Province in China, where other subspecies occur. Common in China, the tree is rare in cultivation. Samaras usually abort in cultivation but a tree at Borde Hill Gardens, England, produced viable seed in the 1970s. Zone 6 (Europe 7)

Acer lucidum. September, courtesy of J. R. P. van Hoey Smith

Acer lucidum

Section *Palmata*, series *Penninervia.* A tree up to 6 m (20 feet) but smaller in cultivation; branches red-brown. Leaves 8–10 cm (3⅛–4 inches) long and 4–6 cm (1½–2⅜ inches) wide, unlobed, persistent, dark glossy green. Flowers yellow. Samaras 3 cm (1⅛ inches) long, erect. Native to Guangdong Province in China, 800–1200 m (2600–3900 feet). Described by Franklin Post Metcalf in 1932. The few plants in cultivation in the Netherlands died and the species is probably extinct in cultivation. Zone 7 (Europe 8)

Acer macrophyllum. May, Arboretum Belmonte

Acer macrophyllum

Section *Lithocarpa*, series *Macrophylla.* A stately tree up to 25 m (82 feet) or more, in Europe usually less, with crown to 15 m (50 feet) wide; branches and shoots greenish brown or reddish. Leaves to 35 cm (14 inches) wide, five-lobed, lobes with large obtuse teeth, pubescent when young, base cordate. Flowers in pendulous racemes 35–40 cm (13¾–15¾ inches) long, yellow.

Acer macrophyllum. September, Arboretum Belmonte

Samaras 4–7 cm (1½–2¾ inches) long, horizontal, nutlets firm, brown, beset with prickly hairs. Native to the western coast of North America from Alaska to southern California in mixed coniferous forest. Described by Friedrich Pursh in 1814. Big-leaf maple or Oregon maple has the largest leaves of the genus, rivaled only by *A. velutinum,* and is common in maple collections. It prefers a climate with dry summers. In Europe, vigorously growing shoots tend to suffer in winter because they do not harden early enough. Zone 6 (Europe 7)

Acer mandshuricum

Section *Trifoliata,* series *Mandshurica.* A slender tree up to 10 m (33 feet) but usually smaller; branches and shoots smooth, not peeling as in *A. griseum.* Leaves trifoliolate, leaflets 5–10 cm (2–4 inches) long, oblong, glabrous, margins obtuse-serrate. Flowers in three-flowered corymbs, yellow, plants monoecious. Samaras 3 cm (1⅛ inches) long, spreading horizontally, nutlets hard, rounded. Native to southeastern Gansu Province and Manchuria in China, in thickets along the upper Ussuri River, also in Korea and common near Vladivostok, Russia. Described by Karl Johann Maximowicz in 1867. Manchurian maple is a beautiful but rare maple related to *A. griseum.* Seed, only rarely available, seems to be the only way to grow it. Its narrow habit makes it suitable for small gardens and it has good fall color. Zone 5 (Europe 6)

Acer macrophyllum. May, Herkenrode Gardens

Acer mandshuricum. May, Westonbirt Arboretum

Acer maximowiczianum. July, Von Gimborn Arboretum

Acer maximowiczianum

Section *Trifoliata*, series *Grisea.* Synonym, *A. nikoense.* A tree up to 12 to 15 m (39–50 feet) but usually smaller; bark dark gray to blackish, not peeling as in *A. griseum.* Leaves trifoliolate, leaflets 5–15 cm (2–6 inches) long and 2–5 cm (¾–2 inches) wide, larger than those of *A. griseum,* oblong, petioles 4–6 cm (1½–2⅜ inches) long; fall color usually reddish orange. Flowers yellow-green, appearing before the leaves, plants dioecious. Samaras 4–5 cm (1½–2 inches) long, nutlets woody; the parthenocarpic tendency strong as in *A. griseum.* Formerly widely distributed in Anhui and Hubei Provinces in China and on Honshū, Kyūshū, and Shikoku Islands, Japan, but now rare. Described by Friedrich Anton Wilhelm Miquel in 1867. Given the Royal Horticultural Society's First Class Certificate in 1971. Nikko maple is a beautiful tree for medium-sized and larger gardens but is present mostly in maple collections. Zone 4 (Europe 5)

Acer miaoshanicum juvenile leaves. May 1993, mountain of Emei Shan, Sichuan Province, China, courtesy of K. W. Verboom

Acer miaoshanicum

Section *Palmata*, series *Sinensia.* A shrub or small tree probably up to 7 to 10 m (23–33 feet). Leaves broadly five-lobed, purplish green; juvenile leaves larger and with longer lobes. Native to central China. Described by Fang Wen-pei in 1966. This interesting species is not yet in cultivation. Zone 7 (Europe 8)

Acer miaoshanicum adult leaves. May 1993, mountain of Emei Shan, Sichuan Province, China, courtesy of K. W. Verboom

Acer micranthum

Section *Macrantha*. A small tree, more often a large shrub up to 8 m (26 feet) or somewhat more in favorable conditions; densely branched, young shoots thin, dark purple and inconspicuously striped. Leaves 5–7 cm (2–2¾ inches) long and wide, five-lobed, deeply cleft, central lobe elongated, margins serrate. Flowers very small, hence the name *micranthum*, in terminal racemes 3–5 cm (1⅛–2 inches) long, almost white. Samaras 1–2 cm (⅜–¾ inch) long, horizontal or spreading in a wide angle, nutlets small. Native to mountainous forests on Honshū, Kyūshū, and Shikoku Islands, Japan. Described by Philipp Franz von Siebold and Joseph Gerhard Zuccarini in 1845 and introduced into Europe in 1879 by Charles Maries. Given the Royal Horticultural Society's Award of Garden Merit. It is a beautiful maple but difficult to propagate and viable seeds are almost never available in the nursery trade. Zone 6 (Europe 7)

Acer micranthum 'Candelabrum'

A rather large shrubby tree, larger than individuals of the species. Leaves five- (or seven-) lobed, of the same form as those of the species but larger. A beautiful specimen grows in the Sir Harold Hillier Gardens and Arboretum, England. Unfortunately, it has not been possible to trace the origin of that tree, present in the arboretum long before 1959. Introduced by Hillier's Nurseries before 1965 and propagated by Firma C. Esveld, Netherlands; named 'Candelabrum' in *Maples of the World*, page 153, in 1994. Zone 6 (Europe 7)

Acer miyabei subsp. *miyabei*

Section *Platanoidea*. A tree up to 20 m (66 feet) but often smaller; branches gray and pubescent, often corky as in *A. campestre*. Leaves to 15 cm (6 inches) wide, shape same as in *A. campestre* but larger, five-lobed, olive-green; fall color yellow. Flowers yellow-green in terminal corymbs. Samaras horizontal, slightly pubescent, nutlets flat. Native to Hokkaidō Island in northern Japan, along river banks and in forests, often together with *A. pictum*. Discovered by Kingo Miyabe at a stop during a train journey and described by Karl Johann Maximowicz in 1888. Introduced in 1892 by

Acer micranthum. May, Herkenrode Gardens

Acer micranthum 'Candelabrum'. July

Acer miyabei subsp. *miyabei*. October

Charles Sprague Sargent of the Arnold Arboretum, Massachusetts. Although rather common in maple collections it is rarely seen in public gardens and parks. It is suitable for medium-sized gardens. Subspecies *miaotaiense* is not in cultivation. Zone 4 (Europe 5)

Acer miyabei subsp. *miyabei.* May, Westonbirt Arboretum

Acer monspessulanum subsp. *monspessulanum.* July

Acer monspessulanum subsp. monspessulanum

A medium-sized tree but more often a densely branched shrub up to 10 to 12 m (33–39 feet); bark smooth, dark gray. Leaves 3–5 cm (1⅛–2 inches) wide but quite variable, sometimes a bit leathery, three-lobed, margins entire; petioles not producing milky sap when broken. Flowers in long, pendulous corymbs, yellow to whitish. Samaras 2–3 cm (¾–1⅛ inches) long, parallel, nutlets rounded. Native to the Mediterranean region, northward into the German Eifel and Jura Mountains. Although known in Europe for centuries, Montpellier maple is not commonly seen in gardens though it is well suited for cultivation in all but the smallest. It is often confused with *A. campestre.* Zone 6 (Europe 7)

Acer monspessulanum subsp. *turcomanicum*

Synonym, *A. turcomanicum*. A densely branched shrub up to 4 to 5 m (13–16 feet); bark smooth, dark gray. Leaves 4–6 cm (1½–2⅜ inches) wide, three-lobed, leathery, half-evergreen in very mild localities. Flowers whitish. Samaras parallel, bright red, nutlets hard. Native to the Caucasus. Originally described as a separate species by Antonia I. Pojarkova in 1932. Although subspecies *turcomanicum* grows faster than subspecies *monspessulanum* it does not develop into a tree. It is of interest botanically but is rare in maple collections and almost never seen in gardens. Zone 6 (Europe 7)

Acer morifolium

Section *Macrantha*. Synonym, *A. capillipes* var. *morifolium*. A treelike shrub up to 10 m (33 feet) or more; trunks green with reddish stripes. Leaves unlobed or slightly lobed, cordate, of the same texture as *A. capillipes*. Flowers in short racemes, yellowish. Samaras small. Native to Yaku Shima (Yaku Island) and Ryukyu Islands, Japan. Described by Gen'ichi Koidzumi in 1911. Only more recently introduced into Europe, there is little experience with cultivating this maple. Zone 7 (Europe 8)

Acer negundo

Section *Negundo*, series *Negundo*. Described by John Ray in 1698, by Carl Linnaeus in 1753. Three subspecies are cultivated, *californicum*, *interius*, and *negundo*, in addition to the cultivars. All of these are listed alphabetically. Also, a couple of other notable cultivars are listed at the end of the entries for *A. negundo*. Most cultivars of *A. negundo* have been unjustly neglected in recent decades.

Acer negundo 'Auratum'

A densely branched shrub, sometimes a small tree grafted onto *A. negundo*, up to 6 to 7 m (20–23 feet). Leaves golden yellow in spring, turning greenish yellow later; underside completely smooth, important for identification. Introduced by Späth Nurseries, Germany, in 1892. Given the Royal Horticultural Society's Award of Merit in

Acer monspessulanum subsp. *turcomanicum*. May

Acer morifolium. May, Westonbirt Arboretum

Acer negundo 'Auratum'. June

1901. It is suitable for small gardens and is not to be confused with 'Odessanum', a very rare cultivar supposed to have pubescence underneath the leaf. Zone 5 (Europe 6)

Acer negundo 'Aureomarginatum'. July, Research Station for Nursery Stock

Acer negundo 'Aureomarginatum'. April, Arboretum Belmonte

Acer negundo 'Aureomarginatum'

A tree or large shrub slightly smaller than individuals of the species. Leaf margins creamy yellow, from time to time reverting to green. Flowers sterile. Introduced by Dieck Nurseries, Germany, in 1885. It is common and a good plant for larger gardens and parks. Branches with reverted leaves must be removed. Zone 5 (Europe 6)

Acer negundo subsp. *californicum*. July

Acer negundo subsp. *californicum*

A tree up to 15 to 20 m (50–66 feet), in general appearance similar to subspecies *negundo*. Leaves slightly larger, both sides covered with a velvety pubescence. Flowers in long, drooping racemes, yellowish, plants dioecious. Samaras small, only viable when harvested from a natural stand, nutlets flat. Native to valleys and along riverbanks in central and southern California, also in Arizona. Originally described as a separate species by John Torrey and Asa Gray in 1838. Rare in cultivation, trees labeled as such often are subspecies *negundo*. Pubescence of the foliage is essential for correct identification. It deserves more use; the velvety leaves are especially interesting. Zone 6 (Europe 7)

Acer negundo 'Dr. Herskalt'. June, Westonbirt Arboretum

Acer negundo 'Dr. Herskalt'

A bushy shrub up to 3 to 4 m (10–13 feet). Leaves three- or five-foliolate, pale green. As far as known it is present only in the Westonbirt Arboretum, England. Zone 6 (Europe 7)

Acer negundo 'Elegans'. July

Acer negundo 'Elegans'

A small tree or eventually a multistemmed shrub up to 8 m (26 feet); branches smooth, dark green. Leaves smaller than those of the species, five- or seven-foliolate, leaflets convex, margins yellow. Named by Fritz Graf von Schwerin before 1901. Present especially in older gardens and parks, it is rare in collections. It has been unjustly neglected; it is attractive and suitable for medium-sized gardens. Zone 5 (Europe 6)

Acer negundo 'Flamingo'. July

Acer negundo 'Flamingo'

A large shrub, occasionally a small tree and then usually grafted on a standard, up to 8 to 10 m (26–33 feet); branches gray-green. Leaves white and pink variegated, the variegation especially noticeable in spring. Raised by J. Bastiaanse, Netherlands, in 1976. Given an Award of Merit by the Royal Boskoop Horticultural Society in 1977 and the Royal Horticultural Society's Award of Garden Merit in 1993. Suitable even in small gardens, this is one of the best cultivars developed since the early 1970s. Some pruning is essential to maintain the pink variegation. Zone 6 (Europe 7)

Acer negundo 'Heterophyllum'. October, Hillier Gardens and Arboretum

Acer negundo subsp. *interius*. March

Acer negundo 'Heterophyllum'

Synonyms, *A. negundo* 'Barabits', 'Laciniatum'. A densely branched tree up to 5 to 6 m (16–20 feet) and as wide. Leaves compound and differently shaped from those of the species, pale green, turning yellow in fall. Introduced by Späth Nurseries, Germany, in 1883. Rare in cultivation, this tree presents an aspect quite different from what one would expect of a cultivar of *A. negundo*. Zone 5 (Europe 6)

Acer negundo 'Kelly's Gold'. June, Savill Gardens

Acer negundo 'Kelly's Gold'

A small tree or a shrub up to 8 to 10 m (26–33 feet). Leaves five- or seven-foliolate, greenish yellow. Raised and introduced by Duncan & Davies, New Zealand, in 1989. It is newer than 'Auratum' though it is less attractive but also less apt to sunburn. Zone 6 (Europe 7)

Acer negundo subsp. *interius*

A tree with puberulous branches, rarely glabrous, up to 15 m (50 feet), sometimes multistemmed and shorter. Leaves three- to seven-lobed and more serrate than in subspecies *negundo*, dull green and of thin texture. Native to the Rocky Mountains and central plains of North America, from Saskatchewan, Canada, to New Mexico, U.S.A. Originally described as a separate species by Nathaniel L. Britton in 1908. A tree rare in cultivation though a large specimen grows in the Arnold Arboretum, Massachusetts. It is suitable for large gardens. Zone 6 (Europe 7)

Acer negundo subsp. *negundo*

A tree, sometimes with several trunks, up to 20 to 25 m (66–82 feet) or even more; branches smooth, brittle, covered with a glaucous bloom when young. Leaves three- to seven-foliolate, leaflets 5–10 cm (2–4 inches) long, margins slightly serrate, fresh green; fall color yellow. Flowers produced in abundance in drooping racemes, pale green, plants dioecious. Fruits in drooping racemes, mostly sterile in cultivation, certainly on isolated trees; fruits remaining in quantity on trees after leaves have fallen. Native to Canada where it can form impenetrable thickets, the United States west to the Rocky Mountains, and south to Guatemala (trees from there more tender); naturalized in eastern China. Box elder is one of the most common maples in cultivation. There are quite a few beautiful cultivars available, suitable for medium-sized and larger gardens. It is not suitable as a timber tree, however, because the wood quality is rather poor. Zone 4 (Europe 5)

Acer negundo 'Variegatum'

Synonym, *A. negundo* 'Argenteovariegatum'. A small tree or large shrub up to 10 to 12 m (33–39 feet), sometimes taller; branches smooth, dark gray-green. Leaves with creamy white margins. Flowers in long, drooping racemes, creamy white, plants dioecious. The cultivar is female and fruits usually are all sterile. Introduced by F. A. Wiegers, Germany, in 1809. Given the Royal Horticultural Society's Award of Merit in 1975. Frequently planted, it is one of the best variegated maples. Branches with green leaves may appear and they have to be removed. Zone 5 (Europe 6)

Acer negundo subsp. *negundo.* November, Von Gimborn Arboretum

Acer negundo 'Variegatum'. July, Von Gimborn Arboretum

Acer negundo 'Violaceum'. July

Acer negundo 'Violaceum'

A large tree, differing from the species by the conspicuous bluish color of younger shoots and thin branches. Described by J. Miller in 1826. Too large for the average garden, the tree is not often planted. Vegetative propagation is essential to keep the color of the branches. Zone 5 (Europe 6)

Other Cultivars of *Acer negundo*

In addition to those illustrated or discussed, we mention the following:

'Baron'. A very hardy, vigorously growing plant and a good street tree for cold areas.

'Sensation'. A medium-sized, densely branched tree.

Acer nipponicum. July

Acer nipponicum

Section *Parviflora*, series *Parviflora*. Synonym, *A. parviflorum* in the sense of Franchet and Savatier, not Ehrhart. A tree with a rather large crown up to 10 m (33 feet) in cultivation, in its habitat up to 20 m (66 feet); bark smooth or slightly fissured, blackish brown. Leaves 15–25 cm (6–10 inches) wide, shallowly five-lobed, rusty pubescent underneath. Flowers in long, drooping racemes with as many as 400 flowers. Samaras 3–5 cm (1⅛–2 inches) long, nutlets thick; only a few fruits per raceme ripening. Native to mountainous regions on Honshū, Kyūshū, and Shikoku Islands, Japan; not common. Originally described by Adrien René Franchet and Paul Amedée Ludovic Savatier in 1878. A tree in the Zuiderpark, The Hague, has produced many seeds and its offspring have been sent to a number of botanical gardens and parks. Thus present in several collections, Nippon maple is otherwise rare in cultivation. Zone 6 (Europe 7)

Acer oblongum. September, Savill Gardens

Acer obtusifolium. June

Acer oblongum

Section *Pentaphylla*, series *Trifida*. Synonym, *A. albopurpurascens*. A tree up to 25 m (82 feet) in its habitat, much smaller in cultivation. Leaves 6–12 cm (2⅜–4¾ inches) long and 4–5 cm (1½–2 inches) wide, unlobed but young leaves sometimes bearing three-lobed leaves (the lobes often underdeveloped), evergreen, leathery. Flowers yellow-green. Samaras erect, nutlets angular. Native to mountainous forest, 600–1500 m (2000–4900 feet), in the Himalayas, Nepal, Kashmir in India, and southwestern China. Described by Nathaniel Wallich and Augustin Pyramus de Candolle in 1824. Planted as a street tree in southeastern China, some gnarled specimens of flying-moth tree grow in British collections. Otherwise, it is a plant for the cool greenhouse and can be seen in some botanical gardens. Zone 7 (Europe 8)

Acer olivaceum

Section *Palmata*, series *Sinensia*. In its habitat a tree up to 10 m (33 feet). Leaves 7–8 cm (2¾–3⅛ inches) wide, five-lobed, lobes very regular and margins slightly serrate, olive-green. Flowers small, purplish green. Samaras 3 cm (1⅛ inches) long, spreading at a wide angle. Native to Anhui, Jiangxi, and Zhejiang Provinces in China, 200–1000 m (650–3300 feet). Described by Fang Wen-pei and Chiu Pao-ling in 1979. Extremely rare, little is known about its behavior in cultivation. Zone 7 (Europe 8)

Acer obtusifolium

Section *Acer*, series *Monspessulana*. Synonyms, *A. orientale*, *A. syriacum*. A densely branched shrubby tree up to 10 to 12 m (33–39 feet) in cultivation but often smaller. Leaves 6–9 cm (2⅜–3½ inches) long, unlobed or three-lobed (the lobes often underdeveloped), margins mostly entire, usually evergreen and of firm texture. Flowers in short umbels, greenish yellow. Samaras divergent, nutlets small. Native to coastal mountainous regions of eastern Turkey, Syria, Lebanon, and Cyprus. Originally described (as *A. orientale*) by Carl Linnaeus in 1767. Due to its tenderness it is rare in gardens though present in major collections. Zone 7 (Europe 8)

Acer olivaceum. May

Acer oliverianum

Section *Palmata,* series *Sinensia.* Described by Ferdinand Albin Pax in 1889. Two subspecies are recognized, *formosanum* and *oliverianum.*

Acer oliverianum subsp. *formosanum.* May

Acer oliverianum subsp. *oliverianum.* October, Valley Gardens

Acer oliverianum subsp. *formosanum*

Synonym, *A. serrulatum.* A large tree in its habitat, much larger than subspecies *oliverianum,* much smaller in cultivation; branches and shoots purplish green. Leaves about 10 cm (4 inches) long and 7 cm (2¾ inches) wide, five-lobed, central lobe distinctly longer, margins finely serrate, leaves less leathery than those of subspecies *oliverianum.* Flowers in terminal corymbs, yellow. Samaras almost 3 cm (1⅛ inches) long, horizontal. Native to Taiwan, common in forests from 1000 to 2000 m (3300–6500 feet). Originally described as a subvariety by Gen'ichi Koidzumi in 1911. It is the largest maple on Taiwan but is usually not present in Western collections because of its tenderness. Zone 7 (Europe 8)

Acer oliverianum subsp. *oliverianum*

A medium-sized tree, more often a large shrub up to about 10 m (33 feet) and as wide; branches and shoots purplish green. Leaves 7–12 cm (2¾–4¾ inches) wide, five-lobed, palmate, somewhat leathery, dark green, turning a good yellow in fall. Flowers in small corymbs, whitish. Samaras 2.5–3 cm (1–1⅛ inches) long, spreading at a wide angle. Native to Hubei and Yunnan Provinces in China, 1500–2000 m (4900–6500 feet). *Acer oliverianum* is also reported to inhabit western Sichuan Province but it is likely that those plants are actually *A. campbellii* subsp. *sinense.* Present in several collections, *A. oliverianum* subsp. *oliverianum* is otherwise rare. It is suitable for sheltered, medium-sized gardens. A huge tree planted early in the twentieth century grows in the Zuiderpark, The Hague. Large specimens are also present in the Westonbirt Arboretum and in Valley Gardens, England. Zone 6 (Europe 7)

Acer opalus subsp. *obtusatum.* July

Acer opalus subsp. *hispanicum.* July

Acer opalus subsp. *hispanicum*

Synonyms, *A. granatense, A. hispanicum.* A small tree or densely branched shrub up to 10 m (33 feet), smaller than subspecies *opalus.* Leaves small, five-lobed, lobes blunt, margins shallowly incised. Flowers in small terminal umbels, yellow. Samaras small, nutlets woody. Distributed in the Pyrenees Mountains of northern Spain and southwestern France. Originally described as a separate species by Pierre André Pourret de Figeac in 1788. When seen in an arboretum it is usually labeled as *A. granatense.* Zone 6 (Europe 7)

Acer opalus subsp. *opalus*

Synonyms, *A. italum, A. montanum.* Sometimes a tree up to 20 m (66 feet), more often a large shrub; branches brown-gray, variable in size. Leaves 7–12 cm (2¾–4¾ inches) wide, leathery, five-lobed, lobes rounded, glaucous underneath when young. Flowers in short terminal umbels, yellow. Samaras 2–3 cm (¾–1⅛ inches) long, nutlets thick. Native to southeastern Europe, north to the Jura Mountains in Switzerland and east to the Caucasus, also in Italy, France, Spain, and Morocco. Although usually present in

Acer opalus subsp. *obtusatum*

Synonyms, *A. obtusatum, A. opulifolium.* A tree or dense shrub up to 10 to 13 m (33–46 feet); branches smooth, dark brown-gray. Leaves five-lobed, lobes smaller and more obtuse than those of subspecies *opalus.* Flowers in short terminal umbels, yellow. Samaras small, nutlets rounded, strong tendency to parthenocarpy. Native to Hungary, the Balkans, southern Italy, and Morocco. Originally described as a separate species by Karl Ludwig Willdenow in 1806. It is not uncommon in arboretums but rare in public parks and gardens. In cultivation subspecies *obtusatum* is often mixed with subspecies *opalus.* It is strange that subspecies *obtusatum* is not more frequently planted because it has a good habit and good fall color. It is suitable as a solitary tree in medium-sized gardens. Zone 5 (Europe 6)

Acer opalus subsp. *opalus.* June

collections, Italian maple is much less common in gardens. It is one of the few European maples but it is, unfortunately, not readily available in the nursery trade. It has good golden yellow fall color. Zone 4 (Europe 5)

Acer opalus subsp. *opalus.* October, Royal Botanic Gardens, Kew

ACER PALMATUM

Section *Palmata,* series *Palmata.* Described by Carl Peter Thunberg and Johan Andreas Murray in 1784. This Japanese maple has by far the largest number of cultivars, more than a thousand, not all currently in cultivation and many not in cultivation in the Western world. Many of the cultivars are of Japanese origin. Documentation of the early existence of some of these cultivars is provided in the following Japanese books:

1710: *Zōho Chikinshō* by Ibei Itō, 8 volumes (Volume 4 includes maples)
1719: *Kōeki Chikinshō* by Ibei Itō, 8 volumes (Volume 3 includes maples)
1733: *Chikinshō Furoku* ("supplement") by Ibei Itō
1882: *Kaede Binran* by Seigorō Oka, Isaburō Itō, and Gosaburō Itō
1891: *Kaede Rui Zukō* ("maples with illustrations"), 3 volumes
1898: *Maples of Japan,* catalog issued by the Yokohama Nursery Company

Reference is made to these lists (for example, "list of 1710") in the following descriptions of *Acer palmatum* cultivars. Confusion has resulted because Japanese names in different transliterations and Western names have been applied to the same cultivar in a number of instances. As explained in our chapter "Classification of Maples," under the heading "Cultivars," we have attempted to avoid confusion through careful translation and transliteration of Japanese cultivar names. Additional comments on names and features that may be useful in distinguishing plants are also offered in the cultivar descriptions below.

Cultivars of *Acer palmatum* may be divided into groups and a number of the groups correspond to the three subspecies recognized, *palmatum* (Groups 1 and 5), *amoenum* (Group 2), and *matsumurae* (Groups 3 and 4). Descriptions of the many cultivars (without subspecies name but with Group number given in each description) and the three subspecies are organized alphabetically for ease of reference. In addition, a few other notable cultivars are listed at the end of the entries for *A. palmatum.*

GROUP 1, PALMATUM

Cultivars in Group 1 are usually upright-growing shrubs or small trees. Leaves are usually five-lobed, sometimes seven-lobed, and relatively small. Samaras are small. Several subgroups may be recognized:

Group 1a. Leaves green or green with reddish margins
Group 1b. Leaves purple, sometimes fading to dark green
Group 1c. Leaves variegated, pink, white, yellow, cream, or entirely of the different color

A number of these cultivars may be further identified as belonging to one of the following four groups:

Aureum Group. Group 1a cultivars, densely branched shrubs, leafing out clear yellow to orange, fading to yellow-green or light green in summer, turning yellow again in fall, not variegated

Corallinum Group. Group 1b cultivars, densely branched shrubs up to 3 to 4 m (10–13 feet), young shoots thin, leaves five-lobed, 4–6 cm (1½–2⅜ inches) wide, when unfolding brilliant scarlet to red, later turning bluish green

Roseomarginatum Group. Group 1c cultivars, densely branched shrubs occasionally up to 6 to 8 m (20–26 feet), leaves five- or seven-lobed with white, pink, or bicolored margins, not speckled, tending to revert to entirely green foliage

Versicolor Group. Group 1c cultivars, densely branched shrubs occasionally up to 7 to 8 m (23–26 feet), leaves five- or seven-lobed, white and pink speckled all over, some leaves perhaps entirely white or pink

GROUP 2, AMOENUM

Cultivars in Group 2 are upright-growing shrubs or small trees but are usually less densely branched and have larger leaves. Leaves are seven- (to nine-) lobed, divided to half the leaf blade or somewhat more. Samaras are 4–5 cm (1½–2 inches) long, larger than those of Group 1, and often beautifully colored. Several subgroups may be recognized:

Group 2a. Leaves green or green with reddish margins
Group 2b. Leaves purple-red or purple fading to dark green
Group 2c. Leaves variegated, pink, white, or cream

GROUP 3, MATSUMURAE
Cultivars in Group 3 are mostly large shrubs, rarely trees. Leaves are large, deeply divided, usually cleft almost to the base, and margins are serrate or incised. Samaras are about 4 cm (1½ inches) long, often colorful. Several subgroups may be recognized:

Group 3a. Leaves green or green with reddish margins
Group 3b. Leaves purple or purple fading to dark green
Group 3c. Leaves variegated, red, pink, yellow, or cream

GROUP 4, DISSECTUM
Cultivars in Group 4 are all of garden origin and are sufficiently different in shape that it is worthwhile to separate them from Group 3. All are mushroom-shaped plants, sometimes very large but almost always wider than tall. Leaves are finely dissected, cleft to the leaf base, with lobes also finely dissected. Several subgroups may be recognized:

Group 4a. Leaves green
Group 4b. Leaves purple or purple-brown, sometimes fading to dark green
Group 4c. Leaves variegated

GROUP 5, LINEARILOBUM
Cultivars in Group 5 are upright, slow-growing shrubs. Leaves are usually five-lobed, the lobes threadlike and not more than 0.5 cm (³⁄₁₆ inch) wide. Plants with such threadlike leaves have not been found in the wild. Two subgroups may be recognized:

Group 5a. Leaves green
Group 5b. Leaves purple or purple-brown

GROUP 6, BONSAI
Cultivars in Group 6 are dwarf forms suitable for growing as penjing, that is, trained small trees usually in shallow containers (bonsai) or used in the creation of miniature scenes incorporating rocks or other plants. Three subgroups may be recognized:

Group 6a. Leaves green
Group 6b. Leaves purple or rusty brown
Group 6c. Leaves variegated

GROUP 7
The few cultivars in Group 7 do not fit into the system defining the other groups. They are upright-growing shrubs that have unusual leaf forms or colors.

Acer palmatum 'Aka ne'. June

Acer palmatum 'Aka ne'
Group 1a (Aureum Group). A bush probably up to 2 to 3 m (6½–10 feet); young branches coral red. Leaves orange-yellow in spring, turning golden yellow and greenish back to intense yellow. Origin Japanese, before 1990. It is similar to *A. palmatum* 'Katsura', 'Orange Dream', and 'Sode nishiki' but smaller, and it is yellower in spring and summer than *A. palmatum* 'Aureum'. The foliage of *A. palmatum* 'Beni zuru' is similar to that of 'Aka ne' but is a bit less bright orange in spring. Zone 6 (Europe 7)

Acer palmatum 'Aka shigitatsu sawa'. June, Savill Gardens

Acer palmatum 'Aka shigitatsu sawa'

Group 3c. A shrub up to 5 m (16 feet) and even wider. Leaves dark reddish green, flamed with pink and white; fall color spectacular. Flowers rarely produced. Fruits mostly sterile. Origin Japanese, before 1960 and probably much older. It has been confused with *A. palmatum* 'Beni shigitatsu sawa' because *aka* and *beni* both mean "red" in Japanese but the two cultivars are different; 'Beni shigitatsu sawa' is slightly darker than 'Aka shigitatsu sawa'. 'Aka shigitatsu sawa' is similar to *A. palmatum* 'Ariadne' and 'Kasagi yama' and is an excellent plant for larger gardens. Zone 6 (Europe 7)

Acer palmatum 'Aka shigitatsu sawa'. June, Savill Gardens

Acer palmatum 'Aka shime no uchi'. May, Valley Gardens

Acer palmatum 'Akita yatsubusa'. October, Foliage Gardens, courtesy of H. Olsen

Acer palmatum 'Aka shime no uchi'
Group 5b. A narrow shrub up to 4 to 5 m (13–16 feet). Leaves almost linear, dark red in spring, becoming greener in summer. An old cultivar, appearing in the list of 1710. It is rare; many plants believed to be 'Aka shime no uchi' are actually *A. palmatum* 'Atrolineare', with which it may be confused. *Acer palmatum* 'Enkan' and 'Red Pygmy' are smaller. Zone 6 (Europe 7)

Acer palmatum 'Akita yatsubusa'
Group 6b. A small plant with salmon-red leaves in spring, fading to greenish yellow. Raised and introduced by TC Plants, Oregon, about 1990. It is very much like *A. palmatum* 'Sharp's Pygmy' in form. The leaves of 'Akita yatsubusa' are, however, much finer, and fall color is more brilliant, orange through red. Zone 6 (Europe 7)

Acer palmatum 'Akegarasu'. June

Acer palmatum 'Akegarasu'
Group 3b. An upright-growing shrub, openly branched, up to 5 to 6 m (16–20 feet). Leaves dark purple-red in spring, large, deeply divided, margins green in summer. Flowers profusely. Seeds germinate poorly. Mentioned in the list of 1882 and by Gen'ichi Koidzumi in 1911. 'Akegarasu' has the largest leaves of Group 3b. Petioles are long and red. *Acer palmatum* 'Taihai' is similar but has smaller leaves. It is not common in cultivation but then it is not particularly attractive. Zone 6 (Europe 7)

Acer palmatum subsp. *amoenum*. June, Valley Gardens

Acer palmatum subsp. *amoenum*
Synonym, *A. amoenum*. A shrub up to 10 to 12 m (33–39 feet), rarely a tree and if so multistemmed. Leaves 8–12 cm (3⅛–4¾ inches) wide, seven-lobed, divided to half

the leaf blade, margins serrate, color fresh green, becoming yellow in fall. Flowers in pendulous racemes, reddish white. Samaras to 4 cm (1½ inches) long, nutlets rounded. Native to mountainous regions of Japan, Korea, and China, mixed with subspecies *palmatum*. Originally described as a separate species by Elie Abel Carrière in 1867. It is in wider cultivation than believed because it is often incorrectly labeled and cultivars of this particular subspecies are often not recognized as such. Zone 6 (Europe 7)

Acer palmatum subsp. *amoenum*. June, Valley Gardens

Acer palmatum 'Angustilobum'. June

Acer palmatum 'Angustilobum'

Group 5b. Synonym, *A. palmatum* 'Angustilobum Purpureum'. Named by Gen'ichi Koidzumi in his efforts to latinize Japanese names. It is a member of the *A. palmatum* 'Linearilobum' group of cultivars and may be identical to 'Aka shime no uchi' or 'Atrolineare' itself. It is also similar to 'Enkan' and 'Red Pygmy'. Zone 6 (Europe 7)

Acer palmatum 'Ao ba jō'. November

Acer palmatum 'Ao ba jō'

Group 6a. Alternatively, *A. palmatum* 'Ao ba joh'. A dwarf shrub. Leaves rather large, lobes acuminate, color orange-green in spring, turning bronze-green in summer, yellow in fall. It is suitable for bonsai; *A. palmatum* 'Ryūzu' is similar. Zone 6 (Europe 7)

Acer palmatum 'Ao kanzashi'. August

Acer palmatum 'Ao meshime no uchi'. September, Castle Gardens Arcen

Acer palmatum 'Ao shidare'. July

Acer palmatum 'Ao kanzashi'

Group 1c (Roseomarginatum Group). A vase-shaped shrub up to 7 to 8 m (23–26 feet), densely branched. Leaves five- or seven-lobed, lobes somewhat convex, green with slight greenish white variegation. Origin Japanese. *Acer palmatum* 'Chirimen nishiki', 'Fūjin' (alternatively, 'Fuhjin'; leaves more pointed and starlike than those of 'Ao kanzashi'), 'Kokubunji nishiki', and 'Taiyō nishiki' (alternatively, 'Taiyoh nishiki') are similar. The leaves of *A. palmatum* 'Hiryū' (alternatively, 'Hiryuh') are similar to those of 'Ao kanzashi' but 'Hiryū' grows slower, reaching 3.4 m (11⅛ feet), and the variegated parts of its leaves shrivel, giving it a peculiar appearance. Zone 6 (Europe 7)

Acer palmatum 'Ao meshime no uchi'

Group 5a. A vase-shaped shrub up to 3 to 3.5 m (10–11 feet), rather densely branched. Leaves narrowly lobed, color fresh green, becoming yellow in fall. Origin Japanese. It is sometimes considered to be identical with the better known *A. palmatum* 'Shinobu ga oka', which is not identical to 'Linearilobum'. *Acer palmatum* 'Ao shichigo-san' is similar 'Ao meshime no uchi' and probably synonymous. Group 5a includes a large number of very similar cultivars, some which may in fact be identical. Zone 6 (Europe 7)

Acer palmatum 'Ao shidare'

Group 4a. A mushroom-shaped shrub up to 2 to 2.5 m (6½–8 feet) and even wider. Leaves bright green, deeply dissected, turning yellow in fall. Described by Gen'ichi Koidzumi in 1911. 'Ao shidare' may be confused with several slightly different cultivars, *A. palmatum* 'Dissectum', 'Kiri nishiki', 'Ōgon shidare' (alternatively, 'Ohgon shidare'), and 'Waterfall'. The leaves of 'Ao shidare' tend to be darker green. Zone 6 (Europe 7)

Acer palmatum 'Ao yagi'

Group 1a. A pleasing, upright-growing shrub or small tree up to 8 m (26 feet) or more; bark glistening fresh green and conspicuous in winter. Leaves small, five-lobed, bright green, turning yellow in fall. Mentioned in the list of 1882. It is similar to *A. palmatum* 'Dezome irizome' (leaves more deeply cleft), 'Ukon' (leaves somewhat larger; not to be confused with a cultivar of *A. pictum* of the same name), and 'Volubile' (which lacks the good green color of the branches). *Ao yagi* means "green willow" and a good companion plant is 'Sango kaku', which has coral-red bark. Zone 6 (Europe 7)

Acer palmatum 'Ao yagi'. April

Acer palmatum 'Ara kawa'. October, courtesy of H. Olsen

Acer palmatum 'Ara kawa'. July, Boxleitner

Acer palmatum 'Ara kawa'

Group 1a. A vigorous, shrubby tree up to 8 to 10 m (26–33 feet). Introduced by Jiro Kobayashi, Japan, about 1970. Sometimes called "rough bark maple," it has a very attractive corky bark that becomes more prominent with age. It may be compared with *A. palmatum* 'Nishiki gawa', which also has conspicuous bark. Zone 6 (Europe 7)

Acer palmatum 'Ara tama'. April, courtesy of H. Olsen

Acer palmatum 'Ara tama'
Group 6b. A slow-growing medium-sized shrub with thin branches. Leaves five-lobed, dark purple in spring, turning lighter red in late summer. It is said to be a bud sport of 'Ko murasaki'. It is a true dwarf. Zone 6 (Europe 7)

Acer palmatum 'Ariadne'. April

Acer palmatum 'Ariadne'
Group 3c. A shrub up to 3 m (10 feet) and almost as wide. Leaves deeply divided, margins coarsely serrate, reddish purple with pink variegation not unlike *A. palmatum* 'Beni shigitatsu sawa' but becoming much larger. Discovered in a seedbed of *A. palmatum* of garden origin, named for Vezna Ariadne van Gelderen, daughter and grand-daughter of the authors of the present book, and introduced by Firma C. Esveld, Netherlands, in 1991. It has attractive color in summer and the variegation remains visible in fall. It is similar to *A. palmatum* 'Kasagi yama' but has a different habit. Zone 6 (Europe 7)

Acer palmatum 'Ariake nomura'. May

Acer palmatum 'Ariake nomura'
Group 2b. A narrowly growing shrub up to 7 to 8 m (23–26 feet) with dark red branches. Leaves 4–6 cm (1½–2⅜ inches) wide, five-lobed, dark purple, becoming shinier in fall. It is reported to be a seedling of 'Nomura', but that means little. Similar cultivars are *A. palmatum* 'Fireglow', 'Moonfire', and 'Nure sagi'. Zone 6 (Europe 7)

Acer palmatum 'Asahi zuru'
Group 1c (Versicolor Group). Synonym, *A. palmatum* 'Asahi juru'. A vase-shaped shrubby tree up to 10 m (33 feet), densely branched. Leaves pink and white variegated. Introduced by Koichiro Wada, Japan, in 1938. *Asahi zuru* means "maple of the morning sun." It grows vigorously and tends to revert to entirely green leaves. To maintain the variegation, plant it on a poor place. There are several similar cultivars, usually finer but also more fragile, such as *A. palmatum* 'Karasu gawa' and 'Oridono nishiki'. Also similar are *A. palmatum* 'Hanazono nishiki', 'Honō' (alternatively, 'Honoh'; prone to reversion to completely green leaves), 'Miyabi nishiki' (variegation less sharply defined than in 'Asahi zuru'), and

Acer palmatum 'Asahi zuru'. September, Arboretum Trompenburg

'Mugiwara nishiki' and 'Ryūmon nishiki' (alternatively, 'Ryuhmon nishiki'; less variegated than 'Asahi zuru'). Zone 6 (Europe 7)

Acer palmatum 'Atrolineare'. June, Valley Gardens

Acer palmatum 'Atrolineare'. June, Valley Gardens

Acer palmatum 'Atrolineare'

Group 5b. Synonyms, *A. palmatum* 'Linearilobum Atropurpureum', 'Scolopendrifolium Purpureum'. A shrub up to 4 m (13 feet), usually higher than wide. Leaves five-lobed, linear, dark red in spring, becoming dark green in late summer. Fritz Graf von Schwerin introduced the name 'Atrolineare' in 1893 and it is the oldest published name. There are several similar forms in cultivation, all very much alike. It is difficult to decide whether they are identical as the circumstances in which they are grown are often different. Similar cultivars are *A. palmatum* 'Aka shime no uchi', 'Angustilobum', 'Curtis Strapleaf', 'Enkan', and 'Red Pygmy'. Zone 6 (Europe 7)

Acer palmatum 'Atropurpureum'. May, Herkenrode Gardens

Acer palmatum 'Atropurpureum'

Group 1b. An upright-growing treelike shrub, sometimes up to 10 m (33 feet) or more. Leaves 5–8 cm (2–3⅛ inches) wide, five- or seven-lobed, margins serrate, color dark wine-red; fall color glistening red. 'Atropurpureum' of Dutch or German origin is usually grown from cuttings or grafted from a superior clone selected by Constant Wattez, Netherlands, before 1910. The cultivar breeds almost true from seed, however, and the plants in cultivation have thus become a grex instead of a clone. The leaf color of seedlings varies, some turning dark green in fall. Several selections have been made and named in past decades, the plants usually being sold as *A. palmatum* f. *atropurpureum.* The true clonal cultivar needs a new name, in fact, but renaming would cause confusion. Similar cultivars include *A. palmatum* 'Bloodgood', 'Fireglow', and 'Nure sagi'. Zone 6 (Europe 7)

Acer palmatum 'Aureum'. July

Acer palmatum 'Aureum'

Group 1a (Aureum Group). Synonym, *A. palmatum* 'Sunrise'. A rather tall, vase-shaped shrub, densely branched. Leaves small, five-lobed, margins finely serrate, color butter-yellow when leafing out, later turning soft yellow-green. Flowers and fruits not seen, even on a 20-year-old plant. Named by George Nicholson, England, in 1881. Some similar but yellower cultivars are *A. palmatum* 'Katsura', 'Orange Dream', 'Sode nishiki', and 'Ueno homare'. Zone 6 (Europe 7)

Acer palmatum 'Attraction'. July

Acer palmatum 'Attraction'

Group 1b. Synonym, *A. palmatum* 'Atropurpureum Superbum'. A vase-shaped shrubby tree up to 10 m (33 feet) or more. Leaves slightly darker than those of 'Atropurpureum', the same color as those of 'Bloodgood'. Origin Japanese. *Acer palmatum* 'Bloodgood' and 'Fireglow' are very similar. Zone 6 (Europe 7)

Acer palmatum 'Azuma murasaki'. September, Savill Gardens

Acer palmatum 'Azuma murasaki'

Group 3b. A sparsely branched shrubby tree up to 5 to 6 m (16–20 feet). Leaves 6–10 cm (2⅜–4 inches) wide, deeply divided, margins incised, color dark purple in spring, new growth in summer light green, turning dark green; fall color good. Flowers dark red. Samaras red, adding to the plant's beauty in fall. Name first found in the list of 1882. *Acer palmatum* 'Atropurpureum Novum' (bold brown-purple leaves), 'Hinata yama' (leaves bold, purplish with some green spots), and 'Sumi nagashi' (with smaller leaves) are similar. Also see the discussion under *A. palmatum* 'Toshi'. Zone 6 (Europe 7)

Acer palmatum 'Azuma murasaki'. May

Acer palmatum 'Banda hime'

Group 1c (Roseomarginatum Group). A slow-growing shrub. Leaves heavily variegated, mainly brownish red with white, reverting to green somewhat. This rare plant could not be traced in the Japanese lists. Similar cultivars are *A. palmatum* 'Beni shichi henge' and 'Kara ori nishiki' but those two cultivars grow faster and have less of the brownish red color in their leaves. Hisao Nakajima lists a cultivar, 'Kuchibeni nishiki', which is similar. 'Banda hime' appears to be desirable but it is not yet available in the nursery trade. Zone 6 (Europe 7)

Acer palmatum 'Banda hime'. May, Valley Gardens

Acer palmatum 'Beni fushigi'

Group 6b. A shrub probably up to 2 m (6½ feet) or even larger, densely branched, branchlets and shoots thin. Leaves finely dissected, light red when leafing out, becoming darker with age; young plants presenting a bicolored appearance. Introduced by Greer Gardens, Oregon, in 1988. 'Beni fushigi' deserves attention because it grows well and forms a nice plant. It is comparable to *A. palmatum* 'Kamagata' but has red foliage. It is also similar to 'Beni komachi' but that plant is more fragile and difficult to propagate. Zone 6 (Europe 7)

Acer palmatum 'Beni fushigi'. May

Acer palmatum 'Beni hime'. June, Fratelli Gilardelli

Acer palmatum **'Beni hime'**

Group 6b. One of the smallest forms of *A. palmatum*. Leaves reddish at the margins. Origin probably Japanese, before 1960. *Beni hime* means "dwarf red." It is a very attractive plant but only rarely seen due to problems with its propagation. Zone 6 (Europe 7)

Acer palmatum 'Beni kawa'. October

Acer palmatum 'Beni kagami'. May, Valley Gardens

Acer palmatum **'Beni kagami'**

Group 3b. A treelike shrub sometimes up to 10 m (33 feet) or more, growing vigorously when young and needing trimming in order to form a good plant. Leaves 6–10 cm (2⅜–4 inches) wide on vigorous shoots, otherwise somewhat smaller, seven-lobed, deeply incised, almost to the base, margins serrate, color dark wine-red. Flowers red. Samaras red, adding to the beauty of the plant. A selection from the Angyō Maple Nursery, Japan, introduced in 1930. *Beni kagami* means "red mirror." Similar cultivars are *A. palmatum* 'Inazuma' (less wine-red), and 'Matsukaze'. 'Inazuma' and 'Matsukaze' are less purple-red in spring but also have good fall color. *Acer palmatum* 'Momiji gawa' is similar to 'Beni kagami'. Zone 6 (Europe 7)

Acer palmatum **'Beni kawa'**

Group 1a. A strongly growing shrub or small tree up to 10 to 12 m (33–39 feet); bark coral-red in winter, yellowish in summer. Leaves smaller than those of the species, fresh green in summer, turning yellow in fall. Origin Japanese, introduced by Greer Gardens, Oregon, about 1987. 'Beni kawa' is similar to the well-known *A. palmatum* 'Sango kaku' but it is not yet possible to say whether 'Sango kaku' is superior to that cultivar. Zone 6 (Europe 7)

Acer palmatum 'Beni kawa'. January

Acer palmatum 'Beni komachi'. May

beautiful little girl." Still rare in cultivation, this nice dwarf plant is unfortunately difficult to propagate; the scion wood is very thin. A similar cultivar is *A. palmatum* 'Beni fushigi'. Zone 6 (Europe 7)

Acer palmatum 'Beni maiko'. July

Acer palmatum 'Beni maiko'

Group 1b (Corallinum Group). A medium-sized shrub, usually wider than high, densely branched with thin branchlets and shoots. Leaves 3–5 cm (1⅛–2 inches) wide, five-lobed, brilliant scarlet when unfolding, later becoming dull dark red to bluish green; fall color not spectacular. Origin Japanese, before 1970. *Beni maiko* means "red-haired dancing girl." Similar cultivars are *A. palmatum* 'Beni chidori', 'Chishio', 'Deshōjō', 'Glowing Embers' (bright red leaves, holding its color during the summer), 'Otome zakura', 'Shin deshōjō', and 'Tanba seigai' (leaves small, coral-red when unfolding, later turning dull green). Zone 6 (Europe 7)

Acer palmatum 'Beni komachi'

Group 6b. A dwarf shrub possibly to 2 m (6½ feet) wide and of the same height, densely branched, with long, thin branchlets. Leaves somewhat curly, deeply dissected, unusually bright red when unfolding, turning bluish red or green; fall color red. Named and introduced by J. D. Vertrees, Oregon, before 1975. Given a Silver Medal by the Royal Boskoop Horticultural Society in 1978. *Beni komachi* means "red-haired,

Acer palmatum 'Beni ōtaki'. November, Foliage Gardens, courtesy of H. Olsen

Acer palmatum 'Beni ōtaki'

Group 5b. Alternatively, *A. palmatum* 'Beni ohtaki'. Synonym, *A. palmatum* 'Beni ōtake'. The outstanding feature of this plant is its bamboo-like appearance. Leaves five- or seven-lobed, long and narrow, deep scarlet-red. Named by Edward Wood and introduced by TC Plants, Oregon, in 1980. Only rarely available in the nursery trade, it is an attractive plant, suitable for small gardens. Zone 6 (Europe 7)

Acer palmatum 'Beni shidare'. May, Herkenrode Gardens

Acer palmatum 'Beni shichi henge'. June

Acer palmatum 'Beni shichi henge'

Group 1c (Roseomarginatum Group). A narrow, upright-growing shrub, reaching 4–5 m (13–16 feet) with age, rather poorly branched. Leaves 4–5 cm (1½–2 inches) wide, five-lobed, white and rosy brown variegated, sometimes wrinkled. Named and introduced by the Angyō Maple Nursery, Japan, in 1967. *Beni shichi henge* means "red and changeful." Rather difficult to propagate, it is similar to *A. palmatum* 'Butterfly' but that cultivar lacks the brownish pink color. *Acer palmatum* 'Beni kosode' (pink variegated leaves), 'Geisha' (larger leaves and more variegated, sometimes all white, pink, and brownish), 'Hatsukoi' (lighter pink than 'Beni shichi henge'), 'Kuchibeni nishiki' and 'Ori zuru' (both more variegated than 'Beni shichi henge' and the colors of 'Ori zuru' markedly more intense), and 'Ueno nishiki' (lighter pink variegated than 'Beni shichi henge') are similar cultivars. Zone 6 (Europe 7)

Acer palmatum 'Beni shidare'

Group 4b. A mushroom-shaped shrub up to 3 to 4 m (10–13 feet) and sometimes much broader. Leaves deeply divided and dissected, warm brown-red in spring, turning greenish and green, later becoming orange-red to yellow. Introduced by the Yokohama Nursery Company, Japan, in 1896. *Beni shidare* means "red and pendulous." This pretty plant is similar to the well-known *A. palmatum* 'Ornatum', still often wrongly called 'Dissectum Atropur-

Acer palmatum 'Beni shidare'. May, Herkenrode Gardens

Acer palmatum 'Beni tsukasa'. May, Westonbirt Arboretum

pureum'. It is perhaps a bit more cascading than that cultivar. *Acer palmatum* 'Mutsu beni shidare' is very similar to 'Beni shidare'. Zone 6 (Europe 7)

Acer palmatum 'Beni tsukasa'

Group 1c. A slow-growing, vase-shaped shrub reaching 3–4 m (10–13 feet), densely branched. Leaves 4–6 cm (1½–2⅜ inches) wide, five-lobed, spectacularly colored salmon-pink, red, and greenish, changing in summer to somewhat more green. Origin Japanese, before 1970. This very desirable form is only rarely available in the nursery trade because it is difficult to propagate. *Acer palmatum* 'Coral Pink' is even more fragile. The foliage of *A. palmatum* 'Beni otome' is similar to that of 'Beni tsukasa' but is more intensely colored at the margins of the leaves. Zone 6 (Europe 7)

Acer palmatum 'Beni tsukasa'. April

Acer palmatum 'Bloodgood'. June, Arboretum Belmonte

Acer palmatum 'Bloodgood'

Group 1b. A treelike shrub reaching 10–12 m (33–39 feet) or occasionally more, rather sparsely branched. Leaves 5–8 cm (2–3⅛ inches) wide, five- or seven-lobed, margins serrulate, color dark wine-red and not fading to brown or greenish; fall color shining red. Samaras glowing red. Introduced by Bloodgood Nurseries, New York, before 1950. Given the Royal Horticultural Society's Award of Garden Merit in 1993. One of the darkest of all the "Atropurpureum" cultivars, the fruits are especially attractive Suitable in gardens with little space because it grows higher than wide, it is easy to grow and is generally available in the nursery trade. *Acer palmatum* 'Flushing' is similar to 'Bloodgood' in leaf shape and color; 'Italy Red' is about half the size, otherwise very much like 'Bloodgood'; 'Crimson

Acer palmatum 'Bloodgood'. June, Arboretum Belmonte

Prince', 'Fireglow', and 'Moonfire' also have dark foliage like that of 'Bloodgood'; 'Christy Ann' and 'Murakumo' have dark purple leaves; and 'Red Spray' grows fast. Zone 6 (Europe 7)

Acer palmatum 'Bonfire'. October, Foliage Gardens, courtesy of H. Olsen

Acer palmatum 'Bonfire'. April, Foliage Gardens, courtesy of H. Olsen

Acer palmatum 'Bonfire'

Group 1c. This is a cultivar with variegated leaves. Another cultivar with coral-red foliage is also called 'Bonfire'. *Acer palmatum* 'Akaji nishiki," a name also used for a plant with coral-red leaves, does in fact not exist. The name 'Akaji nishiki' is used for a cultivar of *A. truncatum* with yellow variegated leaves. It is most likely that plants with coral red spring leaves called "Akaji nishiki" or "Bonfire" are in fact *A. palmatum* 'Seigai' and that the true 'Bonfire' is a rather poor representative of Group 1c (Versicolor Group). We note that Harry Olsen does not agree with this interpretation. Zone 6 (Europe 7)

Acer palmatum 'Boskoop Glory'. June

Acer palmatum 'Boskoop Glory'

Group 2b. Leaves somewhat less dark than those of 'Bloodgood' and with more fall color. Samaras also red. Named and introduced by Greer Gardens, Oregon, in 1985. In spite of what the name suggests, that this cultivar might be the Dutch, Constant Wattez type of 'Atropurpureum', it is not; the leaves are darker than that. Zone 6 (Europe 7)

Acer palmatum 'Brandt's Dwarf'. October, Foliage Gardens, courtesy of H. Olsen

Acer palmatum 'Brandt's Dwarf', 7 years old and 1 m (3 feet) high. October, Foliage Gardens, courtesy of H. Olsen

Acer palmatum 'Brandt's Dwarf'

Group 6b. A witches'-broom, mature size unknown. Probably a sport of *A. palmatum* 'Bloodgood', the leaves much smaller than those of that cultivar. Introduced by Henry Hohman, Kingsville Nurseries, Maryland. A specimen dating to the 1950s grows at the U.S. National Arboretum, Washington, D.C. Witches'-brooms such as this one tend to be very much alike and are practically indistinguishable without proper labeling. They are suitable for bonsai. Zone 6 (Europe 7)

Acer palmatum 'Burgundy Lace'

Group 3b. A shrub up to 8 m (26 feet) and as wide, heavily branched. Leaves seven-lobed and deeply divided, almost to the base, margins coarsely dissected, color dark red; fall color not spectacular because the red summer color is quite strong. Samaras reddish. Introduced by Vermeulen & Son, New Jersey, in 1958. Given an Award of Merit by the Royal Boskoop Horticultural Society in 1977 and the Royal Horticultural Society's Award of Garden Merit in 1993. Similar forms are *A. palmatum* 'Inabuchi' and 'Sherwood Flame'. Zone 6 (Europe 7)

Acer palmatum 'Burgundy Lace'. May, Herkenrode Gardens

Acer palmatum 'Butterfly'

Group 1c (Roseomarginatum Group). A vase-shaped shrub up to 6 to 7 m (20–23 feet); branches and shoots thin, sometimes branching a second time in the same summer. Leaves five-lobed, margins white variegated, sometimes reverting to green. In-

Acer palmatum 'Butterfly'. June, Fratelli Gilardelli

troduced by Koichiro Wada, Japan, in 1938
but the form is probably much older and its
Japanese name might be 'Kochō nishiki'
(alternatively, 'Kochoh nishiki'), which
appears in the list of 1882; *kochō* means
"butterfly." Given an Award of Merit by
the Royal Boskoop Horticultural Society in
1977 and the Royal Horticultural Society's
Award of Garden Merit in 1993. 'Butterfly'
is a useful plant for smaller gardens but reverted shoots must be removed. 'Beni shichi henge' is more variegated with pink.
Zone 6 (Europe 7)

Acer palmatum 'Chishio'. May, Herkenrode Gardens

Acer palmatum 'Chikumano'. July

Acer palmatum 'Chikumano'

Group 2b. A shrub tending to become
broader than high, occasionally a tree up
to 6 to 7 m (20–23 feet). Leaves to 15 cm (6
inches) wide, usually seven-lobed, dark purple-red, fading to greenish brown; fall color
orange to orange-yellow. Origin probably
Japanese, before 1970. According to Ver-
rees, *Japanese Maples,* 'Chikumano' is one
of the best cultivars for landscaping in the
western United States. Zone 6 (Europe 7)

Acer palmatum 'Chishio'

Group 1b (Corallinum Group). Synonym,
A. *palmatum* 'Shishio'. A densely branched
shrub up to 4 to 5 m (13–16 feet); branchlets
and shoots thin. Leaves 4–5 cm (1½–2
inches) wide, five-lobed, brilliant scarlet
when unfolding, later fading to pinkish,
afterward bluish green with reddish mar-

Acer palmatum 'Chishio'. May, Herkenrode Gardens

gins. Introduced by the Yokohama Nursery
Company, Japan, in 1896. *Chishio* means
"blood" and the cultivar has been called
"Sanguineum," an illegitimate name. 'Chishio' needs a sheltered place in the garden.
It is often used for bonsai. Similar cultivars
are A. *palmatum* 'Beni maiko', 'Corallinum',
and 'Deshōjō'. Zone 6 (Europe 7)

Acer palmatum 'Chishio Improved'. May, Weston-birt Arboretum

Acer palmatum 'Chishio Improved'

Group 1b (Corallinum Group). Closely related to *A. palmatum* 'Chishio', the main difference is the stronger growth and somewhat firmer branchlets and shoots of 'Chishio Improved'. Origin Japanese, introduced through Belgium to the Netherlands with this undocumented name about 1965. It is now well established in horticulture. Similar to the other cultivars of the Corallinum Group, it is the strongest growing and needs more space. Zone 6 (Europe 7)

Acer palmatum 'Chishio Improved'. May, Savill Gardens

Acer palmatum 'Chitose yama'

Group 3b. A slow-growing shrub up to about 3 to 4 m (10–13 feet) and as wide. Leaves 5–8 cm (2–3⅛ inches) wide, seven-lobed, margins serrate, color dark purple-red; fall color a lighter, shiny red. Flowers red. Samaras red. First described in the list of 1882. A different maple with olive-green leaves (given the Royal Horticultural Society's Award of Garden Merit in 1993) has also appeared in the trade under the name 'Chitose yama'. Those plants came from Exbury Gardens, England. The Japanese expert Jiro Kobayashi has made it clear that true 'Chitose yama' has dark purple, not olive, leaves. 'Chitose yama' is suitable for medium-sized gardens. *Acer palmatum* 'Koba shōjō' (alternatively, 'Koba shohjoh') is similar. Zone 6 (Europe 7)

Acer palmatum 'Chitose yama'. May, Valley Gardens

Acer palmatum 'Coonara Pygmy'

Group 6a. A densely branched shrub up to 1 m (3¼ feet) or more. Leaves small, five-lobed, fresh green, young leaves yellow. Found in Australia, introduced by Yamina Rare Plants (Don Teese), Victoria, before 1965. A witches'-broom, it is difficult to propagate. As often seen in witches'-brooms, it is short-lived and dies back suddenly. It is only rarely available in the nursery trade due to its fragility, otherwise it would be one of the few maples suitable for rock gardens. Zone 6 (Europe 7)

Acer palmatum 'Coonara Pygmy'. June

Acer palmatum 'Corallinum'. June

Acer palmatum 'Corallinum'

Group 1b (Corallinum Group). Synonym, *A. palmatum* 'Spring Fire'. A slow-growing shrub usually not higher than 2 to 3 m (6½–10 feet); branches dark purple, shoots thin. Leaves five-lobed, brilliant red when unfolding, later turning light red and pink, afterward bluish green; fall color not very impressive, usually yellow. Introduced by Hillier's Nurseries, England, before 1900. It is also known in the trade as "Carminium" and "Sanguineum," both names illegitimate. 'Corallinum' needs a sheltered place for best results. Similar cultivars are *A. palmatum* 'Beni maiko', 'Chishio', and 'Deshōjō'; 'Yama shiro' has coral-red leaves in spring, like those of 'Corallinum', but the leaf shape is like that of 'Kamagata' with a somewhat more serrated margin. Zone 6 (Europe 7)

Acer palmatum 'Coral Pink'. April

Acer palmatum 'Coral Pink'

Group 6c. A dwarf form of upright habit, reaching 2 m (6½ feet) in 25 years; branches dark gray. Leaves five-lobed, salmon-pink when unfolding, keeping the color a fairly long time. Raised and introduced by Robert de Belder, Belgium, about 1970 and named in 1985. For collectors only, it needs a very well sheltered place as it is apt to sunburn, and shrivels in strong winds. The salmon-pink color is very conspicuous and there are few similarly colored cultivars, for example, *A. palmatum* 'Beni tsukasa', 'Tōhoku shichi henge' (alternatively, 'Tohhoku shichi henge'), 'Wilson's Pink Dwarf', and 'Yūzuki' (alternatively, 'Yuhzuki'). Zone 6 (Europe 7)

Acer palmatum 'Crimson Queen'. June, Valley Gardens

Acer palmatum 'Crimson Queen'

Group 4b. A mushroom-shaped shrub not exceeding 2 m (6½ feet) in height but becoming much broader, up to 3 m (10 feet) in 25 years, fairly densely branched. Leaves finely dissected, very dark purple-red, not fading in summer; fall color shiny red. Raised and introduced by Cascio, U.S.A., in 1965. Given a First Class Certificate by the Royal Boskoop Horticultural Society in 1971 and the Royal Horticultural Society's Award of Garden Merit in 1993. It is fit for any but the smallest gardens and is one of the best cultivars in its group. 'Crimson Queen' may be compared with *A. palmatum* 'Garnet', which has the same color but grows faster. Zone 6 (Europe 7)

Acer palmatum 'Crippsii'. May, Savill Gardens

Acer palmatum 'Crippsii'

Group 6a. An upright-growing dwarf shrub not exceeding 2.5 m (8 feet) in height, densely branched. Leaves small, five-lobed, fresh green but individual leaves differing. Introduced by Hillier's Nurseries, England, in 1928. It tends to die back suddenly without any apparent reason. It is a rare plant, comparable only to the much better known *A. palmatum* 'Shishi gashira', which grows better and becomes taller. Zone 6 (Europe 7)

Acer palmatum 'Deshōjō'. May, Westonbirt Arboretum

Acer palmatum 'Deshōjō'

Group 1b (Corallinum Group). Alternatively, *A. palmatum* 'Deshohjoh'. A fairly well growing shrub, up to 3 to 4 m (10–13 feet) with thin branchlets and shoots. Leaves 4–5 cm (1½–2 inches) wide, five-lobed, brilliantly red when unfolding, later turning dark pink and bluish green to green; fall color not spectacular. Origin Japanese, before 1900. Requiring a sheltered place in the garden, it is popular for bonsai. Similar cultivars include *A. palmatum* 'Chishio Improved', 'Otome zakura', and 'Shin deshōjō'. Zone 6 (Europe 7)

Acer palmatum 'Dissectum'

Group 4a. Synonym, *A. palmatum* 'Dissectum Viride'. A mushroom-shaped shrub, even a small tree up to 4 m (13 feet) and often much wider. Leaves seven-lobed, divided to the leaf base and every lobe finely dissected, summer color sumptuous green, turning dark yellow with some orange in fall. Originally described as *A. dissectum* by Carl Peter Thunberg in 1784 but not found in the wild. Given the Royal Horticultural Society's Award of Garden Merit in 1984. One of the most well known Japanese maples, there is a problem with the name 'Dissectum'. The most common 'Dissectum' seen in gardens is almost always the same clone but the cultivar sometimes sets seed, seedlings arise from time to time, and eventually the name has ended up being applied to a mixture of similar plants. The same problem has happened to *A. palmatum* 'Atropurpureum' but renaming would cause much confusion. Cultivars similar to 'Dissectum' include *A. palmatum* 'Dissectum Paucum', 'Ellen', 'Green Mist' (grows well, foliage light green), 'Kiri nishiki', 'Seki mori', and 'Waterfall'. Zone 6 (Europe 7)

Acer palmatum 'Dissectum'. May, Valley Gardens

Acer palmatum 'Dissectum'. May

Acer palmatum 'Dissectum Flavescens'. April

Acer palmatum **'Dissectum Flavescens'**

Group 4a. Closely related to *A. palmatum* 'Dissectum', somewhat more spreading. Leaves yellowish when unfolding, later turning light green; fall color clear yellow. Raised and introduced by Hillier's Nurseries, England, in 1928. Zone 6 (Europe 7)

Acer palmatum 'Dissectum Nigrum'. April

Acer palmatum **'Dissectum Nigrum'**

Group 4b., Synonym, *A. palmatum* 'Ever Red'. A plant of irregular mushroom shape to 3 m (10 feet) wide. Leaves dark red in spring, turning dull brown-green in summer, young leaves unfolding with a silvery coating of hairs, no other 'Dissectum'-type cultivars showing this feature; fall color

usually shiny red. Introduced by Koichiro Wada, Japan, in 1938. Similar, even better forms are *A. palmatum* 'Crimson Queen', 'Garnet', 'Inaba shidare', and 'Stella Rossa'. Zone 6 (Europe 7)

Acer palmatum 'Dissectum Paucum'. May, Savill Gardens

Acer palmatum 'Dissectum Paucum'. July

Acer palmatum **'Dissectum Paucum'**

Group 4a. Synonyms, *A. palmatum* 'Dissectum Palmatifidum', 'Palmatifidum'. A fast-growing, mushroom-shaped shrub up to 3 to 4 m (10–13 feet) and as wide. Leaves somewhat larger, less finely dissected, darker green than those of 'Dissectum'. Introduced by a Dutch nursery before 1900. The form is common in the United States as "Palmatifidium" (sic). Similar cultivars include *A. palmatum* 'Kiri nishiki' and 'Seki mori'. See also 'Washi no o'. Zone 6 (Europe 7)

Acer palmatum 'Dissectum Rubrifolium'. May, Arboretum Belmonte

Acer palmatum 'Dissectum Rubrifolium'. October

Acer palmatum 'Dissectum Rubrifolium'

Group 4a. A shrub of mushroom habit, about 3 m (10 feet) high and 4 m (13 feet) wide. Leaves brownish green when unfolding, turning dark green; fall color orange-yellow. Originally described as a botanical entity by Friedrich Anton Wilhelm Miquel in 1865. An old cultivar, now only rarely met with, it has been surpassed by the well-known 'Ornatum', still often wrongly called 'Dissectum Atropurpureum'. It is similar to *A. palmatum* 'Dissectum Rubrum'. *Acer palmatum* 'Berrima Bridge' (leaves green in spring, turning red in fall), 'Bronze Wing' (dissected bronze leaves), and 'Filigree Rouge' (leaves reddish in spring, soon turning dark green-brown) are similar. Zone 6 (Europe 7)

Acer palmatum 'Dissectum Rubrum'. May

Acer palmatum 'Dissectum Variegatum'. May, Valley Gardens

Acer palmatum 'Dissectum Rubrum'

Group 4a or Group 4b. Similar to *A. palmatum* 'Dissectum Rubrifolium'. Leaves more dissected, less brown in spring, turning green early in summer; fall color orange-yellow. Introduced by W. Barron, England, about 1875. Zone 6 (Europe 7)

Acer palmatum 'Dissectum Variegatum'

Group 4c. A mushroom-shaped shrub up to 3 m (10 feet) and as wide. Leaves brownish green, most white variegated, some almost green. Introduced by the Lawson Seed and Nursery Company, Great Britain, in 1874. Branches without variegated leaves appear often and should be removed. 'Dissectum Variegatum' is similar to *A. palmatum* 'Ornatum' but with some variegation. Now quite rare in gardens, similar, more strongly variegated cultivars are *A. palmatum* 'Goshiki shidare', 'Ruth Murray', and 'To yama nishiki'. Zone 6 (Europe 7)

Acer palmatum 'Eagle's Claw'
Group 6a. A small shrub, probably a witches'-broom. Leaves green, turning yellow, and crinkled and overlapping, hence 'Eagle's Claw'. It is suitable for bonsai. Zone 6 (Europe 7)

Acer palmatum 'Eagle's Claw'. November, Foliage Gardens, courtesy of H. Olsen

Acer palmatum 'Eddisbury'. May, Westonbirt Arboretum

Acer palmatum 'Eddisbury'
Group 1a. A strongly growing vase-shaped shrub up to 8 to 10 m (26–33 feet); branches coral-red in winter like those of the well-known *A. palmatum* 'Sango kaku'. Leaves sturdier than those of 'Sango kaku', more leathery and dark green; fall color less spectacular, usually greenish yellow. Raised and introduced by Morray & Sons, Great Britain, in 1970. 'Eddisbury' is not generally available in the nursery trade. Similar cultivars are 'Beni kawa' and 'Sango kaku'. Zone 6 (Europe 7)

Acer palmatum 'Eimini'. June

Acer palmatum 'Eimini'
Group 6a. A small dwarf, barely more than 1 m (3¼ feet) wide; densely branched with thin branchlets. Leaves 1–2 cm (⅜–¾ inch) wide, five-lobed, green. Found in the gardens of Villa Taranto, Italy, and introduced by Otto Eisenhut, Switzerland, about 1985. It is among the smallest cultivars of *A. palmatum* and is suitable for bonsai. *Acer palmatum* 'Coonara Pygmy' is similar in habit and 'Yatsubusa' is equally small, with tiny leaves. Zone 6 (Europe 7)

Acer palmatum 'Elegans'

Group 2a. Synonym, *A. palmatum* 'Septem-lobum Elegans'. A shrub or even a multi-stemmed tree up to 10 m (33 feet) and 5–6 m (16–20 feet) wide. Leaves seven-lobed, incised to half the leaf blade, sturdy, olive-green with hints of brown-red at the margins, unfolding leaves also brownish but soon turning green; fall color yellow with orange. Introduced by R. Smith and Company, Nursery, England, in 1874. A very desirable plant for larger gardens, there are only a few cultivars with similar habit and leaves, perhaps *A. palmatum* 'Kihachijō'. Zone 6 (Europe 7)

Acer palmatum 'Ellen'

Group 4a. A shrub of the mushroom type not exceeding 1 m (3¼ feet) in height but much wider. Leaves larger than those of similar cultivars, very lacy and dissected, fresh green, turning yellow in fall. Named for Mrs. Ellen van Weely, wife and daughter-in-law of the authors of the present book, introduced by Firma C. Esveld, Netherlands, in 1992. A selection from among seedlings of *A. palmatum* 'Dissectum', it is similar to 'Dissectum' or 'Waterfall', but both of those cultivars are taller. Zone 6 (Europe 7)

Acer palmatum 'Enkan'

Group 5b. An elegant, vase-shaped shrub up to 2 to 3 m (6½–10 feet), growing slowly. Leaves about 3 to 4 cm (1⅛–1½ inches) wide, dark wine-red, lobes linear. Supplied by Jiro Kobayashi, Japan, and imported to the Netherlands in 1991. It is similar to *A. palmatum* 'Red Pygmy' but keeps its wine-red color better. *Acer palmatum* 'Beni ubi gohon' is a similar cultivar with purple leaves. Zone 6 (Europe 7)

Acer palmatum 'Elegans'. September, Collingwood Grange

Acer palmatum 'Ellen'. July

Acer palmatum 'Enkan'. July

Acer palmatum 'Felice'. June

Acer palmatum 'Felice'

Group 4c. A bushy shrub probably to 2 m (6½ feet) wide. Leaves finely dissected, differently colored, young growth usually greenish orange-red, later turning dark brownish green, the bicolor effect maintained during most of summer. A chance seedling arising from open-pollinated 'Dissectum', named for Felice Renée van Gelderen, daughter and granddaughter of the authors of the present book, and introduced by Firma C. Esveld, Netherlands, in 1998. 'Felice' must prove its value but is promising and different. *Acer palmatum* 'Lemon Lime Lace' is similar but has light yellow-green foliage, turning orange in fall, with the leaves closely set at the ends of the shoots. Zone 6 (Europe 7)

Acer palmatum 'Filigree'. May

Acer palmatum 'Filigree'. May, Savill Gardens

Acer palmatum 'Filigree'

Group 4c. A slow-growing, mushroom-shaped shrub up to 2 m (6½ feet) and 3 m (10 feet) wide, densely branched. Leaves very finely dissected and incised, more so than in similar cultivars, light green with a silvery hue, turning yellow in fall. Introduced by Joel Spingarn, New York, in 1955. One of the best introductions of recent decades and deserving much more attention. It is suitable for small gardens and there are only a few maples that are both easy to grow and that do not grow fast. It is very similar to *A. palmatum* 'Suisei', possibly identical, and to 'Shigi no mai'. Zone 6 (Europe 7)

Acer palmatum 'Fior d'Arancio'. July

Acer palmatum 'Fior d'Arancio'

Group 2b. A shrub up to 7 to 8 m (23–26 feet), becoming treelike with age. Leaves unfolding wine-red but soon turning greenish brown; in July there is a bicolor effect. Origin unknown but first cultivated by Fratelli Gilardelli, Italy, and now propagated by Firma C. Esveld, Netherlands. A similar cultivar is *A. palmatum* 'Shinonome'. Zone 6 (Europe 7)

Acer palmatum 'Fireglow'

Group 1b. Synonym, *A. palmatum* 'Effegi'. A well-branched shrub, treelike with age, up to 10 m (33 feet) or more. Leaves 6–8 cm (2³⁄₈–3¹⁄₈ inches) wide, five- or seven-lobed, dark wine-red, keeping the color well during summer. Raised by Fratelli Gilardelli, Italy, and named by W. J. Spaargaren, Netherlands, in 1977. It can be compared with *A. palmatum* 'Bloodgood', 'Moonfire', or 'Nure gagi' but those cultivars usually grow into rather leggy treelike shrubs; 'Fireglow' seems to retain its shape better. 'Kingsville Red' is another erect shrub. Zone 6 (Europe 7)

Acer palmatum 'Fireglow'. July, Research Station for Nursery Stock

Acer palmatum 'Garnet'. May, Valley Gardens

Acer palmatum 'Garnet'

Group 4b. Synonym, *A. palmatum* 'Dissectum Garnet'. A vigorously growing shrub up to 3 m (10 feet) and 4–5 m (13–16 feet) wide with age, somewhat less branched than other similar cultivars but forming a nice plant that is easily grown. Leaves dark wine-red and keeping their color into fall unless fading in very dry situations; fall color shiny red. Found among a large number of seedlings imported from Italy to serve as rootstocks, introduced by Guldemond Brothers, Netherlands, in 1959. Given an Award of Merit by the Royal Boskoop Horticultural Society in 1959 and the Royal Horticultural Society's Award of Garden Merit in 1993. Perhaps the most widely grown 'Dissectum'-type cultivar of all, this popular maple is generally available in the nursery trade and is suitable for every garden save the smallest. Similar forms are *A. palmatum* 'Hatsu shigure' (leaves dark purple), 'Inaba shidare', 'Stella Rossa', and 'Sumi shidare' (leaves dark purple and deeply dissected). Zone 6 (Europe 7)

Acer palmatum 'Garnet'. October

Acer palmatum 'Garyū'. July, courtesy of H. Olsen

Acer palmatum 'Garyū'

Group 6b. Alternatively, *A. palmatum* 'Garyuh'. A slowly growing shrublet perhaps up to 1.5 m (5 feet). Leaves 3–4 cm (1⅛–1½ inches) wide, irregularly linear, distinctive, three-, five-, or seven-lobed. Origin Japanese, before 1960. *Garyū* means "one's own style or manner." It is a delicate plant, suitable for bonsai. Propagation is difficult due to the thin scion wood. Foliage of *A. palmatum* 'Beni fushigi' and 'Beni komachi' is similar but the habit is not. Zone 6 (Europe 7)

Acer palmatum 'Golden Pond'. October

Acer palmatum 'Golden Pond'

Group 3a. A shrub to 4 to 6 m (13–16 feet)
wide, usually wider than high. Leaves
greenish yellow in summer, turning brilliant yellow in fall. Imported from Japan as
'Shigure zome' but turning out to be entirely different, named and introduced by Firma
C. Esveld, Netherlands, in 1997. Zone 6
(Europe 7)

Acer palmatum 'Golden Pond'. October

Acer palmatum 'Goshiki shidare'. June

Acer palmatum 'Green Globe'. June, Fratelli Gilardelli

Acer palmatum 'Goshiki shidare'

Group 4c. A slow-growing plant of mushroom shape up to 2 m (6½ feet) and eventually 3 m (10 feet) wide. Leaves brown-red, cream and white variegated, deeply dissected. Origin Japanese. Suitable for small and sheltered gardens, it is a somewhat fragile plant, not easy to grow and only rarely available in the nursery trade. *Acer palmatum* 'Beni shidare Tricolor', with an illegitimate name, is very similar if not the same. Zone 6 (Europe 7)

Acer palmatum 'Green Globe'

Group 4a. A fast-growing shrub probably up to 4 to 5 m (13–16 feet) and about as wide, rounded rather than of the usual mushroom form. Leaves seven-lobed, very deeply divided, margins dissected, emerald-green in summer, turning yellow. Named and introduced by Fratelli Gilardelli, Italy, about 1980. It is similar to *A. palmatum* 'Demisec', and in the catalog of Fratelli Gilardelli 'Green Globe' is also called 'Viridis Olandese', which suggests close affinity to the Dutch type of 'Dissectum'. Zone 6 (Europe 7)

Acer palmatum 'Green Lace'. June, Fratelli Gilardelli

Acer palmatum 'Green Lace'

Group 4a. With a flat, mushroom habit, growing much wider than high. Leaves finely dissected, fresh green, turning golden yellow in fall. Named and introduced by Fratelli Gilardelli, Italy, about 1980. It is good for grafting on a standard in which case it develops a cascading habit. Zone 6 (Europe 7)

Acer palmatum 'Green Lace'. June, Fratelli Gilardelli

Acer palmatum 'Green Trompenburg'. August

Acer palmatum 'Hagoromo'. July

Acer palmatum 'Green Trompenburg'

Group 3a. A shrub, almost treelike, up to 10 m (33 feet), sparsely branched. Leaves seven-lobed, lobes with convex margins similar to those of *A. palmatum* 'Trompenburg', color fresh green; fall color orange-yellow. Found as a chance seedling in the Esveld Aceretum, Netherlands, sent to J. D. Vertrees, Oregon, registered by him, raised and introduced by Firma C. Esveld in 1980. There are no very similar cultivars. Zone 6 (Europe 7)

Acer palmatum 'Hagoromo'

Group 7. Synonyms, *A. palmatum* 'Hagaromo', 'Sessilifolium'. An upright shrub up to 10 m (33 feet), rather sparsely branched. Leaves three-, five-, or seven-lobed, sometimes without petioles, irregularly formed, giving an feathery impression, dark green. Originally described (as *A. sessilifolium*) by Carl Peter Thunberg, cultivated since at least 1845, and mentioned in the list of 1882. The name 'Hagoromo' has priority over 'Sessilifolium' because the latter name covers more than one clone. Said to be found as a sport on *A. palmatum*, it sometimes reverts to plain *A. palmatum*. It is suitable for medium-sized gardens. *Acer palmatum* 'Koshi mino', 'Momenshide', and 'Tsukuma no' are similar. Zone 6 (Europe 7)

Acer palmatum 'Hama otome'. October

Acer palmatum 'Hanami nishiki'. May, Savill Garden

Acer palmatum 'Hama otome'

Group 1c. A shrub up to 3 m (10 feet), densely branched. Leaves five-lobed, variable in form and size, texture thin, young leaves yellowish, later turning light green but with an undertone of yellow. Origin Japanese, before 1970. It is somewhat fragile, needing some shade in summer. Zone 6 (Europe 7)

Acer palmatum 'Hanami nishiki'

Group 6a. A slowly growing, densely branched shrub up to about 2 m (6½ feet) high and as wide. Leaves small, five-lobed, green, turning yellow in fall. Origin Japanese. *Hanami nishiki* means "flower viewing." This choice dwarf plant is rare in cultivation. As a young plant it sometimes develops vigorous shoots but this character-

Acer palmatum 'Hanami nishiki'. May, Savill Garden

stic soon disappears. It is also a bit tender.
Its habit is not unlike that of *A. palmatum*
'Kashima' or 'Tama hime' but those cultivars are more strongly growing. It is good
for bonsai. Zone 6 (Europe 7)

Acer palmatum 'Harusame'. July

Acer palmatum 'Harusame'

Group 2a. A sturdy shrub up to 4 m (13
feet) and as wide. Leaves seven-lobed, margins sharply serrate, color green in summer,
turning red with yellowish margins. Introduced by Koichiro Wada, Japan, in 1938.
Harusame means "spring rain." It is good
for large gardens but rare, sometimes misspelled as "Marusame." According to Vertrees, *Japanese Maples*, some leaves are
variegated but we have not observed that.
Zone 6 (Europe 7)

Acer palmatum 'Hazeroino'. June

Acer palmatum 'Hazeroino'

Group 7. A rather weakly growing upright
shrub up to 4 m (13 feet). Leaves of the
same shape as those of *A. palmatum* 'Ha-

goromo' but white and pink variegated.
Year of introduction unknown but certainly
before 1930, the original plant growing in
the Research Station, Boskoop, Netherlands, for many years. All plants in the
nursery trade and in cultivation are derived
from that tree, which is no longer present.
A collector's item. Zone 6 (Europe 7)

Acer palmatum 'Heptalobum'. July, Arboretum Belmonte

Acer palmatum 'Heptalobum'

Group 2a. Synonyms, *A. palmatum* var.
heptalobum, *A. palmatum* 'Septemlobum'.
A strongly growing shrubby tree up to 10 m
(33 feet) or occasionally more. Leaves seven-lobed, hence the name 'Heptalobum',
dark green, turning yellow-orange in fall.
Year of introduction unknown but certainly
long before 1900; described by Alfred Rehder in 1938. Not to be confused with the
obsolete name *A. heptalobum*, which is a
synonym of *A. campbellii* subsp. *flabellatum*. 'Heptalobum' is very close to true *A.
palmatum* subsp. *amoenum*. Often planted
in parks, many large specimens of 'Heptalobum' can be found in British gardens. It is
not impossible that there is more than one
clone in cultivation, however. Related
forms include *A. palmatum* 'Ōsakazuki',
with darker leaves, 'Hōgyoku', and 'Killar-
ney'. Zone 6 (Europe 7)

Acer palmatum 'Heptalobum Rubrum'. May

Acer palmatum 'Herbstfeuer'. June

Acer palmatum 'Heptalobum Rubrum'

Group 2b. A shrubby tree similar to *A. palmatum* 'Heptalobum' except for the leaves, rich purple in spring, fading to dull brown-green, afterward turning glowing orange-red. A Dutch cultivar introduced before 1900 but named later, a large plant was present in the collection of the Research Station in Boskoop, Netherlands, before 1950. Similar treelike forms include *A. palmatum* 'Ōgon sarasa', 'Ōsakazuki', and 'Toshi'. Zone 6 (Europe 7)

Acer palmatum 'Herbstfeuer'

Group 2a. A broad and densely growing treelike shrub. Leaves seven- or nine-lobed, texture firm, dark green; fall color often very good hence the German name *Herbstfeuer*, which means "autumn fire." Arose as a chance seedling at Andreas Bärtels's garden in Waake, Germany, and named by Firma C. Esveld, Netherlands, in 1985. In general appearance it combines the characteristics of *A. palmatum* with those of *A. circinatum* and may be a hybrid. Zone 6 (Europe 7)

Acer palmatum 'Hessei'

Group 2b. Synonym, *A. palmatum* 'Elegans Purpureum'. A shrub up to 5 to 6 m (16–20 feet) and wider than high. Leaves dull brown red, turning greenish brown in summer; fall color attractive shiny brown-red. Described by Fritz Graf von Schwerin and introduced by Hesse Nurseries, Germany, in 1893. 'Hes

Acer palmatum 'Hessei'. May, Von Gimborn Arboretum

sei' is fairly commonly cultivated. Similar forms are *A. palmatum* 'Rubrum', which is slower growing, and 'Tsukushi gata'. Zone 6 (Europe 7)

Acer palmatum 'Higasa yama'

Group 1c. A vase-shaped plant up to 7 to 8 m (23–26 feet) in sheltered locations, densely branched. Leaves five-lobed, somewhat crinkled and heavily yellow variegated in the best individuals. Introduced by the Yokohama Nursery Company, Japan, in 1901. It is a well-known plant but good specimens are rare. Unfortunately, it reverts easily. Branches bearing green leaves should be removed as soon as possible, otherwise the entire plant becomes green in a short time. Green-leaved shoots may develop variegated leaves the next spring but it is an unstable plant in this respect. *Acer palmatum* 'Shin higasa yama' is pink rather than yellow variegated. Zone 6 (Europe 7)

Acer palmatum 'Hōgyoku'

Group 2a. Alternatively, *A. palmatum* 'Hohgyoku'. A large shrubby tree up to 6 to 7 m (20–23 feet) and becoming as wide. Leaves 6–8 cm (2⅜–3⅛ inches) wide, seven-lobed, margins only finely serrate, sturdy; fall color brilliant yellow. Origin Japanese, mentioned in the list of 1882. It is an easy plant to grow but rather uncommon. *Acer palmatum* 'Heptalobum' and 'Golden Pond' (leaves smaller than those of 'Hōgyoku' and turning orange) are similar. Zone 6 (Europe 7)

Acer palmatum 'Higasa yama'. May, Valley Gardens

Acer palmatum 'Hōgyoku'.

Acer palmatum 'Hōgyoku'. October

Acer palmatum 'Hohman's Variegated'. October, Foliage Gardens, courtesy of H. Olsen

Acer palmatum 'Hohman's Variegated'

Group 1c (Roseomarginatum Group). A strongly growing shrub. Leaves pink and white variegated. Raised and introduced by Henry Hohman, Kingsville Nurseries, Maryland. Zone 6 (Europe 7)

Acer palmatum 'Hondoshi'. August

Acer palmatum 'Hondoshi'

Group 2a. A strongly growing shrubby tree probably up to 8 to 10 m (26–33 feet). Leaves 8–10 cm (3⅛–4 inches) wide, five- or seven-lobed, texture firm, dark green; young growth often pink. Introduced in the Netherlands in 1994 from Milim Botanic Garden, Korea. Similar cultivars are *A. palmatum* 'Heptalobum' and 'Kihachijō'. Zone 6 (Europe 7)

Acer palmatum 'Hupp's Dwarf'. May

Acer palmatum 'Hupp's Dwarf'

Group 6a. A small shrub, possibly up to 1 m (3¼ feet) and as wide. Leaves small but well developed, five-lobed, green, turning yellow. Found as a chance seedling by Barbara Hupp, Oregon, and named and introduced by J. D. Vertrees in 1976. It is suitable for bonsai. Similar dwarfs are *A. palmatum* 'Sharp's Pygmy' and, somewhat different, 'Koto hime'. Zone 6 (Europe 7)

Acer palmatum 'Ibo nishiki'. May

Acer palmatum 'Ibo nishiki'

Group 1a. With the same habit and foliage as *A. palmatum* subsp. *palmatum* but not the bark, which develops rough fissures. Fall color red. Origin very likely Japanese. Similar forms are *A. palmatum* 'Ara kawa' and 'Nishiki gawa', but 'Ibo nishiki' remains smaller. Zone 6 (Europe 7)

Acer palmatum 'Ide no sato'. May, Savill Gardens

Acer palmatum 'Iijima sunago'. May

Acer palmatum 'Ide no sato'

Group 2a. A shrub about 4 m (13 feet) in height. Leaves seven-lobed, brownish green, turning orange in fall. Origin Japanese. It is a rare form, not particularly attractive. *Acer palmatum* 'Kinran' and 'Shigarami' are similar but have larger leaves. Zone 6 (Europe 7)

Acer palmatum 'Iijima sunago'

Group 3b. A slender, upright-growing tree-like shrub. Leaves 8–12 cm (3⅛–4¾ inches) wide, incised almost to the base, margins serrate, color a mixture of green and brown in summer; fall color orange-red or orange-yellow. Fruits almost white, an exceptional color. Origin Japanese, mentioned in the list of 1882. *Sunago* means "dusted." The cultivar is noted for its fall color. Zone 6 (Europe 7)

Acer palmatum 'Inaba shidare'. November

Acer palmatum 'Inaba shidare'

Group 4b. A strongly growing, mushroom-shaped shrub up to 3 m (10 feet) and even wider. Leaves very dark wine-red, not fading to a lighter color; fall color almost absent unless planted in dry situations. Introduced from the Yokohama Nursery Company, Japan, through John Henny's nursery, Oregon, and Messrs K. Wezelenburg & Sons, Netherlands. Given the Royal Horticultural Society's Award of Garden Merit in 1993. It has open habit and when grafted on a stan-

Acer palmatum 'Inaba shidare'. June, Fratelli Gilardelli

dard forms a small tree with cascading branches. It is now surpassed by *A. palmatum* 'Garnet', which has a better habit. Other similar forms are *A. palmatum* 'Red Dragon' and 'Stella Rossa'. Zone 6 (Europe 7)

Acer palmatum 'Inazuma'. July

Acer palmatum 'Issai nishiki kawazu'. July

Acer palmatum 'Issai nishiki kawazu'

Group 1a. A slow-growing shrub probably not more than 2 m (6½ feet) high, usually much less; bark very rigid and appearing as though wounded and healed again. Origin Japanese. Other rough bark maples are *A. palmatum* 'Ara kawa' and 'Nishiki gawa' but both of those grow faster and the rough bark is differently textured. Suitable for bonsai and mainly a collector's item, 'Issai nishiki momiji' grows weakly and is quite rare. *Acer palmatum* 'Amime nishiki' is similar to 'Issai nishiki kawazu' if not identical. Zone 6 (Europe 7)

Acer palmatum 'Inazuma'. October

Acer palmatum 'Inazuma'

Group 3b. A treelike shrub up to 8 to 10 m (26–33 feet). Leaves deeply divided, almost to the base, purple when unfolding, turning soft brown and dark green, later becoming brilliant orange-red. Origin Japanese, mentioned in the list of 1882. *Inazuma* means "thunder." One of the best for fall color, this beautiful maple should be planted more frequently but it needs much space. Similar cultivars are *A. palmatum* 'Matsukaze' and, to a lesser extent, 'Beni kagami'. Zone 6 (Europe 7)

Acer palmatum 'Itami nishiki'. July, Foliage Gardens, courtesy of H. Olsen

Acer palmatum 'Itami nishiki'

Group 1c (Roseomarginatum Group). A small shrub. Leaves tricolored: pink, white, and green-red. Origin Japanese or Korean. There is little experience in cultivation with this rare cultivar. Zone 6 (Europe 7)

Acer palmatum 'Jirō shidare'

Group 7. Alternatively, *A. palmatum* 'Jiroh shidare'. A mushroom-shaped shrub of beautiful form up to 2 m (6½ feet) or more with cascading branches. Leaves 4–5 cm (1½–2 inches) wide, five-lobed, fresh green, turning a good yellow in fall. Introduced by the Shibamichi Honten Nursery, Japan, before 1965. It is one of the very few mushroom-shaped maples with leaves shaped as those in the species. Almost all others have dissected leaves. Zone 6 (Europe 7)

Acer palmatum 'Kaba'

Group 7. A small shrub, more or less growing erectly. Leaves narrow, lobes dark green but occasionally some leaves reddish. Found by John Gibbons, Doncaster, England, and introduced by Firma C. Esveld, Netherlands. *Kaba* means "hippopotamus" and the name was given by Mrs. Ellen van Weely. Similar cultivars include *A. palmatum* 'Maiko' and 'Wabito'. Zone 6 (Europe 7)

Acer palmatum 'Kagiri nishiki'

Group 1c (Roseomarginatum Group). Synonym, *A. palmatum* 'Roseomarginatum'. A strongly growing shrub up to 8 m (26 feet), higher than wide and densely branched. Leaves 3–5 cm (1⅛–2 inches) wide, five-lobed, margins white and pink. Origin Japanese, mentioned in the list of 1710, in cultivation in Europe by 1865, and reported under the name 'Roseomarginatum' by Fritz Graf von Schwerin in 1893. Given the Royal Horticultural Society's First Class Certificate in 1865. Since the name 'Roseomarginatum' is sometimes used for other cultivars, the name 'Kagiri nishiki' is much preferred. 'Kagiri nishiki' develops branchlets with reverted green leaves and such branchlets should be removed carefully. Similar, less fast growing cultivars are *A. palmatum* 'Beni shichi henge', 'Butterfly', and 'Kara ori nishiki', most pink variegated. Also similar are *A. palmatum* 'Kagiri', with leaf margin color even more clearly defined than in 'Kagiri nishiki', and 'Tsuru'. Zone 6 (Europe 7)

Acer palmatum 'Jirō shidare'. July

Acer palmatum 'Kaba'. September, van der Maat

Acer palmatum 'Kagiri nishiki'. June

Acer palmatum 'Kamagata'. June

Acer palmatum 'Kara ori nishiki'. July

Acer palmatum 'Kamagata'

Group 6a. A dwarf, densely and healthily branched, up to 1.5 m (5 feet) in 20 to 25 years. Leaves five-lobed, split to the leaf base, brownish green, later turning green; fall color yellow. Selected by J. D. Vertrees, Oregon, in 1970. This neatly formed plant, desirable for bonsai, is similar to *A. palmatum* 'Beni fushigi' and 'Beni komachi'. Zone 6 (Europe 7)

Acer palmatum 'Kara ori nishiki'

Group 1c (Roseomarginatum Group). A slender, upright-growing treelike shrub up to 4 to 5 m (13–16 feet). Leaves 3–5 cm (1⅛–2 inches) wide, five-lobed, margins white, speckled with brown-red. Origin Japanese, mentioned in the list of 1733. It is an uncommon cultivar that can be compared with *A. palmatum* 'Butterfly', which is better known. Individual leaves of 'Butterfly' are difficult to distinguish from those of 'Kara ori nishiki' but the habits of the plants are different. *Acer palmatum* 'Kagiri nishiki' is also similar but grows faster, and 'Oregon' is of the same habit and color as 'Kara ori nishiki'. Zone 6 (Europe 7)

Acer palmatum 'Karasu gawa'

Group 1c (Versicolor Group). A plant up to 4 m (13 feet), densely branched, branchlets pinkish green, young branchlets often tending to die back in winter. Leaves 4–5 cm (1½–2 inches) wide, five-lobed, irregularly formed, green with large pink and white variegation. Introduced by the Angyō Maple Nursery, Japan, in 1930. One of the most spectacular cultivars in the Versicolor Group, this beautifully variegated maple is for collectors. Although less beautifully variegated there are better growing cultivars such as *A. palmatum* 'Asahi zuru', 'Oridono nishiki', and 'Wakō nishiki' (alternatively, 'Wakoh nishiki'). *Acer palmatum* 'Murasaki Shikibu', the cultivar name honoring a person, is a good pink variegated plant. Zone 6 (Europe 7)

Acer palmatum 'Karasu gawa'. June

Acer palmatum 'Kasagi yama'

Group 3c. An openly growing shrub up to 4 to 5 m (13–16 feet) and about as wide. Leaves seven-lobed, divided to the base, brownish red, pink variegated; fall color orange-reddish. Origin Japanese, before 1960. It is a spectacular plant, unfortunately not easy to propagate. There are a few similar forms such as *A. palmatum* 'Ariadne' and 'Beni shigitatsu sawa'. Zone 6 (Europe 7)

Acer palmatum 'Kasen nishiki'

Group 1c (Versicolor Group). A shrubby tree up to 5 to 6 m (16–20 feet). Leaves with some creamy white variegation, reverting easily. Origin Japanese, mentioned in the list of 1882. It is less conspicuously variegated than some other cultivars. Similar cultivars include *A. palmatum* 'Kagerō' (alternatively, 'Kageroh') and 'Kyū ei nishiki' (alternatively, 'Kyuh ei nishiki'; leaves yellow variegated), 'Ō iso nishiki' (alternatively, 'Oh iso nishiki'; greenish, variegated with a few white spots), 'Suruga nishiki' (some white variegation), and 'Tama nishiki' (somewhat more pink variegated than 'Kasen nishiki'). Zone 6 (Europe 7)

Acer palmatum 'Kashima'

Group 6a. Synonym, *A. palmatum* 'Chiba'. A densely branched shrub up to 3 to 4 m (13–16 feet) after many years, becoming at least as wide. Leaves smaller than those of the species. Origin Japanese. *Chiba*, the

Acer palmatum 'Kasagi yama'. April

Acer palmatum 'Kasen nishiki'. June

Acer palmatum 'Kashima'. July

Acer palmatum 'Kashima'. July, Castle Gardens Arcen

name under which this cultivar sometimes appears in the nursery trade, means "dwarf." In the United States a more compactly growing plant is called 'Kashima' but it is probably *A. palmatum* 'Kashima yatsubusa'. 'Kashima' gives the impression of being a giant bonsai. *Acer palmatum* 'Tama hime' is similar but grows higher and wider; 'Kashima yatsubusa' is more compact. *Acer palmatum* 'Dwarf Shishi' is a miniature form of 'Kashima'. Zone 6 (Europe 7)

Acer palmatum 'Katsura'
Group 1a (Aureum Group). A treelike shrub up to 10 m (33 feet) or sometimes more, densely branched. Leaves 3–5 cm (1⅛–2 inches) wide, five-lobed, orange when unfolding, turning golden yellow with a hint

Acer palmatum 'Katsura'. May, Herkenrode Gardens

of green in summer but turning back to orange in fall. Origin Japanese, before 1960. *Katsura* is a girl's name. One of the most spectacular Japanese maples, it is widely available in the nursery trade and commonly planted. Similar cultivars are *A. palmatum* 'Akebono', 'Katsura nishiki' (with a hint of pink in the unfolding orange-yellow leaves), 'Orange Dream', 'Sode nishiki', and 'Ueno homare'. Zone 6 (Europe 7)

Acer palmatum 'Katsura'. May, Savill Gardens

Acer palmatum 'Kihachijō'. May, Valley Gardens

Acer palmatum 'Kihachijō'

Group 3a. Alternatively, *A. palmatum* 'Kihachijoh'. A sturdy, strong-growing shrub up to 6 to 7 m (20–23 feet) or sometimes more and 4–5 m (13–16 feet) wide. Leaves seven-lobed, divided to the base, somewhat leathery, summer color green, turning red, orange, and yellow in fall. Origin Japanese, mentioned in the list of 1733, the name spelled in different ways. It is distinctive, with no very similar cultivars. *Acer palmatum* 'Meoto' has strongly serrated leaves somewhat like those of 'Kihachijō', which is less serrate, however; the leaves of 'Ō izu' (alternatively, 'Oh izu') are more like those of 'Kihachijō'. Zone 6 (Europe 7)

Acer palmatum 'Kihachijō'. October

Acer palmatum 'Kinran'. May, Valley Gardens

Acer palmatum 'Kiri nishiki'. October

Acer palmatum 'Kinran'

Group 3b. A shrub up to 4 m (13 feet) and as wide, sparsely branched, not unusual in Group 3. Leaves large, seven-lobed, deeply divided, shiny brown-red when unfolding, turning dull greenish brown in summer; fall color good. Origin Japanese, mentioned in the list of 1733. Similar forms are *A. palmatum* 'Beni gasa', 'Hessei' and 'Nomura'. Zone 6 (Europe 7)

Acer palmatum 'Kiri nishiki'

Group 4a. A low-growing shrub, wider than high, with an irregular habit. Leaves deeply divided, the lobes dissected but less so than in other similar cultivars, summer color green, turning orange-yellow in fall. Origin Japanese, mentioned in the list of 1710. Rare in cultivation, a similar form is *A. palmatum* 'Seki mori'. Zone 6 (Europe 7)

Acer palmatum 'Kinshi'. October, Wezelenburg & Sons

Acer palmatum 'Kishūzan'. August

Acer palmatum 'Kinshi'

Group 5a. A modestly growing shrub probably up to 3 m (10 feet). Leaves 5–6 cm (2–2⅜ inches) wide, seven-lobed, lobes narrow but not as linear as those of *A. palmatum* 'Koto no ito', color fresh green; fall color yellow to orange. Introduced by the Shibamichi Honten Nursery, Japan, in 1984 but possibly in cultivation much longer. *Kinshi* means "with golden threads." It is similar to *A. palmatum* 'Ao meshime no uchi'. Zone 6 (Europe 7)

Acer palmatum 'Kishūzan'

Group 3a. Alternatively, *A. palmatum* 'Kishuhzan'. A rather large shrub with spreading habit. Leaves deeply divided and the margins again deeply serrate, color dark green; fall color yellow to orange. Introduced in 1993 or 1994 to the the Netherlands from Korea. It is similar to *A. palmatum* 'Rufescens'. Zone 6 (Europe 7)

Acer palmatum 'Kiyo hime'. June

Acer palmatum 'Kogane nishiki'. July

Acer palmatum 'Kiyo hime'

Group 6a. A low and slowly growing shrub, densely branched. Leaves small, five-lobed, dark green with reddish margins and tips; fall color orange-yellow. Origin Japanese. Much in use as a bonsai plant but it tends to die back suddenly, longer and vigorous shoots especially suffering from this phenomenon. It has an even smaller counterpart, *A. palmatum* 'Murasaki kiyo hime'. Also similar are *A. palmatum* 'Beni yatsubusa' (margins and apexes of leaves reddish in spring, turning green), 'Hime tsuma gaki' (leaves like those of 'Tsuma gaki' but smaller and more deeply incised), and 'Suzu maru'; 'Komachi hime' is almost identical to 'Kiyo hime'. Zone 6 (Europe 7)

Acer palmatum 'Kogane nishiki'

Group 1a. A shrubby plant up to 5 to 6 m (16–20 feet), in habit much like the species. Leaves five- or seven-lobed, green; fall color yellow-orange. Introduced by Jiro Kobayashi, Japan, before 1970. *Kogane nishiki* means "golden brocade." Zone 6 (Europe 7)

Acer palmatum 'Koko'. June, Villa Taranto

Acer palmatum 'Koko'

Group 1a. A densely branched shrub up to 7 to 8 m (23–26 feet). Leaves small, five-lobed, often somewhat deformed, olive-green. The plant grows in the gardens of Villa Taranto, Italy, and the name could not be traced further. Zone 6 (Europe 7)

Acer palmatum 'Koreanum'. September

Acer palmatum 'Koreanum'

Group 2a. A treelike shrub up to 12 to 15 m (39–50 feet), openly branched, bark dark. Leaves seven-lobed, dark green in summer, turning to tones of yellow, red, and orange in fall. Samaras large, nicely colored. Given the Royal Horticultural Society's Award of Garden Merit in 1993. A botanical entity *coreanum*, a synonym of *A. palmatum* subsp. *amoenum*, was originally described by Takenoshin Nakai in 1914 but it is not certain that 'Koreanum' is the same plant. 'Koreanum' is similar to *A. palmatum* 'Ōsaka-zuki' and 'Taihai'. Zone 6 (Europe 7)

Acer palmatum 'Koriba'. August

Acer palmatum 'Koriba'

Group 1b. An erect, slow-growing shrub up to 4 to 5 m (13–16 feet). Leaves five-lobed, purple in spring, dull green in summer, turning brilliant orange-yellow in fall. Received from Jiro Kobayashi, Japan, and imported to the Netherlands in 1992. Its red petioles add to its beauty. Zone 6 (Europe 7)

Acer palmatum 'Koriba'. October

Acer palmatum 'Ko shibori nishiki'

Group 1c. A shrub up to 2.5 m (8 feet), densely branched with thin twigs. Leaves small, five-lobed, usually fully green but some slightly variegated with yellow dots; fall color yellow. Introduced by Koichiro Wada, Japan, in 1938. The original plant may have been much more variegated. *Acer palmatum* 'Kasen nishiki' is somewhat similar. Zone 6 (Europe 7)

Acer palmatum 'Koshi mino'

Group 7. Synonym, *A. palmatum* 'Sessilifolium'. A fast-growing shrubby tree of erect habit up to 7 to 8 m (23–26 feet) or occasionally more. Leaves irregularly, usually five-lobed, dark green, turning orange-yellow or bronze in fall. Introduced by Brian O. Mulligan, Seattle, Washington, in 1938 but originally probably of Japanese origin. It is very similar if not identical to *A. palmatum* 'Hagoromo', which is also called 'Sessilifolium'. In Japan there is also the variegated *A. palmatum* 'Koshi mino nishiki', which may be very similar to 'Hazeroino'. Zone 6 (Europe 7)

Acer palmatum 'Koto hime'

Group 6a. A dwarf with very short but stout branchlets, up to 1.5 m (5 feet) after many years. Leaves small, five-lobed, densely set on short branchlets, usually green or brownish green, turning yellow or orange in fall. It is a very desirable dwarf but hard to grow as the scions are short and the mother plant is easily destroyed if too much scion wood is cut off. There is a variegated form, *A. palmatum* 'Goshiki koto hime', which reverts readily (as true for 'Mikata nishiki') and is probably now lost to commercial cultivation. Zone 6 (Europe 7)

Acer palmatum 'Ko shibori nishiki'. May

Acer palmatum 'Koshi mino'. June

Acer palmatum 'Koto hime'. April

Acer palmatum 'Koto maru'. May, Valley Gardens

Acer palmatum 'Koto no ito'. April

Acer palmatum 'Koto maru'

Group 6a. A slow-growing rounded dwarf bush up to 1.5 m (5 feet). Leaves green, middle lobe distinctly shorter than the side lobes. Origin probably Japanese, in cultivation since 1980 in the Netherlands, much longer in Britain in view of the fact that the plant in Savill Gardens, England, is quite old. It is a fragile plant, tending to die back suddenly. *Acer palmatum* 'Hama no maru' (probably a dwarf like other cultivars with a reduced central apex), 'Renjaku maru' (leaf apexes red), and 'Sharp's Pygmy' are similar. Zone 6 (Europe 7)

Acer palmatum 'Koto no ito'

Group 5a. A shrub up to 3 m (10 feet) or occasionally more. Leaves five- or seven-lobed, lobes threadlike, summer color fresh green, turning yellow in fall. Introduced by Koichiro Wada, Japan, in 1938. Similar cultivars include *A. palmatum* 'Linearilobum' and 'Shinobu ga oka', also 'Ao meshime no uchi', with somewhat wider lobes, but 'Koto no ito' has the narrowest lobes of all. It can happen that leaf growth reverts to producing leaves with wider lobes. Such branchlets may produce narrow-lobed leaves the next spring but if not they must be removed. *Acer palmatum* 'Iso shibuki', 'Kansai koto no ito', and 'Moto koto no ito', the latter with leaves broader than those of 'Koto no ito', are similar. Zone 6 (Europe 7)

Acer palmatum 'Kōya san'

Group 6a. Alternatively, *A. palmatum* 'Kohya san'. A spreading shrublet probably not more than 1.5 m (5 feet) high. Leaves five-lobed with somewhat elongated tips, green, second summer growth orange. Named after a Japanese mountain and introduced by D. van der Maat, Netherlands, in 1996. Zone 6 (Europe 7)

Acer palmatum 'Kōya san'. August, van der Maat

Acer palmatum 'Kurabu yama'. October

Acer palmatum 'Kurabu yama'

Group 3a. Synonym, *A. palmatum* 'Kurabe-yama'. A spreading shrub up to 5 m (16 feet) and as wide, sparsely branched. Leaves deeply divided, rusty brown in spring, fresh green in summer; fall color spectacular yellow and orange. Origin Japanese, mentioned in the list of 1882. It is a distinctive maple; there are no very similar cultivars. Zone 6 (Europe 7)

Acer palmatum 'Linearilobum'. April

Acer palmatum 'Linearilobum'

Group 5a. Synonyms, *A. palmatum* 'Lineare', 'Linearifolium'. A treelike shrub up to 10 m (33 feet) or more but usually smaller, densely branched. Leaves five- or seven-lobed, lobes very narrow and divided to the leaf base, color fresh green; fall color a beautiful yellow. Originally described as a botanical entity by Friedrich Anton Wilhelm Miquel in 1867. Given the Royal Horticultural Society's Award of Garden Merit in 1993. This maple appears under a variety of names in the nursery trade and it is difficult

Acer palmatum 'Kurui jishi'. July

Acer palmatum 'Kurui jishi'

Group 6a. A stiff, upright-growing plant up to 4 m (13 feet), densely branched. Leaves dark gray-green, lobes strongly incurved. Origin Japanese, first mentioned in the list of 1882. Sometimes confused with *A. palmatum* 'Okushimo', 'Kurui jishi' has less incurved leaves. *Acer palmatum* 'Crippsii' is also similar but grows more slowly. Zone 6 (Europe 7)

Acer palmatum 'Linearilobum'. May, Valley Gardens

to decide which forms are identical. *Acer palmatum* 'Scolopendrifolium' is probably a synonym; 'Shinobu ga oka' is similar but has pinkish fruits. Other similar cultivars are *A. palmatum* 'Ao meshime no uchi' and 'Koto no ito' but the latter has leaves with narrower lobes. Zone 6 (Europe 7)

Acer palmatum 'Little Princess'. July

Acer palmatum 'Lozita'. July

Acer palmatum 'Lozita'

Group 2b. A sturdy shrub up to 4 to 5 m (13–16 feet) and almost as wide. Leaves seven-lobed, margins finely serrate, color dark purplish red. Raised and introduced by Vermeulen & Son, New Jersey, in 1984. It is one of the darkest forms but has no significant fall color. It may be compared with a number of other dark-leaved forms such as *A. palmatum* 'Bloodgood', 'Fireglow', 'Shōjō', and 'Tsukushi gata'. Zone 6 (Europe 7)

Acer palmatum 'Little Princess'

Group 6a. Synonym, *A. palmatum* 'Mapi no machi hime'. A dwarf shrub of irregular habit, sparsely branched. Leaves five- or seven-lobed, somewhat wrinkled, fresh green; fall color usually yellow but not outstanding. Named by J. Russell, Great Britain, about 1988. The name 'Mapi no machi hime' may be the correct one but documentation is insufficient to decide. There is confusion regarding this cultivar. Two clones are in cultivation, bearing the same name. The one illustrated resembles *A. palmatum* 'Chiyo hime'. The other resembles *A. palmatum* 'Kiyo hime'. *Acer palmatum* 'Kiyo hime' has similar leaves but grows more vigorously. Zone 6 (Europe 7)

Acer palmatum 'Lutescens'

Group 2a. A vigorously growing shrub up to 6 to 8 m (20–23 feet) and wider than high. Leaves seven-lobed, sturdy, yellowish in spring, turning fresh green in summer; fall color outstanding, yellow and gold. Raised and introduced by Hillier's Nurseries, England, in 1928. The leaf shape is different from that of other cultivars, being more acuminate. It is rarely seen in cultivation. Similar cultivars are *A. palmatum* 'Heptalobum' and 'Samidare', both with greener leaves and good fall color. Zone 6 (Europe 7)

Acer palmatum 'Maiko'

Group 7. A narrow, almost columnar tree up to 5 to 6 m (16–20 feet). Leaves seven-lobed, differently shaped, sometimes quite narrow and irregularly deeply cleft to the base, bright green; fall color yellow. Introduced by J. D. Vertrees, Oregon. *Maiko* means "dancing doll" and the cultivar name is sometimes misspelled "Maoka" or "Miaoka." It should not be confused with 'Beni maiko', an entirely different cultivar. *Acer palmatum* 'Mama' is similar but larger; 'Yūshide' (alternatively, 'Yuhshide') has leaves that are more irregularly formed than those of 'Maiko'. Zone 6 (Europe 7)

Acer palmatum 'Mai mori'

Group 1c (Versicolor Group). A modest shrub about 4 m (13 feet) high and wide, densely branched. Leaves five-lobed, dark green but some leaves completely pink or whitish, other leaves variegated in part. Origin Japanese, imported to the Netherlands in 1990. It reverts easily so it is wise to remove completely green-leaved branches in order to maintain the variegation. *Acer palmatum* 'Ao ba nishiki' (leaves with sharp lobes and white variegated), 'Deshōjō nishiki' (alternatively, 'Deshohjoh nishiki'; leaves with whitish spots, pinkish in spring), 'Kippō nishiki' (alternatively, 'Kippoh nishiki'; leaves light green and pink variegated), 'Sango nishiki' (leaves yellow-green variegated), and 'Shin tsuzure nishiki' (leaves yellowish green variegated) are similar. Zone 6 (Europe 7)

Acer palmatum 'Lutescens'. October, Savill Gardens

Acer palmatum 'Maiko'. May, Herkenrode Gardens

Acer palmatum 'Mai mori'. June

Acer palmatum 'Mama'. August, van der Maat

Acer palmatum 'Margaret Bee'. June, Westonbirt Arboretum

Acer palmatum 'Marjan'. August, van der Maat

Acer palmatum 'Mama'

Group 1a. A rounded, bushy shrub, 5–6 m (16–20 feet) high and wide. Leaves differently shaped, according to Vertrees, *Japanese Maples*, no two alike, color fresh green. Origin Japanese, mentioned in the list of 1733. *Mama* means "doing as one pleases," which is appropriate considering the variable foliage. Unfortunately, the variable foliage reverts from time to time to normal foliage. It is important to control this phenomenon by removing reverted twigs and branches because they grow more strongly. *Acer palmatum* 'Kaba', 'Maiko', and 'Wabito' have similar irregular foliage. Zone 6 (Europe 7)

Acer palmatum 'Margaret Bee'

Group 2b. A shrub up to 7 to 8 m (23–26 feet). Leaves 6–8 cm (2⅜–3⅛ inches) wide, seven-lobed, rather sturdy, dark purple. Introduced by Peter A. Gregory, England, before 1990. It is similar to *A. palmatum* 'Lozita' and 'Moonfire', for example, but 'Margaret Bee' produces long shoots with juvenile-form foliage. Zone 6 (Europe 7)

Acer palmatum 'Marjan'

Group 2b. An erect shrubby tree up to 7 to 8 m (23–26 feet) with age. Leaves dark purple in spring, turning somewhat lighter in summer; fall color shiny red. Found among a large batch of seedlings by Mrs. Marjan van der Maat and named for her. After 10 years of observation, introduced by D. van der Maat, Netherlands, in 1998. Zone 6 (Europe 7)

Acer palmatum 'Masu kagami'

Group 2c. A spreading shrub, wider than high. Leaves deeply divided, almost crimson when unfolding, turning reddish green with slight, sometimes absent, white or yellow-pink variegation. Origin Japanese, mentioned in the list of 1733. Rarely seen in cultivation, it is a fragile plant and needs protection against wind. Zone 6 (Europe 7)

Acer palmatum 'Masu murasaki'

Group 2b. A shrubby tree up to about 7 to 8 m (23–26 feet). Leaves purple, keeping the color well in summer; fall color inconspicuous. Origin Japanese, mentioned in the list of 1719. This rather rare plant is similar to many cultivars of the type, such as *A. palmatum* 'Beni kagami' and 'Shōjō', and lacks outstanding qualities. Zone 6 (Europe 7)

Acer palmatum 'Masu kagami'. May, Savill Gardens

Acer palmatum 'Masu murasaki'. May, Herkenrode Gardens

Acer palmatum 'Matsu ga e'. June

Acer palmatum 'Matsukaze'. October

Acer palmatum subsp. *matsumurae.* May, Herkenrode Gardens

Acer palmatum 'Matsu ga e'

Group 1c (Roseomarginatum Group). A rather narrowly growing tree, usually not more than 4 to 5 m (13–16 feet) tall. Leaves small, five-lobed, attractively white and pink variegated. Origin doubtless Japanese, named by Fritz Graf von Schwerin in 1893. An attractive plant but rare, its appearance it is between that of *A. palmatum* 'Beni shichi henge' and 'Kagiri nishiki' and is similar to that of 'Kara ori nishiki'. Zone 6 (Europe 7)

Acer palmatum 'Matsukaze'. May, Valley Gardens

Acer palmatum 'Matsukaze'

Group 3b. A sturdy and firm shrubby tree up to 7 to 9 m (23–30 feet), sparsely branched. Leaves seven-lobed, firm, purplish red when unfolding, turning an inconspicuous greenish brown; fall color spectacular glistening red and orange-red. Origin Japanese, mentioned in the list of 1710. It is not commonly planted. Similar cultivars are *A. palmatum* 'Inazuma' and 'Nicholsonii'. Zone 6 (Europe 7)

Acer palmatum subsp. *matsumurae*

A large shrubby tree about as wide as high. Leaves deeply divided, fresh green. Native to moist forests, usually, of Japan, mixed with subspecies *palmatum*. Described by Gen'ichi Koidzumi in 1911. Material from the wild is rare and plants in cultivation are usually clones. Zone 6 (Europe 7)

Acer palmatum 'Matsuyoi'. October, Foliage Gardens, courtesy of H. Olsen

Acer palmatum 'Matsuyoi'

Group 2a. A shrub to 5 m (16 feet) wide. Leaves unusual, some hanging, others bent or lobes twisted, color at first yellowish, turning green when mature. Origin doubtless Japanese. Zone 6 (Europe 7)

Acer palmatum 'Matthew'. October, Foliage Gardens, courtesy of H. Olsen

Acer palmatum 'Mikawa yatsubusa'. July

Acer palmatum 'Mikawa yatsubusa'

Group 6a. An attractive small bush up to 1.5 m (5 feet), densely branched. Leaves crowded on short twigs, five-lobed, with a long central lobe, color fresh green. Introduced by J. D. Vertrees, Oregon, before 1970. This dwarf plant is one of the very best cultivars for bonsai. It is rather difficult to propagate, as usual for most dwarfs. *Acer palmatum* 'Seiun kaku' is similar but grows much faster; 'Shishi yatsubusa', a

Acer palmatum 'Matthew'. October, Foliage Gardens, courtesy of H. Olsen

Acer palmatum 'Matthew'

Group 6a. A witches'-broom. Leaves small, green, turning yellow in fall. Found as a seedling, introduced by William Schwartz, Green Mansions Nursery, Pennsylvania, about 1976. Witches'-brooms can be very similar and 'Matthew' is almost indistinguishable from *A. palmatum* 'Coonara Pygmy', for example. Zone 6 (Europe 7)

Acer palmatum 'Mikawa yatsubusa'. October

good dwarf but rarely seen, has smaller leaves that are less star-shaped than those of 'Mikawa yatsubusa'. Zone 6 (Europe 7)

Acer palmatum 'Mirte'

Group 3a. A shrubby tree up to 10 m (33 feet) and almost as wide, openly branched. Leaves seven-lobed, deeply divided almost to the base, having a peculiar chocolate color in spring, later olive-green, turning dark blackish green in summer, fading back to olive in fall. Named for Mirte Yasemin van Gelderen, daughter and granddaughter of the authors of the present book. Raised and introduced by Firma C. Esveld, Netherlands, in 1986. 'Mirte' has an unusual combination of colors. Zone 6 (Europe 7)

Acer palmatum 'Mirte'. May, Herkenrode Gardens

Acer palmatum 'Mizu kuguri'. April

Acer palmatum 'Mizu kuguri'

Group 3a. A shrub up to 2 to 3 m (6½–10 feet), usually wider than high, regularly branched. Leaves seven-lobed, colors changing, in spring green with an orange hue, later green to olive-green with pinkish hue; fall color golden yellow to brown-yellow with some orange hue. Origin Japanese, mentioned in the list of 1733. Its attractive change of colors is distinctive. Zone 6 (Europe 7)

Acer palmatum 'Mizu kuguri'. April

Acer palmatum 'Momiji gasa'. May, Savill Gardens

Acer palmatum 'Mon zukushi'. April

Acer palmatum 'Moonfire'. May

Acer palmatum 'Momiji gasa'

Group 2a. Synonyms, *A. japonicum* 'Momiji gasa', *A. shirasawanum* 'Momiji gasa', *A. sieboldianum* 'Momiji gasa'. A sturdy shrub or tree up to 4 to 5 m (13–16 feet) and about 3 m (10 feet) wide. Leaves seven- or nine-lobed, covered with white hairs when unfolding, pubescence less prominent when leaves mature in summer, color reddish purple; fall color golden with red. Origin probably Japanese. A rare maple, cultivated in Korea and in Europe seen only at Savill Gardens, England. *Acer shirasawanum* 'Gloria' and 'Yasemin' are similar. Zone 6 (Europe 7)

Acer palmatum 'Mon zukushi'

Group 1a. A well-branched shrub up to 4 m (13 feet) and about as wide. Leaves yellowish green in spring, turning green in summer, becoming orange-yellow in fall. Origin Japanese, mentioned in the list of 1719. It has many seven-lobed leaves and thus might also be included in Group 2a. There are a few similar cultivars such as *A. palmatum* 'Ko shibori nishiki' and 'Shikage ori nishiki'. Zone 6 (Europe 7)

Acer palmatum 'Moonfire'

Group 2b. A compact shrub up to 4 m (13 feet). Leaves seven-lobed, wine-red, turning purple, second growth in summer fiery red, not much fall color. Introduced by Richard P. Wolff, Pennsylvania, in 1970. It is not easy to propagate. This good purple-leaved plant grows slowly, remaining smaller than *A. palmatum* 'Bloodgood', and is suitable for smaller gardens. *Acer palmatum* 'Nigrum' and 'Nure sagi' are similar, also dark purple. Zone 6 (Europe 7)

Acer palmatum 'Murasaki kiyo hime'. April

Acer palmatum 'Murasaki kiyo hime'

Group 6a. A neat dwarf shrub usually not more than 1.5 m (5 feet) high, occasionally to 2.5 m (8 feet) wide, densely branched. Leaves small, five-lobed, dark green with a purplish hint and with purple apexes and margins, this color disappearing later in the year. Origin Japanese. It is suitable for bonsai and for small gardens. *Acer palmatum* 'Kiyo hime' is similar but grows taller. Zone 6 (Europe 7)

Acer palmatum 'Murasaki kiyo hime'. April

Acer palmatum 'Mure hibari'. May, Valley Gardens

Acer palmatum 'Mure hibari'. May, Valley Gardens

Acer palmatum 'Mure hibari'

Group 3a. An upright-growing shrubby tree up to 4 to 5 m (13–16 feet), later becoming more spreading, not very densely branched. Leaves deeply divided, lobes pointing forward, margins irregularly incised, dark green. Origin Japanese, mentioned in the list of 1882 and documented by Gen'ichi Koidzumi in 1911. *Mure hibari* means "a flock of skylarks." It is a rare form and a somewhat aberrant member of Group 3a. Zone 6 (Europe 7)

Acer palmatum 'Muro gawa'. May, Valley Gardens

Acer palmatum 'Nanase gawa'. July

Acer palmatum 'Muro gawa'

Group 3a. A strongly growing shrub up to 8 to 10 m (26–33 feet) and as wide, densely branched, later cascading to the ground. Leaves large, seven-lobed, purple in spring, turning olive-green; fall color orange-red. Origin Japanese. Not a bad choice for use in landscaping but it remains inconspicuous for a long time. *Acer palmatum* 'Kinran' and 'Nomura' are somewhat similar but do not cascade as much. Zone 6 (Europe 7)

Acer palmatum 'Nanase gawa'

Group 7. A plant up to 4 m (13 feet). Leaves deeply divided but margins not incised, color purplish to dark green, turning crimson in fall. Origin Japanese, mentioned in the list of 1733. It does not fit well into the group system, falling between Group 3 and Group 4. Zone 6 (Europe 7)

Acer palmatum 'Nicholsonii'

Group 3a. A shrubby tree up to 5 m (16 feet) and even wider. Leaves rather large, seven-lobed, unfolding olive-green to olive-brown, turning green or olive in summer; fall color brilliant orange and red. Named by Fritz Graf von Schwerin in 1893, honoring George Nicholson. It is one of the best cultivars in the group and is readily available in the nursery trade. *Acer palmatum* 'Heiwa' (leaves incised to the base, silvery bronze in spring), 'Inazuma', and 'Mon Papa' (a spreading shrub, leaves purplish brown in spring, becoming olive-green) are some of the few similar forms. Zone 6 (Europe 7)

Acer palmatum 'Nicholsonii'. May, Herkenrode Gardens

Acer palmatum 'Nicholsonii'. Arboretum Belmonte

Acer palmatum 'Nigrum'. July

Acer palmatum 'Nigrum'

Group 1b. A shrub reaching 4 m (13 feet) in height with age and becoming perhaps 3 m (10 feet) wide. Leaves five-lobed, very dark purple and not turning lighter. Fruits green-white, contrasting well with the dark foliage. Introduced by Hillier's Nurseries, England, in 1928. Not to be confused with *A. palmatum* 'Dissectum Nigrum', which is very different. 'Nigrum' is useful for the small garden. It is a smaller expression of *A. palmatum* 'Atropurpureum' or 'Bloodgood'. Zone 6 (Europe 7)

Acer palmatum 'Nishiki gasane'. May

Acer palmatum 'Nishiki gawa'. November

Acer palmatum 'Nishiki gasane'

Group 1c. A slowly growing shrub up to 2 m (6½ feet) or somewhat more with age. Leaves five- or seven-lobed, green with yellow dots and stripes. Mentioned in the list of 1882, introduced by the Yokohama Nursery Company, Japan, in 1896. It is a difficult plant to grow and would be forgotten if there were more strongly yellow variegated cultivars. It needs shade to avoid sunburn. *Acer palmatum* 'Sagara nishiki' is very similar if not identical. *Acer palmatum* 'Kasane jishi', 'Meihō' (alternatively, 'Meihoh'), 'Meihō nishiki' (alternatively, 'Meihoh nishiki'; more variegated than 'Meihō', some leaves completely yellow), 'Shiro fu nishiki' and 'Yōdo nishiki' (alternatively, 'Yohdo nishiki') are also similar. Zone 6 (Europe 7)

Acer palmatum 'Nishiki gawa'. November

Acer palmatum 'Nishiki gawa'

Group 1a. A shrubby tree up to 8 to 10 m (26–33 feet), densely branched; bark corky. Leaves fresh green; fall color red, unusual for green-leaved *A. palmatum* cultivars. Origin Japanese. Its main feature is the corky bark with longitudinal coarse creases, present even on young branches. It is called "pine bark maple." *Acer palmatum* 'Ara kawa' is similar and is called "rough bark maple." 'Ibo nishiki' is also a rough bark maple and all three cultivars can be used for bonsai. *Acer palmatum* 'Ara kawa ukon' has yellow fall color; 'Tobiosho' is like 'Nishiki gawa' except that it does not develop a rough bark. Zone 6 (Europe 7)

Acer palmatum 'Nomura'. May

Acer palmatum 'Nomura'

Group 2b. A fast-growing shrubby tree up to 8 m (26 feet) and almost as wide. Leaves seven-lobed, bold and shiny, purple when leafing out, with a minute pubescence soon disappearing, summer color brownish green; fall color good. Introduced by the Yokohama Nursery Company, Japan, in 1896. Sometimes found in the nursery trade, it is present in several maple collections. Similar cultivars are *A. palmatum* 'Daimyō nishiki' (alternatively, 'Daimyoh nishiki'; a compact shrub with brownish purple leaves), 'Kinran', 'Muro gawa', 'Musashino' (leaves less deeply cleft), 'Nikkō shichihenge' (alternatively, 'Nikkoh shichihenge'), 'Nomura kōyō' ('Nomura kohyoh'; leaves somewhat lighter than those of 'Nomura' when unfolding), 'Nomura ōba' (alternatively, 'Nomura ohba'; leaves lighter yet), and 'Nomura ōjō (alternatively, 'Nomura ohjoh'; leaves somewhat narrower, spring color lighter red). Zone 6 (Europe 7)

Acer palmatum 'Nure sagi'

Group 1b. A slow-growing upright shrub up to 4 to 5 m (13–16 feet). Leaves small, five- or seven-lobed, when unfolding with a light pubescence, soon disappearing, color dark purple, fading very little, turning glowing red in fall. Origin Japanese, mentioned in the list of 1882. *Nure sagi* means "wet heron." It is nice, similar to *A. palmatum* 'Moonfire' or 'Shōjō'. *Acer palmatum* 'Bloodgood' is also similar but grows more quickly and becomes taller, and 'Hi no tsukasa' has leaves that are less dark purple. Zone 6 (Europe 7)

Acer palmatum 'Nomura nishiki'. June

Acer palmatum 'Nomura nishiki'

Group 4b. A low, mushroom-shaped plant. Leaves dark purple, becoming dark green-purple in early fall, later turning scarlet; Vertrees, *Japanese Maples,* states that fall color is orange-red, as usual in drier climates. Other sources suggest the leaves should be bronze or green with yellow spots. The name 'Nomura nishiki' has not been traced in Hisao Nakajima's records. It is strange that the cultivar does not match other forms whose names include the word *nomura.* Although the name must be mistrusted, the plant is very attractive. When staked it develops cascading branches. Zone 6 (Europe 7)

Acer palmatum 'Nure sagi'. October

Acer palmatum 'Ōgon sarasa'. October, Castle Gardens Arcen

Acer palmatum 'Ōjishi'. July

Acer palmatum 'Ōgon sarasa'

Group 3b. Alternatively, *A. palmatum* 'Ohgon sarasa'. A treelike shrub up to 10 m (33 feet) or more, sparsely branched. Leaves seven-lobed, purplish when unfolding, turning bronze or moss-green; fall color usually orange to orange-red. Reported to be a seedling of 'Nomura', named by Brian O. Mulligan, and introduced through the Washington Park Arboretum, University of Washington, Seattle, in 1958. *Ōgon sarasa* means "gold calico cloth." It is rare in cultivation. Similar cultivars are *A. palmatum* 'Yūgure', which is darker purple, and 'Shikage ori nishiki'. Zone 6 (Europe 7)

Acer palmatum 'Ōjishi'

Group 6a. Alternatively, *Acer palmatum* 'Ohjishi'. Growing only a few centimeters per year, perhaps up to 1 m (3¼ feet) after 25 years. Leaves similar to but less wrinkled than those of *A. palmatum* 'Shishi gashira', a plant that becomes much taller. Origin certainly Japanese. One of the most dwarfed forms in the entire range of cultivars of *A. palmatum*, it is a desirable plant but only rarely available in the nursery trade due to the fact that almost no scions are available. Zone 6 (Europe 7)

Acer palmatum 'Ōkagami'

Group 2b. Alternatively, *A. palmatum* 'Ohkagami'. A beautiful shrub up to 4 to 5 m (13–16 feet). Leaves seven-lobed, deeply divided, margins slightly serrated, color dark purple; fall color glowing red. Introduced by Angyō Maple Nursery, Japan, in 1930. It is only occasionally seen in cultivation. Similar forms are *A. palmatum* 'Moon fire' and 'Nure sagi' but those cultivars are slightly more upright; 'Hyōtei' (alternatively 'Hyohtei') is also similar to 'Ōkagami'. Zone 6 (Europe 7)

Acer palmatum 'Ōkagami'. May

Acer palmatum 'Okukuji nishiki'. October

Acer palmatum 'Okukuji nishiki'

Group 1c (Roseomarginatum Group). A densely branched shrub up to 4 to 5 m (13–16 feet) and almost as wide, occasionally more. Leaves small, five-lobed, heavily white and cream variegated; fall color not conspicuous. Origin most probably Japanese. There are several similar cultivars, such as *A. palmatum* 'Beni shichi henge', 'Butterfly', and 'Kara ori nishiki'. Zone 6 (Europe 7)

Acer palmatum 'Okushimo'. July

Acer palmatum 'Okushimo'

Group 1a. A vase-shaped shrub up to 5 m (16 feet) but only 2–3 m (6½–10 feet) wide, densely branched. Leaves five- or seven-lobed, radiating outward, each lobe ending in a tapering point; fall color may be very nice but this is not always so. Origin Japanese, mentioned in the list of 1719. *Okushimo* means "pepper and salt." 'Okushimo' has been called many wrong names, such as "Chishio" (not to be confused with true *A. palmatum* 'Chishio'), "Crispa," "Crispum," and "Cristatum." There is a similar cultivar, *A. palmatum* 'Kurui jishi', with even more curled leaves. Zone 6 (Europe 7)

Acer palmatum 'Omato'. August

Acer palmatum 'Omato'

Group 2a. A shrub or tree up to 7 to 8 m (23–26 feet) and almost as wide. Leaves about 10 cm (4 inches) wide, seven-lobed, brownish green in spring, turning green in summer; fall color very good, mostly orange-red to red. Introduced by Angyō Maple Nursery, Japan, in 1930. It is rare in cultivation due to competition with more well known cultivars such as *A. palmatum* 'Ōsakazuki'. *Acer palmatum* 'Mure suzume', with dark green-purplish leaves, good fall color, and reddish leaf apexes, is similar to 'Omato'. Zone 6 (Europe 7)

Acer palmatum 'Omure yama'. September

Acer palmatum 'Orange Dream'. April

Acer palmatum 'Omure yama'

Group 3a. Synonym, *A. palmatum* 'Omurayama'. A tree up to 7 to 8 m (23–26 feet) and becoming even wider. Leaves seven-lobed, deeply divided, fresh green, turning brilliant golden orange and red in fall. Raised and introduced by Koichiro Wada, Japan, in 1938. Distinctive, it is a highlight among spreading trees with cascading branches. It needs much space and is suitable only for large gardens. *Acer palmatum* 'Myoi' is similar but its leaves are somewhat larger and pendulous and the plant remains smaller. Zone 6 (Europe 7)

Acer palmatum 'Orange Dream'

Group 1a (Aureum Group). A strongly growing shrub up to 6 to 8 m (20–26 feet), densely branched. Leaves golden yellow when unfolding, becoming somewhat greenish in summer, then turning to orange-golden hues in fall. Raised and introduced by Fratelli Gilardelli, Italy, before 1991. A plant for medium-sized gardens, this cultivar has a very good future. Similar forms are the well-known *A. palmatum* 'Katsura' and the more recent introductions, 'Sode nishiki' and 'Ueno homare'. Zone 6 (Europe 7)

Acer palmatum 'Orange Dream'. April

Acer palmatum 'Orangeola'. October, Foliage Gardens, courtesy of H. Olsen

Acer palmatum 'Orangeola'. July

Acer palmatum 'Orangeola'

Group 4b. A large shrub with cascading branches, when staked perhaps reaching several meters (yards) in height. Leaves finely dissected, orange-red when unfolding, changing to brown-red or even dark green; fall color glistening red and orange. Introduced by Greer Gardens, Oregon, about 1988. Given an Award of Merit by the Royal Boskoop Horticultural Society in 1996. This spectacular shrub is one of the finest of the more recent introductions. The leaves often persist until mid-November so fall color is present for a long time. Zone 6 (Europe 7)

Acer palmatum 'Orangeola'. July

Acer palmatum 'Oridono nishiki'

Group 1c (Versicolor Group). Synonyms, *A. palmatum* 'Orido nishiki', 'Versicolor' (in nurseries). An upright-growing shrub up to 5 to 6 m (16–20 feet), densely branched, thin twigs prone to some dieback, which is also usual in similar cultivars. Leaves 5–6 cm (2–2³⁄₈ inches) wide, five-lobed, green but heavily pink and white variegated; not much fall color. Mentioned in the list of 1882 and introduced by the Yokohama Nursery Company, Japan, in 1896. The variegation is not completely stable; green-leaved twigs appear rather frequently and must be removed. 'Oridono nishiki' is also sensitive to late spring frosts. Similar cultivars are *Acer palmatum* 'Asahi zuru' (stronger but less variegated), 'Diana Verkade' (foliage similar to 'Oridono nishiki' but the plant

Acer palmatum 'Oridono nishiki'. June

tending to become as broad as tall), 'Hikaru Genji' (the cultivar name honoring a person and the plant with some yellow leaves among the pink-and-green foliage), 'Izu no odoriko' (strongly growing), 'Karasu gawa', and 'Rokugatsuen nishiki' (leaf lobes slightly convex). Zone 6 (Europe 7)

Acer palmatum 'Ornatum'. October, Wisley Garden

Acer palmatum 'Ornatum'

Group 4b. Synonym, *A. palmatum* 'Dissectum Atropurpureum'. A large shrub of mushroom shape, up to 3 m (10 feet) and 5–6 m (16–20 feet) wide after many years. Leaves deeply dissected and incised, dark brown when unfolding, turning through brown, green, and reddish to brilliant orange and yellow fall color. Named by Elie Abel Carrière in 1867, 'Dissectum Atropurpureum' dating from J. Hogg in 1879. 'Ornatum' is a spectacular cultivar that is still often sold under the invalid name 'Dissectum Atropurpureum', which covers several slightly different forms. 'Ornatum' is the best known of all the cultivars with finely dissected leaves and is also one of the finest. *Acer palmatum* 'Beni shidare' is similar if not the same. *Acer palmatum* 'Barrie Bergman' (rusty red leaves), 'Beni kumo no su' (leaves dark red in spring, fading to green; fall color yellow), 'Brocade', and 'Takara yama' (leaves with an underlying greenish color) are also similar to 'Ornatum'. Zone 6 (Europe 7)

Acer palmatum 'Ornatum'. May, Herkenrode Garden

Acer palmatum 'Ōsakazuki'. July, Arboretum Belmonte

Acer palmatum 'Ōsakazuki'. November

Acer palmatum 'Ōsakazuki'

Group 2a. Alternatively, *Acer palmatum* 'Ohsakazuki'. A treelike shrub up to 10 m (33 feet) or even more, tending to become wider in age. Leaves 8–10 cm (3⅛–4 inches) wide, bold, seven-lobed, olive-brown when unfolding, becoming dark brownish green in summer; fall color spectacular orange, red, and dark red. Origin Japanese, mentioned on the list of 1882. Given the Royal Horticultural Society's Award of Garden Merit in 1993. One of the best known Japanese maples, it is widely planted and available from many nurseries. Similar forms include *A. palmatum* 'Ōgon sarasa', 'Omato', 'Ōsakazuki no akame' (alternatively, 'Ohsakazuki no akame'), and 'Taihai'. Zone 6 (Europe 7)

Acer palmatum 'Oshio beni'

Group 2b. A sturdy, upright-growing shrub up to 6 m (20 feet) and as wide. Leaves dark purple when unfolding, becoming brown in summer. Introduced by the Yokohama Nursery Company, Japan, in 1898. Several clones are available in the nursery trade under this name, especially in the United States. 'Oshio beni' is thus a problematic name. Zone 6 (Europe 7)

Acer palmatum 'Oshio beni'. October, Wisley Garden

Acer palmatum 'Oto hime'. August

Acer palmatum 'Otome zakura'. April

Acer palmatum 'Oto hime'

Group 6a. A compact shrublet, nevertheless growing vigorously when young. Leaves fresh green, turning yellow in fall; petioles exceptionally long. Described by J. D. Vertrees, Oregon, before 1987. This semidwarf is also suitable for bonsai. Although no very similar dwarfs are available, *A. palmatum* 'Tama hime' may be mentioned for comparison. Zone 6 (Europe 7)

Acer palmatum 'Otome zakura'. May

Acer palmatum 'Otome zakura'

Group 1b (Corallinum Group). A densely branched shrub up to 2.5 m (8 feet) and about as wide; branchlets thin and fragile. Leaves 4–5 cm (1½–2 inches) wide but size variable, five-lobed, brilliant scarlet when unfolding, later fading bluish pink and green. Origin certainly Japanese, before 1987. Similar forms include *A. palmatum* 'Beni maiko', 'Chishio', 'Deshōjō', and 'Seigai ha' (unfolding leaves reddish brown, later pink). A difference is that 'Otome zakura' usually has both small and large leaves on the same plant. Zone 6 (Europe 7)

Acer palmatum subsp. palmatum

Synonym, *A. polymorphum.* A shrub or tree up to 12 to 15 m (39–50 feet), rarely higher; branches and shoots green-brown with small white markings. Leaves 4–7 cm (1½–2¾ inches) wide, five-lobed, lobes finely serrate, color green; fall color yellow. Flowers in small terminal corymbs, purplish red with white. Samaras 1 cm (⅜ inch) long, nutlets small. Native to mixed forests, 500–1500 m (1600–4900 feet), of Japan, Korea, Taiwan, and eastern China. Cultivars of this species are very common in cultivation. In addition to the many named cultivars, thousands of unnamed seedlings of varying interest are present in many parks and gardens. Zone 5 (Europe 6)

Acer palmatum subsp. *palmatum.* October, Winkworth Arboretum

Acer palmatum 'Peaches and Cream'. September

Acer palmatum 'Peaches and Cream'

Group 3c. A rather compact shrub up to 3 m (10 feet) and about as wide. Leaves densely arranged along the twigs, variegation reticulate, greenish pink and white. Found by Don Teese, Yamina Rare Plants, Australia, as a seedling of 'Reticulatum' in 1980. It is closely related also to *A. palmatum* 'Beni shigitatsu sawa' and, to a lesser extent, 'Ariadne'. Zone 6 (Europe 7)

Acer palmatum subsp. *palmatum.* November, Arboretum Kalmthout

Acer palmatum 'Pendulum Julian'. May

Acer palmatum 'Pendulum Julian'

Group 4b. A mushroom-shaped bush usually not more than 3 m (10 feet) high and 4–5 m (13–16 feet) wide. Leaves much like those of *A. palmatum* 'Ornatum', deeply dissected and incised, dark brown when unfolding, turning through brown, green, and reddish to brilliant orange and yellow fall color, perhaps fading somewhat quicker. Raised by the Yokohama Nursery Company, Japan, about 1935 and introduced by Henry Hohman, Kingsville Nurseries, Maryland, in 1950. Often misspelled "Pendula Julian," in general appearance 'Pendulum Julian' is somewhat similar to a couple of cultivars with brown-red foliage, 'Beni tsukasa shidare' and 'Mioun', the latter named but yet to be released. Zone 6 (Europe 7)

Acer palmatum 'Pink Filigree'. June, Fratelli Gilardelli

Acer palmatum 'Pink Filigree'. June, Fratelli Gilardelli

Acer palmatum 'Pink Filigree'

Group 4b. A slowly growing, mushroom-shaped shrub, probably not more than 2.5 m (8 feet) high. Leaves very finely dissected reddish brown in spring, later turning pinkish brown; fall color outstanding, the brown leaves covered with crimson, giving an exciting look. Introduced by Fratelli Gilardelli, Italy, about 1994 after a long period of observation. It seems destined to become one of the more popular of the more recent introductions. Zone 6 (Europe 7)

Acer palmatum 'Pixie'. October, Foliage Gardens, courtesy of H. Olsen

Acer palmatum 'Purpureum Angustilobum'. April

Acer palmatum 'Pixie'

Group 6b. A shrublet not more than 1.5 m (5 feet) high. Leaves small, seven-lobed, dark purple. Introduced by the Buchholz Nursery, Oregon, in 1990. It is suitable for the smallest garden or for bonsai. Zone 6 (Europe 7)

Acer palmatum 'Purpureum Angustilobum'

Group 5b. A shrub up to 2.5 m (8 feet) and as wide, densely branched. Leaves five-lobed, linear, dark purple when unfolding, later duller purple. *Acer palmatum* 'Enkan' and 'Red Pygmy' are similar but both of them grow more slowly than 'Purpureum Angustilobum'. Zone 6 (Europe 7)

Acer palmatum 'Purpureum'. May

Acer palmatum 'Purpureum'

Group 1b. Synonym, *A. palmatum* 'Purpureum Superbum'. A sturdy shrubby tree up to 6 m (20 feet) with stout branches. Leaves unfolding dark purple, fading quickly to reddish brown, green-brown, to dark green; fall color good, usually bright red. Introduced by the Lawson Seed and Nursery Company, Great Britain, in 1874. Although sometimes confused with *A. palmatum* 'Deshōjō', 'Purpureum' is entirely different. Zone 6 (Europe 7)

Acer palmatum 'Red Autumn Lace'. June

Acer palmatum 'Red Autumn Lace'

Group 4a. A mushroom-shaped shrub about 2.5 m (8 feet) high and about as wide. Leaves finely dissected, green in summer, and as one of the few green-leaved Group 4 cultivars, fall color brilliant red. Raised, named, and introduced after many years of observation by Fratelli Gilardelli, Italy, about 1992. *Acer palmatum* 'Koyō ao shidare' (alternatively, 'Koyoh ao shidare') is similar. Zone 6 (Europe 7)

Acer palmatum 'Red Autumn Lace'. October

Acer palmatum 'Red Filigree Lace'. June

Acer palmatum 'Red Filigree Lace'

Group 6b. Synonym, *A. palmatum* 'Red Lace' A slowly growing plant, twigs thin and fragile. Leaves threadlike, dark purple, not fading. Found by William J. Curtis, Oregon, about 1950 and sold to other nurserymen, first to W. Goddard, British Columbia, who sold it to John Mitsch, Oregon, and finally it came to Iseli Nursery, Oregon, which propagated it and introduced it about 1965. This splendid plant has the finest dissected leaves of all cultivars of Group 4b. It is, unfortunately, difficult to propagate. Zone 6 (Europe 7)

Acer palmatum 'Red Dragon'. May or June, Savill Gardens

Acer palmatum 'Red Dragon'

Group 4b. A large shrub or even a small tree when staked; branches cascading. Leaves finely dissected, intense purple, not fading unless in a dry and hot climate. Introduced by Graham Roberts, New Zealand, in 1990. *Acer palmatum* 'Inaba shidare' and 'Stella Rossa' are similar in most respects. Zone 6 (Europe 7)

Acer palmatum 'Red Flash'. May or June

Acer palmatum 'Red Flash'

Group 1b. An upright and compactly growing shrub up to about 5 to 6 m (16–20 feet), well branched. Leaves five-lobed, dark red, unfolding new leaves scarlet, thus giving a bicolor effect. Raised and introduced by Fratelli Gilardelli, Italy, about 1992. It shows promise. Zone 6 (Europe 7)

Acer palmatum 'Red Pygmy'. May, Savill Gardens

Acer palmatum 'Red Select'. November

Acer palmatum 'Red Pygmy'

Group 5b. A modestly growing shrub up to 3 to 4 m (10–13 feet) and about half that width, densely branched. Leaves five-lobed, linear and dark purple when unfolding, turning greenish brown, becoming reddish in fall; fall color not outstanding. Found nameless in an Italian garden and introduced by Firma C. Esveld, Netherlands, in 1969. Given an Award of Merit by the Royal Boskoop Horticultural Society in 1969 and the Royal Horticultural Society's Award of Garden Merit in 1993. Similar cultivars are *A. palmatum* 'Atrolineare', 'Enkan', 'Kansai aka schichigosan' (leaves dark red-purple), 'Keiser', 'Nimura' (leaves broader than those of 'Red Pygmy'), 'Pung Kill', 'Purpureum Angustilobum', and 'Red Spider'. Zone 6 (Europe 7)

Acer palmatum 'Red Select'

Group 4b. A well-growing, mushroom-shaped plant up to 2 m (6½ feet) and 3–4 m (10–13 feet) wide. Leaves finely dissected, dark purple, turning greenish purple later but losing color in summer; fall color dark red speckled with crimson. Raised and introduced by J. D. Vertrees, Oregon, before 1978. It is similar to *A. palmatum* 'Crimson Queen' and 'Dissectum Nigrum'. Zone 6 (Europe 7)

Acer palmatum 'Reticulatum'. October

Acer palmatum 'Reticulatum'. July

Acer palmatum 'Reticulatum'

Group 2c. Probable synonyms, *A. palmatum* 'Shigitatsu', 'Shigitatsu sawa'. A shrub 4–5 m (13–16 feet) high and about as wide. Leaves seven-lobed, green with white reticulations on the main veins. Origin Japanese but named by Edouard François André, France, in 1870, prior to a Japanese name

Acer palmatum 'Rising Sun'.

Acer palmatum 'Rising Sun'. October

appearing in the list of 1882. Less easy to grow outdoors, it is extremely nice when forced in spring. *Acer palmatum* 'Samuri' (more yellowish green) and 'Sawa chidori' are similar. Zone 6 (Europe 7)

Acer palmatum 'Rising Sun'

Group 1a. A bushy shrub up to 5 to 6 m (16–20 feet), possibly more with age. Leaves five-lobed, fresh green in summer, turning to lovely tones of orange, yellow, and red in fall, the color holding for several weeks when weather permits. Raised and introduced by Firma C. Esveld, Netherlands, in 1997. *Acer palmatum* 'Ichigyoji' is similar. Zone 6 (Europe 7)

Acer palmatum 'Rubrum'. April

Acer palmatum 'Rubrum'

Group 2b. Synonyms, *A. japonicum* 'Purpureum', *A. palmatum* 'Sanguineum' in part. A slow-growing sturdy shrub up to 4 m (13 feet) and at least as wide. Leaves large, seven-lobed, unfolding purple-red, soon fading to greenish purple; fall color usually splendid, orange-yellow to glistening red. Introduced by Philipp Franz von Siebold in 1864 to the Netherlands. Although rare in collections this beautiful plant is suitable for smaller gardens. *Acer palmatum* 'Taimin nishiki' is practically identical except for some pink variegated leaves. Zone 6 (Europe 7)

Acer palmatum 'Ruby Stars'. May, Foliage Gardens, courtesy of H. Olsen

Acer palmatum 'Ruby Stars'

Group 6b. A dwarf. Leaves star-shaped, the central lobe longer. Found as a witches'-broom on *A. palmatum* 'Bloodgood'. Zone 6 (Europe 7)

Acer palmatum 'Ruby Stars'. May, Foliage Gardens, courtesy of H. Olsen

Acer palmatum 'Rufescens'. August

Acer palmatum 'Rufescens'

Group 3a. A shrub up to 5 to 6 m (16–20 feet) and 6–8 m (20–26 feet) wide, sparsely branched. Leaves seven-lobed, deeply divided, margins wavy and conspicuously serrate, green; fall color orange-red to yellow. Named and introduced by J. A. Siesmayer, Germany, in 1888. The name 'Rufescens' is sometimes used as a substitute for 'Nicholsonii', which is not correct. There appears to be a plant sold as 'Rufescens' the leaves of which unfold purple and soon become green but the correct name for that form is unknown to us. Zone 6 (Europe 7)

Acer palmatum 'Rugose Select'. June

Acer palmatum 'Rugose Select'

Group 3c. A shrub up to 2.5 m (8 feet), openly branched. Leaves seven-lobed, lobes irregularly shaped, texture rugose, color brown-purple with some pink. Found by J. D. Vertrees, Oregon, and sent for trial to the Netherlands about 1980. The name was provisional but a provisional name often persists. In spring it is almost like *A. palmatum* 'Kasagi yama' but later in the season 'Rugose Select' is less attractive. Zone 6 (Europe 7)

Acer palmatum 'Ryoku ryū'. June

Acer palmatum 'Ryūzu'. May

Acer palmatum 'Ryoku ryū'

Group 6a. Alternatively, *A. palmatum* 'Ryoku ryuh'. A semidwarf up to 2 m (6½ feet) or a little more, well and densely branched. Leaves five-lobed, lobes long tapering, color fresh green, turning yellow in fall. Origin Japanese, imported to the Netherlands in 1991. *Acer palmatum* 'Ao kanzashi' (a bit variegated), 'Ōgi nagashi' (alternatively, 'Ohgi nagashi'; traces of yellowish variegation and leaves incised and a bit crinkled), and 'Okina' (young shoots purple, leaves very small, narrow, dissected, and crinkled) are similar. Zone 6 (Europe 7)

Acer palmatum 'Ryūzu'

Group 6a. Alternatively, *A. palmatum* 'Ryuhzu'. A neat, dwarf shrub up to 1.5 m (5 feet) or somewhat more, densely branched. Leaves 3–4 cm (1⅛–1½ inches) wide, five-lobed, lobes rather long, color orange-yellow in spring, later dark green with a bronze hue; fall color again orange-yellow. Origin Japanese, J. D. Vertrees, Oregon, introduced it before 1970. This shrublet is useful for bonsai. *Acer palmatum* 'Ao ba jō' is similar, possibly identical. Somewhat similar cultivars include *A. palmatum* 'Globosum' (an illegitimate name in use at the former nursery of Messrs K. Wezelenburg & Sons, Netherlands; with smaller leaves, always green), 'Hime yatsubusa' (leaves green with reddish margins), 'Ryūtō' (alternatively, 'Ryuhtoh'; leaf color more contrasting, brown-red at apex with green blade, fading to one color in summer), and 'Suzu kaze' (leaves small with red apexes). Zone 6 (Europe 7)

Acer palmatum 'Samidare'. August

Acer palmatum 'Samidare'

Group 2a. A beautiful shrubby tree up to 6 to 8 m (20–26 feet) and as wide, densely branched. Leaves about 8 cm (3⅛ inches) wide, seven-lobed, texture sturdy, color emerald green, turning brilliant orange-yellow in fall. Origin Japanese, mentioned in the list of 1882. It is a very desirable plant. *Acer palmatum* 'Heptalobum' and 'Tatsuta gawa' are similar. Zone 6 (Europe 7)

Acer palmatum 'Sango kaku'. October

Acer palmatum 'Sango kaku'

Group 1a. Synonym, *A. palmatum* 'Senka-ki'. A shrub sometimes up to 10 m (33 feet) or more, young branches and twigs fiery coral-red in winter, turning yellowish red in summer, a conspicuous feature and very ornamental in winter. Leaves turning golden yellow in fall. Introduced by Daisy Hill Nurseries, Ireland, about 1920. Given the Royal Horticultural Society's Award of Garden Merit in 1993. It is prone to some dieback in the younger branches, usually caused by the young branches not ripening enough. *Acer palmatum* 'Beni kawa', 'Eddisbury', 'Japanese Sunrise', 'Japanese Sunset', and 'Red Wood' are similar. *Acer palmatum* 'Fjellheim' is a witches'-broom with the characteristics of 'Sango kaku' but much more compact, and 'Winter Flame' is also more compact. In some older publications the name "Corallinum" has erroneously been used for 'Sango kaku'. Zone 6 (Europe 7)

Acer palmatum 'Sango kaku'. October, Valley Gardens

Acer palmatum 'Sango kaku'. March

Acer palmatum 'Saoshika'. May, Valley Gardens

Acer palmatum 'Saoshika'

Group 2a. A shrub up to 3 to 4 m (10–13 feet) and as wide. Leaves seven-lobed, margins slightly serrate, texture good, color fresh green; fall color usually orange-yellow. Origin Japanese, mentioned in the list of 1882. *Acer palmatum* 'Sa otome' is similar as is, to a lesser degree, 'Samidare'. Zone 6 (Europe 7)

Acer palmatum 'Satsuki beni'. April

Acer palmatum 'Satsuki beni'

Group 2a. Synonym, *A. palmatum* 'Satzuki beni'. An upright, strongly growing shrub up to 5 m (16 feet) or even more. Leaves seven-lobed, structure firm, color dark green, turning glistening scarlet in fall. Mentioned by Vertrees, *Japanese Maples, Second Edition*, introduced before 1985. *Beni* means "red" but there is only a trace of red in the unfolding leaves in spring, as in *A. palmatum* 'Tsuma gaki'; the coloring soon disappears. *Acer palmatum* 'Gasshō' (alternatively, 'Gasshoh'; apexes of the leaves somewhat less red), 'Ōgi tsuma gaki' (alternatively, 'Ohgi tsuma gaki'), and 'Shuzenji' are similar. Zone 6 (Europe 7)

Acer palmatum 'Sa otome'

Group 2a. A shrub up to 2.5 to 3 m (8–10 feet), rather densely branched. Leaves five-lobed, fresh green with a purplish overtone in spring; fall color yellow-orange but not spectacular. Origin Japanese, mentioned in the list of 1882. *Sa otome* means "rice-planting girl." It is similar to *A. palmatum* 'Kaga kujaku', 'Kantō hime yatsubusa' (alternatively, 'Kantoh hime yatsubusa'), and 'Saoshika'. Zone 6 (Europe 7)

Acer palmatum 'Sa otome'. May

Acer palmatum 'Sazanami'

Group 3a. A strongly growing shrubby tree up to 6 m (20 feet) and about 4 m (13 feet) wide. Leaves deeply divided, distinctly and sharply seven-lobed with an almost horizontal leaf base, color dark green with red petioles, unfolding leaves orange-purplish but turning green quite soon; fall color also interesting. Origin Japanese, mentioned in the list of 1733. *Sazanami* means "ruffles." It is a distinctively different cultivar. Zone 5 (Europe 7)

Acer palmatum 'Seigen'

Group 1b (Corallinum Group). A shrub up to 2 to 3 m (6½–10 feet), young branchlets tending to die back. Leaves five-lobed, small, brilliant silvery pink when unfolding, turning dull green very soon. Origin Japanese, the year of introduction unknown but must have long been cultivated, mentioned in the literature for the first time by S. G. Hinkul in 1956. The name 'Seigen' is much better known than the plant itself, which is quite rare. It is the most famous pink-leaved form in Japan, much in demand by lovers of bonsai. In the Western world many plants traded under the name are other, stronger growing cultivars of the Corallinum Group. 'Seigen' is a difficult plant to grow and there are better cultivars such as *A. palmatum* 'Beni maiko', 'Otome zakura', or even 'Corallinum'. The habit of 'Seigen' is like that of 'Corallinum' but 'Seigen' grows more slowly. There is a whitish hue over the unfolding leaves, as in 'Coral Pink'. See also the discussion under *A. palmatum* 'Bonfire'. Zone 6 (Europe 7)

Acer palmatum 'Sazanami'. October, Valley Gardens

Acer palmatum 'Seigen'. May

Acer palmatum 'Seiryū'. June, Herkenrode Gardens

Acer palmatum 'Seiryū'

Group 7. Alternatively, *A. palmatum* 'Seiryuh'. An almost treelike shrub up to 8 to 10 m (26–33 feet) and 3–5 m (10–16 feet) wide. Leaves like those of all 'Dissectum'-type cultivars (Group 4), fresh green, turning dark reddish purple in fall, which is unusual for Group 4a. Origin Japanese, mentioned in the list of 1882. Given an Award of Merit by the Royal Boskoop Horticultural Society in 1978 and the Royal Horticultural Society's Award of Garden Merit in 1993. A very good plant for larger gardens, it is the only Group 4a maple that grows upright and not in the mushroom form. It is a popular cultivar and is widely available in the nursery trade. Zone 6 (Europe 7)

Acer palmatum 'Seiryū'. May, Herkenrode Gardens

Acer palmatum 'Seiun kaku'. May

Acer palmatum 'Seiun kaku'

Group 1a. A flat-topped shrub up to 2 to 3 m (6½–10 feet) and even wider, densely branched. Leaves five-lobed, lobes slightly convex, which is unusual, color fresh green, petioles red. Origin doubtless Japanese. An old plant present in the former nursery of Messrs K. Wezelenburg & Sons, Netherlands, has been moved to the Esveld Acereum. It is good for bonsai, more vigorous than *A. palmatum* 'Mikawa yatsubusa', its closest relative, which also has overlapping leaf lobes, like roof tiles. Zone 6 (Europe 7)

Acer palmatum 'Seiun kaku'. May

Acer palmatum 'Sekka yatsubusa'. October

Acer palmatum 'Sekka yatsubusa'

Group 1a. An upright-growing medium-sized shrub, many branches abnormally enlarged and flattened at the ends of twigs, conspicuous in winter. Leaves small, five-lobed, dark green, somewhat crinkled and arranged in whorls instead of the usual opposite arrangement; fall color usually yellow. Probably found by J. D. Vertrees, Oregon, before 1960. *Acer palmatum* 'Kyōryū' (alternatively, 'Kyohryuh') also has twig ends enlarged and flattened. Zone 6 (Europe 7)

Acer palmatum 'Seki mori'. August

Acer palmatum 'Seki mori'

Group 4a. A mushroom-shaped shrub much wider than high. Leaves dark green; fall color clear butter-yellow. Origin Japanese, mentioned in the list of 1719. Rare in cultivation, *A. palmatum* 'Ao shidare', 'Dissectum Paucum', and 'Kiri nishiki' are similar. Zone 6 (Europe 7)

Acer palmatum 'Semi no hane'. May, Westonbirt Arboretum

Acer palmatum 'Shaina'. July

Acer palmatum 'Sharp's Pygmy'. July

Acer palmatum 'Semi no hane'

Group 3a. Synonym, *A. palmatum* 'Seme no hane'. A strongly growing shrub about 4 to 5 m (13–16 feet) high and wide. Leaves deeply divided, rusty purple in spring, turning dull green; fall color variable, depending on weather conditions. Origin unknown but before 1950. Similar cultivars are *A. palmatum* 'Inazuma' and 'Ōgon sarasa'. Zone 6 (Europe 7)

Acer palmatum 'Shaina'

Group 6b. A dwarf shrub, a witches'-broom probably to 2 m (6½ feet) high and about as wide; with only 10 years of observation available, difficult to predict eventual growth. Leaves deeply divided, two-toned, dark red and maroon. Found and named by William Schwartz, Green Mansions Nursery, Pennsylvania, in the late 1960s. Given the Royal Horticultural Society's Award of Garden Merit in 1993. It is a mutant of an 'Atropurpureum'. *Acer palmatum* 'Oregon Sunset' is similar, with leaves bunched at the ends of shoots as in 'Ryūzu' or 'Tarō yama'; 'Ruby Stars' is also similar but has leaves with shorter central veins and is not a witches'-broom and grows more strongly than 'Shaina'; 'Kurenai jishi' also has red foliage. Zone 6 (Europe 7)

Acer palmatum 'Sharp's Pygmy'

Group 6a. A compact and slow-growing shrublet not more than 1 m (3¼ feet) high and wide, densely branched. Leaves tiny, five-lobed, green; fall color a nice orange. Raised and introduced by Sharp's Nursery, U.S.A., in 1985. Similar cultivars include *A. palmatum* 'Ikeda yatsubusa', 'Ryoku ryū' (as attractive as 'Sharp's Pygmy' and more open and faster growing), and 'Saihō' (alternatively, 'Saihoh'). Zone 6 (Europe 7)

Acer palmatum 'Sherwood Flame'

Group 3b. A sturdy shrub up to 5 to 6 m (16–20 feet) and about as wide, openly branched. Leaves deeply divided to the base, dark purple, not fading to a lighter color; fall color absent in maritime climates but can be crimson-red in dry situations. Found as a chance seedling, raised and introduced by William J. Curtis, Oregon, before 1970. *Acer palmatum* 'Burgundy Lace' is similar and shows somewhat more fall color. In Europe the two cultivars are in fact inseparable. 'Sherwood Flame' is highly recommended for use in North America, one of the best maples for medium-sized gardens. Zone 6 (Europe 7)

Acer palmatum 'Sherwood Flame'. May

Acer palmatum 'Shichihenge'. April

Acer palmatum 'Shichihenge'

Group 2b. A shrub up to 3 to 4 m (10–13 feet). Leaves sturdy, seven-lobed, the lobes held closely together, dark reddish brown. Mentioned by Vertrees, *Japanese Maples*, introduced before 1970. It is rare in cultivation. Zone 6 (Europe 7)

Acer palmatum 'Shigarami'. May, Savill Gardens

Acer palmatum 'Shigarami'

Group 1a. Synonym, *A. palmatum* 'Saku'. Essentially a tree up to 10 m (33 feet), thinly branched. Leaves five-lobed, fresh green with purple margins, fading in summer, nevertheless a conspicuous plant; fall color yellow to orange. Origin Japanese, mentioned in the list of 1710. It is one of the few really treelike forms in its group. *Acer palmatum* 'Tana' is similar, with smaller leaves. Zone 6 (Europe 7)

Acer palmatum 'Shigure bato'. June

Acer palmatum 'Shigure zome'. November

Acer palmatum 'Shigure bato'

Group 3a. A slowly growing shrub up to 2 m (6½ feet) and as wide. Leaves deeply divided, margins also divided but less than in 'Dissectum'-type cultivars (Group 4), color fresh green, young leaves reddish purple but soon fading; fall color orange to golden. Raised and introduced by Angyō Maple Nursery, Japan, in 1930. Although somewhat fragile and difficult to grow there are few similar forms, except perhaps *A. palmatum* 'Dissectum Paucum'. The leaves of *A. palmatum* 'Chiri hime' are serrate and of the shape of those of 'Shigure bato'. Zone 6 (Europe 7)

Acer palmatum 'Shigure zome'

Group 3b. A shrub up to 4 to 5 m (13–16 feet) and as wide, openly branched. Leaves seven-lobed, bronze-green, divided almost to the base; colors changing in summer, becoming scarlet to purplish in fall. Mentioned in the list of 1719 and documented by Gen'ichi Koidzumi in 1911. There are few similar forms, perhaps *A. palmatum* 'Fior d'Arancio'. Zone 6 (Europe 7)

Acer palmatum 'Shikage ori nishiki'

Group 2b. A vase-shaped shrub up to 6 to 7 m (20–23 feet) and 4–5 m (13–16 feet) wide. Leaves dull purple, fading to olive-green in summer; fall color an attractive warm orange. Origin Japanese, mentioned in the list of 1719. *Acer palmatum* 'Iijima sunago' and 'Nomura' are similar and have interesting fall colors, varying depending on the weather. Zone 6 (Europe 7)

Acer palmatum 'Shikage ori nishiki'

Acer palmatum 'Shin deshōjō'. May, Valley Gardens

Acer palmatum 'Shin deshōjō'

Group 1b (Corallinum Group). Alternatively, *Acer palmatum* 'Shin deshohjoh'. A shrub up to 2.5 to 3 m (8–10 feet), densely branched, branches thin and prone to some dieback in winter. Leaves small, five-lobed, brilliant scarlet when unfolding, later fading to bluish pink and dull green; fall color not spectacular. Origin Japanese, before 1950. *Shin deshōjō* means "a new 'Deshōjō'." It is especially attractive in spring. *Acer palmatum* 'Deshōjō' is similar, as are 'Chishio' and 'Otome zakura'. Zone 6 (Europe 7)

Acer palmatum 'Shin deshōjō'. May, Valley Gardens

Acer palmatum 'Shinobu ga oka'. August

Acer palmatum 'Shinobu ga oka'

Group 5a. An elegant erect shrub reaching a height of 3 m (10 feet) or more. Leaves five- or seven-lobed, linear, fresh green, turning yellow in fall. Origin Japanese, mentioned in the list of 1882. Almost identical to *A. palmatum* 'Linearilobum', 'Shinobu ga oka' seems to be slightly different by having a pinkish second growth when young. Frequently seen in maple collections, other similar cultivars include *A. palmatum* 'Ao meshime no uchi', 'Ao meshime no uchi shidare' (branches pendulous), 'Kansai ao schichigosan', and 'Koto no ito'. Zone 6 (Europe 7)

Acer palmatum 'Shinonome'. July

Acer palmatum 'Shinonome'

Group 3a. An upright-growing shrub up to 4 m (13 feet). Leaves seven-lobed, deeply divided, margins serrate, brown when unfolding, later fading to dull green-brown, the second growth contrasting with the first growth in April; fall color a good crimson. Origin Japanese, mentioned in the list of 1882. *Shinonome* means "dawn." Although little known in cultivation, it is suitable for smaller gardens. *Acer palmatum* 'Heisei nishiki' is like a variegated 'Shinonome', with reddish brown young foliage and white variegated green mature foliage. Zone 6 (Europe 7)

Acer palmatum 'Shishi gashira'

Group 1a or Group 6a. Synonyms, *A. palmatum* 'Cristatum', 'Ribesifolium'. A vase-shaped shrub usually up to 3 m (10 feet) but occasionally more, even up to 5 to 6 m (16–20 feet); branches firm and stout but growth slow. Leaves five-lobed, very dark green and crinkled, not unlike the leaves of *Ribes alpinum*; fall color yellow or golden brown. Origin Japanese, mentioned in the list of 1882 but perhaps much older. *Shishi*

Acer palmatum 'Shishi gashira'. October, Arboretum Belmonte

Acer palmatum 'Shishi gashira'. July, Arboretum Belmonte

gashira means "lion's head." One of the best Japanese maples, it is frequently seen in collections and gardens. There is only one similar cultivar, *A. palmatum* 'Ōjishi', but that plant grows slower and is a true dwarf; 'Meijishi' is probably identical to 'Shishi gashira'. Zone 6 (Europe 7)

Acer palmatum 'Shōjō nomura'

Group 2b. Alternatively, *A. palmatum* 'Shohjoh nomura'. 'Shōjō nomura' in cultivation is sometimes regarded as synonymous with 'Shōjō' bu the two cultivars are in fact different. The plant owned by the former nursery, Messrs K. Wezelenburg & Sons, Netherlands, has been transferred to the Esveld Aceretum for further study. Zone 6 (Europe 7)

Acer palmatum 'Shōjō'. May

Acer palmatum 'Shōjō'

Group 2b. Alternatively, *A. palmatum* 'Shohjoh'. A strong and sturdy shrub up to 5 m (16 feet), more or less vase-shaped. Leaves seven-lobed, dark purple red, holding color in summer and turning crimson in fall. Introduced by Angyō Maple Nursery, Japan, in 1930. It is not certain that 'Shōjō nomura' truly differs from 'Shōjō'. Plants imported from Japan under both names are exactly the same but material is insufficient to make a decision. Good similar cultivars are *A. palmatum* 'Sumi nagashi', and 'Yezo nishiki'. Zone 6 (Europe 7)

Acer palmatum 'Shōjō nomura'. April

Acer palmatum 'Shōjō shidare'. June

Acer palmatum 'Shōjō shidare'

Group 4b. Alternatively, *A. palmatum* 'Shohjoh shidare'. A low mushroom form or a plant with cascading branches when staked. Leaves dark purple in spring, turning a somewhat lighter tone in late summer; fall color usually glistening red-crimson. Not mentioned in the Japanese lists but present in the nursery of Jiro Kobayashi, Japan; described by Vertrees, *Japanese Maples*; introduced before 1970. One of the very best cultivars, there are several similar forms, including *A. palmatum* 'Crimson Queen', 'Red Dragon', and 'Tamuke yama'. Zone 6 (Europe 7)

Acer palmatum 'Shōjō shidare'. June

Acer palmatum 'Shūzankō'. July

Acer palmatum 'Shūzankō'

Group 2a. Alternatively, *A. palmatum* 'Shuhzankoh'. A bushy shrub up to 6 to 10 m (20–33 feet). Leaves (five- or) seven-lobed, green, turning yellow in fall. *Shūzankō*, literally meaning "red mountains in autumn," is the Japanese word for *A. palmatum* subsp. *amoenum* but 'Shūzankō' is a clonal form of the subspecies, as is 'Heptalobum', and that is sufficient reason to maintain the cultivar name instead of sinking it into synonymy under the subspecies. Similar forms include *A. palmatum* 'Harusame' and 'Samidare'. Zone 6 (Europe 7)

Acer palmatum 'Skeeter's Broom'. October, Foliage Gardens, courtesy of H. Olsen

Acer palmatum 'Skeeter's Broom'

Group 6b. A witches'-broom, mature size unknown. A sport of *A. palmatum* 'Bloodgood', the leaves much smaller than those of that cultivar. Introduced by Edward "Skeeter" Rodd, Pennsylvania, in the 1970s. Witches'-brooms like this one tend to be very much alike and are practically indistinguishable without proper labeling. They are suitable for bonsai. Zone 6 (Europe 7)

Acer palmatum 'Sode nishiki'

Group 1a (Aureum Group). A slender, upright-growing shrub eventually up to 6 to 7 m (20–23 feet), densely branched, branchlets thin. Leaves five- or seven-lobed, clear orange-yellow when unfolding, becoming golden yellow with reddish margins in early summer; summer color greener but again turning golden yellow in fall. Origin Japanese, imported to the Netherlands about 1992. Similar cultivars include *A. palmatum* 'Harusame', 'Katsura', 'Ueno homare' (leaves orange-yellow but tending to be greenish), and 'Orange Dream'. Zone 6 (Europe 7)

Acer palmatum 'Sode nishiki'. April

Acer palmatum 'Stella Rossa'. July

Acer palmatum 'Sumi nagashi'. October

Acer palmatum 'Stella Rossa'

Group 4b. A strongly growing plant with cascading branches when staked when young, developing into a more or less mushroom-shaped shrub up to 2.5 m (8 feet) and even wider. Leaves finely dissected, the margins also, color dark purple, not fading in summer; fall color crimson. Raised and introduced by Fratelli Gilardelli, Italy, in 1984. This impressive newer cultivar may be compared with well-known ones such as *A. palmatum* 'Garnet' and 'Inaba shidare'. Zone 6 (Europe 7)

Acer palmatum 'Sumi nagashi'

Group 3b. A shrub, or almost treelike, sometimes up to 10 m (33 feet) and almost as wide. Leaves seven-lobed, deeply incised, dark purplish red in spring and summer, fading to more crimson tones in fall. Samaras abundant, red. Introduced by Angyō Maple Nursery, Japan, in 1930. *Sumi nagashi* means "village on the riverbank." It is one of the best dark purple cultivars for areas with a maritime climate. There are several similar forms such as *A. palmatum* 'Beni kagami', 'Shiraname' (synonym, 'Shiranami'), 'Shōjō', and 'Yezo nishiki'. Zone 6 (Europe 7)

Acer palmatum 'Suisei'. October

Acer palmatum 'Suisei'

Group 4a. A slowly growing shrub up to 1.5 m (5 feet) and about as wide. Leaves finely dissected, green with some white veins. Imported into the Netherlands from Jiro Kobayashi, Japan, about 1992. It is very similar to *A. palmatum* 'Seijaku' and perhaps identical to 'Filigree'. Zone 6 (Europe 7)

Acer palmatum 'Taimin nishiki'. April

Acer palmatum 'Taimin nishiki'

Group 3c. A slowly growing shrub up to 2 to 2.5 m (6½–8 feet) and as wide. Leaves five- or seven-lobed, deeply divided, purple with occasional red and pink variegation.

Origin Japanese, mentioned in the list of
1882. It tends to revert to the original unvariegated color, as happens often with
such forms. *Acer palmatum* 'Hinode nishiki' (brown foliage with pink variegation)
and 'Yūyake nishiki' (alternatively, 'Yuh
yake nishiki'; purple foliage with pink variegation) are similar. A similar plant, without variegation, is *A. palmatum* 'Rubrum'.
Zone 6 (Europe 7)

Acer palmatum 'Tama hime'

Group 1a. A shrub up to 4 to 5 m (13–16
feet) and even wider, densely branched,
resembling a natural bonsai. Leaves five-
lobed, small, green, much like those of subspecies *palmatum* itself; fall color may be a
good yellow. Origin doubtless Japanese. It
can easily be confused with the closely related *A. palmatum* 'Kashima'. Zone 6 (Europe 7)

Acer palmatum 'Tama hime'. April

Acer palmatum 'Tamuke yama'. June

Acer palmatum 'Tamuke yama'

Group 4b. A very attractive, mushroom-
shaped plant up to 2 to 2.5 m (6½–8 feet)
and 3–5 m (10–16 feet) wide, if staked or
grafted on a standard developing gracefully
cascading branches. Leaves deeply divided,
the margins also serrate, of the darkest pur-

Acer palmatum 'Tama hime'. April

Acer palmatum 'Tana'. May, Savill Gardens

Acer palmatum 'Tarō yama'. April

ple in spring, soon fading to a lighter tone. Origin Japanese, mentioned in the list of 1710 and documented by Gen'ichi Koidzumi in 1911. Similar cultivars are *A. palmatum* 'Crimson Queen', 'Irish Lace', and 'Shōjō shidare'. Zone 6 (Europe 7)

Acer palmatum 'Tana'

Group 1a. Synonym, *A. palmatum* 'Tana bate'. A slender, vase-shaped shrub up to 8 to 9 m (26–30 feet) and 2 m (6½ feet) wide. Leaves five- or seven-lobed, green with purple margins, fading in summer; fall color yellow. It is very similar to 'Shigarami', maybe even identical, and both tend to become one-stemmed trees. Not mentioned in the older Japanese lists but present in the nursery of Jiro Kobayashi, Japan; described by Vertrees, *Japanese Maples*; introduced before 1970; and documented in the lists of Masato Yokoi. Zone 6 (Europe 7)

Acer palmatum 'Tarō yama'

Group 6a. Alternatively, *A. palmatum* 'Taroh yama'. A compactly growing bushy plant up to 1.5 to 2 m (5–6½ feet) and as wide, similar to *A. palmatum* 'Ryūzu'. Origin Japanese. 'Tarō yama' produces the same shades of color as *A. palmatum* 'Felice', red with orange, later yellow-green. *Acer palmatum* 'Kuro hime' has redder leaves than 'Tarō yama', mixed with green, and 'Sunset' has the same shades with its 'Dissectum'-type leaves. Zone 6 (Europe 7)

Acer palmatum 'Tarō yama'. May

Acer palmatum 'Tatsuta gawa'. October

Acer palmatum 'Tatsuta gawa'

Group 2a. Synonym, *A. palmatum* 'Tatsuta' in nursery catalogs). A dense, sturdy shrub up to 4 to 5 m (13–16 feet) and as wide. Leaves seven-lobed, rather firm, when unfolding light green, later turning clear green and finally red-crimson. Origin Japanese, mentioned in the list of 1710. It is a good plant but not widely known. There are similar forms such as *A. palmatum* 'Saoshika' and 'Sa otome'. Zone 6 (Europe 7)

Acer palmatum 'Tennyo no hoshi'. May, Savill Gardens

Acer palmatum 'Tennyo no hoshi'

Group 1c. A upright-growing vase-shaped shrub, densely branched, branchlets thin and prone to some dieback when young. Leaves peculiarly formed with more or less incurved margins, dark and light green, turning yellow in fall. Origin Japanese, before 1987. It is a rare form and there are few similar plants. Zone 6 (Europe 7)

Acer palmatum 'The Bishop'. June

Acer palmatum 'The Bishop'

Group 2b. A shrub up to 4 m (13 feet) and about as wide. Leaves rather large, seven-lobed, dull purple; fall color not outstanding. Raised and introduced by Henry Hohman, Kingsville Nurseries, Maryland, before 1960. *Acer palmatum* 'Suru sumi' and 'Teriba' are similar. Many better forms than 'The Bishop' are available in the nursery trade. Zone 6 (Europe 7)

Acer palmatum 'Toshi'. April

Acer palmatum 'Toshi'

Group 3b. A multistemmed treelike shrub up to 8 m (26 feet), in habit very much like *A. palmatum* 'Azuma murasaki' or 'Ōsaka-zuki'. Leaves 6–10 cm (2⅜–4 inches) wide, seven-lobed, dull purple in spring, turning olive-greenish in summer. It is considered to be identical with 'Azuma murasaki' by some but leaves are soft bronze, turning

Acer palmatum 'To yama nishiki'. July

Acer palmatum 'Trompenburg'. May, Valley Gardens

Acer palmatum 'Tsuchi gumo'. May

green. This is possibly due to different conditions of soil and climate. *Acer palmatum* 'Kansai tsukuba ne', bronze-green leaves in spring, turning green, is similar. Zone 6 (Europe 7)

Acer palmatum 'To yama nishiki'

Group 4c. A slowly growing, mushroom-shaped shrub up to 1 m (3¼ feet) or slightly more. Leaves seven-lobed, finely dissected, brown-purple, pink speckled. Origin doubtless Japanese, introduced by J. Dickson & Sons, England, in 1882. *Acer palmatum* 'Goshiki shidare', also a variegated 'Dissectum'-type cultivar, is similar but its variegation is not as dark; 'Hana matoi' has pink and white variegated purple leaves. Zone 6 (Europe 7)

Acer palmatum 'Trompenburg'

Group 3b. A slender, upright-growing tree sometimes up to 10 m (33 feet) or more, sparsely branched, seldom shrubby. Leaves seven-lobed, dark shining purple, lobes strongly convex, making the plant unique. Found and introduced by J. R. P. van Hoey Smith, Trompenburg Arboretum, Rotterdam, Netherlands, in 1965. Given the Royal Horticultural Society's Award of Preliminary Commendation in 1984. One of the outstanding novelties of more recent decades, young plants grow strongly and form long branches with different juvenile leaves with less or almost without convex lobing. Zone 6 (Europe 7)

Acer palmatum 'Tsuchi gumo'

Group 1a. A densely branched shrub sometimes up to 5 m (16 feet) but usually smaller, more or less vase-shaped. Leaves five-lobed, strongly curled, brownish at first, quickly turning fresh green in early summer; fall color yellow to orange. Mentioned in the list of 1882 and by Gen'ichi Koidzumi in 1911. It is not a true dwarf. There are only few more or less similar forms such as *A. palmatum* 'Chiyo hime' and 'Little Princess'. Zone 6 (Europe 7)

Acer palmatum 'Tsukomo'. May, Westonbirt Arboretum

Acer palmatum 'Tsukomo'

Group 6a. Synonym, *A. palmatum* 'Tsuku-no'. A dwarf not exceeding 2 m (6½ feet) in height and about as wide, densely branched. Leaves tightly set together, small, green, turning yellow in fall. Introduced by the Yokohama Nursery Company, Japan, in 1936. It is difficult to grow and rarely seen. Similar forms are *A. palmatum* 'Hupp's Dwarf' and 'Sharp's Pygmy'. Zone 6 (Europe 7)

Acer palmatum 'Tsukuba ne'

Group 2b. A treelike shrub up to 7 to 8 m (23–26 feet) and 3–5 m (10–16 feet) wide, openly branched. Leaves rather large, seven-lobed, purple when unfolding, soon turning green; fall color very conspicuous, a fiery orange-red, giving the impression of a bon-fire. Origin Japanese, mentioned in the list of 1882 and documented by Gen'ichi Koid-zumi in 1911. *Acer palmatum* 'Heptalo-bum', 'Koreanum' (close to subspecies *amoenum*), and 'Miyagino' (outstanding fall color) are similar. Zone 6 (Europe 7)

Acer palmatum 'Tsukuba ne'. October

Acer palmatum 'Tsukushi gata'. November

Acer palmatum 'Tsuma gaki'. May

Acer palmatum 'Tsuma gaki'. June

Acer palmatum 'Tsukushi gata'

Group 2b. A shrub usually 4–5 m (13–16 feet) high and about as wide. Leaves 6–8 cm (2⅜–3⅛ inches) wide, seven-lobed, at first shining purple, becoming dull in summer; fall color crimson. Origin Japanese, mentioned in the list of 1882. *Acer palmatum* 'Goten nomura' (leaves bold, brown-purple) 'Kinran', 'Nomura', and 'Shōjō nomura' are similar. Zone 6 (Europe 7)

Acer palmatum 'Tsuma gaki'. May, Valley Gardens

Acer palmatum 'Tsuma gaki'

Group 1c. Synonym, *A. palmatum* 'Tsuma beni'. A slowly growing shrub up to 2.5 or 3 m (8–10 feet) and as wide, branches spreading. Leaves five- or seven-lobed, yellow-green with attractive red-purple apexes; fall color orange-yellow with less conspicuous margins. Unfortunately, this beautiful maple is difficult to propagate. Some author consider 'Tsuma beni' to be a different cultivar, saying that the leaves of 'Tsuma beni' are not pendulous when leafing out, but the difference is so minor that the two can be considered as one here. Both names may be found in the list of 1882. *Acer palmatum* 'Usu midori' has leaves more deeply divided than those of 'Tsuma gaki'. Zone 6 (Europe 7)

Acer palmatum 'Tsuri nishiki'. July

Acer palmatum 'Tsuri nishiki'

Group 3a. A sturdy shrub up to 4 to 5 m (13–16 feet). Leaves seven- or nine-lobed, deeply cleft, to the base, margins strongly serrate on juvenile leaves, less so on adult leaves, color dark green. The name appears in the list of 1882 without description. Zone 6 (Europe 7)

Acer palmatum 'Ueno yama'. April, Foliage Gardens, courtesy of H. Olsen

Acer palmatum 'Ueno yama'

Group 1a (Aureum Group). An upright-growing shrub of medium size. Leaves brilliant orange in spring when leafing out, turning greenish yellow in summer. Origin Japanese, before 1970, present in Hisao Nakajima's collection and mentioned by Vertrees, *Japanese Maples. Acer palmatum* 'Katsura', 'Orange Dream', and 'Sode nishiki' are similar but less brightly colored. Zone 6 (Europe 7)

Acer palmatum 'Ueno homare'. May

Acer palmatum 'Ueno homare'

Group 1a (Aureum Group). A strongly growing shrub up to 5 to 6 m (16–20 feet) and 3–4 m (10–13 feet) wide, densely branched. Leaves rather small, five-lobed, intense yellow with narrow reddish margins, turning greenish in summer but later again golden yellow. Mentioned by Vertrees, *Japanese Maples*, introduced before 1970. The red margins hold only for a short time but give the plant an intense orange color when unfolding. Similar cultivars include *A. palmatum* 'Gekkō nishiki' (alternatively, 'Gekkoh nishiki'; leaves like those of 'Kiyo hime' but with orange apexes), 'Katsura', 'Katsura hime' (apexes perhaps more reddish), and 'Orange Dream'. Zone 6 (Europe 7)

Acer palmatum 'Uki gumo'. May

Acer palmatum 'Uki gumo'

Group 1c. A slowly growing erect shrub up to 3 to 4 m (10–13 feet) after many years. Leaves small, five-lobed, heavily pink and white speckled; not much fall color. Origin doubtless Japanese, before 1970. *Uki gumo* means "floating clouds." It is distinctively different. Some people love the flamboyant variegation, others cannot abide it. *Acer palmatum* 'Erena' is greener with white spots, 'Komon nishiki' has leaves dusted with tiny pink spots, and 'Shimofuri nishiki' has leaves deeply incised, dotted with dark pink. Zone 6 (Europe 7)

Acer palmatum 'Ume ga e'. June

Acer palmatum 'Ume ga e'

Group 2b. A shrub of rather erect habit up to 5 to 6 m (16–20 feet). Leaves seven-lobed, margins finely serrate, color purple-red, turning a good crimson in fall. Origin Japanese, mentioned in the list of 1882. It is a rare cultivar, similar to *A. palmatum* 'Bloodgood', 'Manyō no sato' (alternatively, 'Manyoh no sato'; foliage bronze with white margins and some green), 'Moonfire', 'Nure sagi', and 'Tsukuma no'. Zone 6 (Europe 7)

Acer palmatum 'Utsu semi'

Group 2a. A shrub up to 4 to 5 m (13–16 feet) and about as wide, sparsely branched. Leaves seven-lobed, texture sturdy, color a beautiful green; fall color scarlet to orange-yellow, quite spectacular. Origin Japanese, mentioned in the list of 1882. In spite of its good characteristics it is rare in cultivation. *Acer palmatum* 'Ichigyōji' (alternatively, 'Ichigyohji') and 'Kihachijō' are similar in their fall color. Zone 6 (Europe 7)

Acer palmatum 'Utsu semi'. May, Herkenrode Gardens

Acer palmatum 'Villa Taranto'

Group 5b. A vase-shaped shrub up to 4 m (13 feet) and 3 m (10 feet) wide, openly branched. Leaves five-lobed, the lobes linear, color a dull purple in spring, turning dark green with a reddish hue, more golden yellow in fall. As of this writing the original plant is still going strong in the gardens of Villa Taranto, Italy, where it was named in 1967 in cooperation with Firma C. Esveld, Netherlands. Other cultivars may be similar in habit but not in leaf color. Only *A. palmatum* 'Ornatum' (Group 4b) has such a display but its leaves are deeply dissected rather than having linear lobes. Zone 6 (Europe 7)

Acer palmatum 'Villa Taranto'. May, Savill Gardens

Acer palmatum 'Wabito'. May, Valley Gardens

Acer palmatum 'Wabito'

Group 1a. A shrub up to 3 to 4 m (10–13 feet) and perhaps 2 m (6½ feet) wide. Leaves of different types, usually seven-lobed, irregularly incised and dissected, sometimes some variegation visible; fall color good, usually golden yellow. Mentioned in the list of 1710 and reintroduced by the Yokohama Nursery Company, Japan, in 1898. It is difficult to propagate and is rare in cultivation. It is somewhat similar to *A. palmatum* 'Maiko', 'Mama', 'Renjaku' (probably smaller than 'Wabito'), and 'Ryū-gū' (alternatively, 'Ryuhguh'; pinkish white variegated). Zone 6 (Europe 7)

Acer palmatum 'Volubile'. July

Acer palmatum 'Volubile'

Group 1a. An upright-growing shrubby tree up to 8 to 10 m (26–33 feet) and about 3 to 4 m (10–13 feet) wide. Leaves five-lobed; fall color yellow. Perhaps a chance seedling, probably of European origin, introduced and named by Fritz Graf von Schwerin, Germany, in 1893. It is similar to *A. palmatum* 'Ao yagi' but lacks the bright green color of the twigs of that cultivar. *Acer palmatum* 'Kochidori' and 'Nose gawa' are similar to 'Volubile'. Zone 6 (Europe 7)

Acer palmatum 'Waka midori'. July

Acer palmatum 'Waka midori'

Group 1a. A compact shrub up to 2 to 3 m (6½–10 feet), young branchlets purplish. Leaves five-lobed, deeply divided, fresh green. It is a more recent introduction from Japan. Zone 6 (Europe 7)

Acer palmatum 'Waka momiji'. October

Acer palmatum 'Waka momiji'

Group 1a. A sturdy shrub up to 6 to 7 m (20–23 feet), differing little from subspecies *palmatum* itself except in its coral-red twigs which are not unlike those of *A. palmatum* 'Sango kaku', but 'Waka momiji' is more strongly growing. Found by a friend of Yoshimichi Hirose, Japan; introduced by him to the West in 1989. Zone 6 (Europe 7)

Acer palmatum 'Waka momiji Variegated'. September

Acer palmatum 'Waka momiji Variegated'

Group 1c (Versicolor Group). A shrub. Foliage partly pink variegated, making it quite similar to *A. palmatum* 'Karasu gawa'. 'Waka momiji Variegated' is a bud sport of 'Waka momiji' and bears a name that is illegitimate by the rules of horticultural nomenclature. Zone 6 (Europe 7)

Acer palmatum 'Wakehurst Pink'. September

Acer palmatum 'Wakehurst Pink'

Group 2c. A shrub up to 4 to 5 m (13–16 feet) and as wide, openly branched. Leaves seven-lobed, deeply divided, lobes narrow, color purple red with flames of pink and near-white all over. Found wrongly labeled as "Roseomarginatum" in Wakehurst Place Garden, England, renamed and introduced by Firma C. Esveld, Netherlands, in 1988.

Unfortunately, the original plant is no longer alive. The foliage flames in young, vigorous plants are not very spectacular. *Acer palmatum* 'Shi en' has leaf blades not very conspicuously pink striped and dotted. Zone 6 (Europe 7)

Acer palmatum 'Washi no o'. September, Bömer

Acer palmatum 'Washi no o'

Group 4b. A mushroom-shaped shrub up to 2 m (6½ feet) and about as wide. Leaves finely dissected, purple when unfolding, later turning dull brown; fall color good. There is confusion concerning the name 'Washi no o'. Some authors consider it a synonym of *A. palmatum* 'Dissectum Paucum' or 'Dissectum Rubrifolium' but that is almost certainly incorrect. The plant photographed originally came from England and it was not possible to identify it without some doubt. Zone 6 (Europe 7)

Acer palmatum 'Whitney Red'

Group 2b. A shrubby tree up to 5 to 6 m (16–20 feet) and 3–4 m (10–13 feet) wide. Leaves seven-lobed, purple-red when unfolding, later becoming dull purple. A chance seedling found and introduced by W. Whitney, Oregon, in 1980. There are similar forms available in the nursery trade, often with better characteristics. *Acer palmatum* 'Ko murasaki' has incised, dark red leaves. Zone 6 (Europe 7)

Acer palmatum 'Waterfall'. May, Herkenrode Gardens

Acer palmatum 'Waterfall'

Group 4a. A mushroom-shaped shrub up to 3 to 3.5 m (10–11 feet) and even wider. Leaves seven-lobed, deeply incised, the margins again incised, color fresh green; fall color yellow. It is almost certainly identical with the European clone known as *A. palmatum* 'Dissectum', grown in the tens of thousands. It seems that it was renamed in 1920 by the Kingsville Nurseries, Maryland. Of course, 'Waterfall' is a more appealing name. That is what happened with 'Dissectum Nigrum', which was renamed 'Ever Red'. Zone 6 (Europe 7)

Acer palmatum 'Whitney Red'. July

Acer palmatum 'Wilson's Pink Dwarf'. May

Acer palmatum 'Wilson's Pink Dwarf'. July

Acer palmatum 'Wilson's Pink Dwarf'

Group 6c. A shrub up to 2 m (6½ feet) and about as wide, densely branched. Leaves small, five-lobed, lobes narrow, color bright pink in spring, later turning other colors, mostly green, whitish. Introduced by James Wilson, Millbrae, California, in 1980. It is a beautiful plant, worthy of increasing popularity. There are few similar forms available in the nursery trade; one is *A. palmatum* 'Kurenai'. Unfortunately, 'Wilson's Pink Dwarf' is not easy to propagate. Zone 6 (Europe 7)

Acer palmatum 'Yezo nishiki'. May

Acer palmatum 'Yezo nishiki'

Group 2b. A treelike shrub sometimes up to 10 m (33 feet) or more, sparsely branched. Leaves 6–8 cm (2⅜–3⅛ inches) wide, seven-lobed, bold and firm, purple in spring, fading to lighter tones, scarlet in fall. Origin Japanese. There are a few similar forms, such as *A. palmatum* 'Beni kagami' and 'Heptalobum Rubrum'. 'Yezo nishiki' differs from its relatives by its refreshing red color during the entire summer. Zone 6 (Europe 7)

Acer palmatum 'Yūba e'. April

Acer palmatum 'Yūba e'

Group 2b. Alternatively, *A. palmatum* 'Yuhba e'. A slender, upright-growing treelike shrub, openly branched. Leaves seven-lobed, deeply divided, sturdy, dark purple. Named by J. D. Vertrees, Oregon, in 1970. *Yūba e* means "evening glow." According to Vertrees, *Japanese Maples,* there should be scarlet variegation but variegation has not been observed in plants in the Netherlands nor as far as we know in ones cultivated elsewhere in Europe. Zone 6 (Europe 7)

Acer palmatum 'Yūgure'. May

Acer palmatum 'Yūgure'

Group 3b. Alternatively, *A. palmatum* 'Yuh-gure'. A sturdy shrub usually higher than wide. Leaves large, seven-lobed, brown in spring, soon turning less dark; fall color often orange-brown. Origin Japanese, mentioned in the list of 1719 and documented by Gen'ichi Koidzumi in 1911. *Yūgure* means "evening cloud." There are few comparable forms; *A. palmatum* 'Rubrum' is similar except for its habit. Zone 6 (Europe 7)

Acer palmatum 'Yurihime'. November, Foliage Gardens, courtesy of H. Olsen

Acer palmatum 'Yurihime'

Group 6a. A shrublet not more than 1 m (3¼ feet) high. Leaves very small, five-lobed, green in summer, turning to reddish tones in fall. Origin Japanese. It is perfectly suitable for bonsai but of little value in the garden except under the best growing conditions. Zone 6 (Europe 7)

Selected Other Cultivars of *Acer palmatum*

In addition to those illustrated or discussed, we mention the following:

'Amagi shigure'. Group 3c. Foliage with pink veins, similar to 'Beni shigitatsu sawa'.

'Autumn Glory'. Group 1a. Foliage intense orange-red in fall.

'Baldsmith'. Group 4a. Foliage orange-red, turning yellow.

'Beni shigitatsu sawa'. Group 3c. Leaves tricolored: green, whitish green, pink.

'Kogane saka e'. Group 2a. Bark striped with green and yellow as in some bamboos.

'Koto ito komachi'. Group 5b. A small shrub with the narrowest threadlike leaves of all cultivars of *A. palmatum*.

'Mitsuba yama'. Group 7. Leaves somewhat convex, central vein conspicuous.

'Ōnishiki' (alternatively, 'Ohnishiki'; synonym, 'Wou nishiki'). Group 3a. An upright shrub, leaves of different shapes, green, margins tinted pink.

'Ōshū shidare' (alternatively, 'Ohshuh shidare'). Group 2b. Almost a tree with pendulous branches and leaves brown-red.

'Shōnan nishiki' (alternatively, 'Shohnan nishiki'). Group 1c. Young leaves yellowish green with darker spots.

'Shōwa no mai' (alternatively, 'Shohwa no mai'). Group 1c. A slender shrub with conspicuously variegated foliage.

'Takao'. Group 1a. A strongly growing shrub, leaves with reddish margins.

'Tendō' (alternatively, 'Tendoh'). Group 7. Similar to 'Mitsuba yama'.

Acer pauciflorum. June

Acer paxii. May

Acer pauciflorum

Section *Palmata*, series *Palmata*. A slow-growing shrub possibly up to 4 to 5 m (13–16 feet) in its habitat, much smaller in cultivation. Leaves five-lobed, palmate, dull green. Flowers few, villous. Native to Zhejiang Province in China, 200–1000 m (650–3300 feet). Described by Fang Wen-pei in 1932. Grown from a packet of seed sent from China, a plant in the Esveld Aceretum is 1 m (3¼ feet) high and growing slowly, otherwise this maple may not be in cultivation. Fall color has not been noted but its ornamental value is not great. It can be grafted onto *A. palmatum*. Zone 6 (Europe 7)

Acer paxii

Section *Pentaphylla*, series *Trifida*. An evergreen tree up to 10 to 12 m (33–39 feet) in its habitat, smaller in cultivation; bark smooth, gray-black. Leaves 5–9 cm (2–3½ inches) long and 3–5 cm (1⅛–2 inches) wide, three-lobed or sometimes unlobed on the same tree, leathery, margins entire. Flowers small, white. Samaras 2 cm (¾ inch) long, nutlets round. Native to mountainous forests in Yunnan Province in China. Described by Adrien René Franchet in 1886. Rather tender, it is rare in cultivation. It is similar to *A. buergerianum* but differs from that species in its persistent leaves. Zone 8 (Europe 9)

Acer pectinatum subsp. *forrestii.* July

Acer pectinatum

Section *Macrantha*. Described by Nathaniel Wallich and George Nicholson in 1881. Five subspecies are recognized, *forrestii, laxiflorum, maximowiczii, pectinatum,* and *taronense.*

Acer pectinatum subsp. forrestii

Synonym, *A. forrestii.* Usually multistemmed treelike shrubs, in their habitat tending to form thickets, up to 10 m (33 feet) or occasionally more; bark with narrow white stripes. Leaves 5–8 cm (2–3⅛ inches) long and 3–6 cm (1⅛–2⅜ inches) wide, three-lobed, central lobe clearly longer than the side lobes, petioles sometimes red. Flowers in long, hanging raemes, cream. Samaras 2–2.5 cm (¾–1 inch) long, nutlets flat. Native to western and central China, Sichuan Province and the Lichiang Range in northern Yunnan Province. Originally described as a separate species by Friedrich Ludwig Emil Diels in 1912. Rather common in maple collections though less so in gardens, plants labeled *A. forrestii*, a synonym, are sometimes actually *A. davidii* 'George Forrest', which has unlobed leaves. *Acer pectinatum* subsp. *forrestii* has three-lobed leaves and thus may be confused only with the rarer subspecies *axiflorum*. Zone 6 (Europe 7)

Acer pectinatum subsp. *forrestii* 'Alice'. July

Acer pectinatum subsp. *forrestii* 'Alice'

Synonym, *A. forrestii* 'Alice'. A well-branched shrub up to 5 to 6 m (16–20 feet); striped bark pinkish. Leaves three-lobed or five-lobed (the outer lobes often underdeveloped), margins incised, color green when unfolding, during summer turning gorgeous white, cream, and dark pink variegated. Flowers in small racemes, cream, only rarely developed. Samaras 2 cm (¾ inch) long, seeds not viable. Raised from a chance seedling of *A. pectinatum* subsp. *forrestii* and introduced by Firma C. Esveld, Netherlands, in 1981. Given an Award of Merit by the Royal Boskoop Horticultural Society in 1987. It is a good plant for medium-sized gardens. Variegation is less significant on older plants so it is important to prune the plant from time to time. Zone 6 (Europe 7)

Acer pectinatum subsp. *forrestii* 'Sirene'. March

Acer pectinatum subsp. *forrestii* 'Sirene'

A shrub of irregular habit up to 7 to 8 m (23–26 feet); trunk and the branches with dark red bark, beautifully striped. Leaves 10–15 cm (4–6 inches) long and 6–10 cm (2⅜–4 inches) wide, three-lobed, central lobe with elongated apex but not tapered, margins serrate, color purple when unfolding, turning very dark green, unusual for the species. Flowers in short racemes, purplish yellow. Raised from a chance seedling found in a bed of *A. pectinatum* subsp. *forrestii* and introduced by Firma C. Esveld, Netherlands, in 1988. The leaf coloration is unusual for *A. pectinatum*. Zone 7 (Europe 8)

Acer pectinatum subsp. *forrestii* 'Sparkling'. June

Acer pectinatum subsp. *forrestii* 'Sparkling'

A slender treelike shrub up to 10 m (33 feet) and 3–4 m (10–13 feet) wide; branches white striped, bark green. Leaves usually three- or five-lobed with an elongated central lobe, the side lobes much shorter and outer lobes often absent in adult foliage, color fresh green, turning yellow in fall; petioles red. Flowers in short racemes, greenish. Discovered in a batch of seedlings of *A. pectinatum* subsp. *forrestii*, named after 10 years of observation, and introduced by Firma C. Esveld, Netherlands, in 1989. It is suitable for small gardens and the fiery red petioles are very conspicuous and unusual for *A. pectinatum*. Zone 6 (Europe 7)

Acer pectinatum subsp. *laxiflorum*. May, Savill Gardens

Acer pectinatum subsp. *laxiflorum*

Synonym, *A. laxiflorum*. A multistemmed treelike shrub, in its habitat up to 10 to 12 m (33–39 feet), smaller in cultivation; bark striped as in subspecies *forrestii*. Leaves 8–10 cm (3⅛–4 inches) long and 4–5 cm (1½–2 inches) wide, three-lobed with inconspicuous (unlike subspecies *forrestii*) side lobes. Flowers in small hanging racemes, cream. Samaras 2–3 cm (¾–1⅛ inches) long, nutlets flat. Native to central and western China, Yunnan Province and in Sichuan Province abundant on Emei Shan and in the valley of the Dadu River near Kangding. Originally described as a separate species by Ferdinand Albin Pax in 1902. Rarely cultivated, most trees labeled as subspecies *laxiflorum* are subspecies *forrestii* or hybridized plants. A few true *laxiflorum* trees can be found at the Royal Botanic Garden, Edinburgh, and at Trewithen and at Valley Gardens in England. The plant in the Esveld Aceretum is a graft of the Valley Gardens tree. Zone 6 (Europe 7)

Acer pectinatum subsp. *maximowiczii*. May

Acer pectinatum subsp. *maximowiczii*. November

Acer pectinatum subsp. *maximowiczii*

Synonym, *A. maximowiczii*. A densely branched shrub up to 6 to 7 m (20–23 feet), almost never a tree; bark inconspicuously striped. Leaves variable in size and shape, 3–8 cm (1⅛–3⅛ inches) long and 2–4 cm (¾–1½ inches) wide, three- or five-lobed, margins serrate, color dark green; fall color yellow. Flowers in small racemes, creamy white. Samaras 2–3 cm (¾–1⅛ inches) long, obtuse. Native to mountainous regions in Gansu, Hubei, and Sichuan Provinces in China. Originally described as a separate species by Ferdinand Albin Pax in 1889. Not to be confused with *A. maximowiczianum*, a different maple. Sometimes incorrectly labeled in collections, it is a pity that *A. pectinatum* subsp. *maximowiczii* is rare in cultivation. Zone 6 (Europe 7)

Acer pectinatum subsp. *pectinatum*. May, Westonbirt Arboretum

Acer pectinatum subsp. *pectinatum*. May, Westonbirt Arboretum

Acer pectinatum subsp. *pectinatum*

In its habitat always treelike, or in cultivation a shrub up to 8 to 10 m (26–33 feet) and half as wide; bark white striped, usually not very conspicuously. Leaves 8–14 cm (3⅛–5½ inches) long and 5–8 cm (2–3⅛ inches) wide, three- or five-lobed, margins doubly serrate; petioles red in summer. Flowers whitish. Samaras 2–3 cm (¾–1⅛ inches) long, almost horizontal. Native to the Himalayas, Bhutan, Nepal, Myanmar (Upper Burma), and possibly Yunnan Province in China. Other subspecies are more frequently planted than subspecies *pectinatum*. Based on observations of plants in the Esveld Aceretum, of wild origin and collected in Bhutan, this rare tree is surprisingly hardy. Zone 6 (Europe 7)

Acer pectinatum subsp. *taronense*

Synonym, *A. taronense*. A tree or shrub up to 12 m (39 feet) or more; bark purplish green and striped with lighter green, not very conspicuously. Leaves 5–10 cm (2–4 inches) long and 4–6 cm (1½–2⅜ inches) wide, five-lobed, the central lobe of the same size as the outer lobes, color green, turning orange-yellow in fall. Flowers in long racemes, cream or yellow-green. Samaras purplish, almost horizontally arranged. Native to mountainous regions in Myanmar (northeastern Burma), Tibet, and Sichuan and Yunnan Provinces in China. Originally described as a separate species by Heinrich Raphael Eduard Freiherr von Handel-Mazzetti in 1924. Subspecies *taronense*

Acer pectinatum subsp. *taronense*. July

Acer pectinatum subsp. *taronense*. July

is rare in cultivation. Most plants are grafts from the tree at Caerhays Castle, England, which was once wrongly labeled as *A. rufinerve*; brought into cultivation by Firma C. Esveld, Netherlands. Such a tree, growing in the Esveld Aceretum, has reached a considerable size after approximately 25 years. Zone 6 (Europe 7)

Acer pensylvanicum. May, Herkenrode Gardens

Acer pensylvanicum

Section *Macrantha*. Synonym, *A. striatum*. A very openly branched shrub or shrublike tree up to 10 m (33 feet) and as wide; bark conspicuously striped with white. Leaves 12–25 cm (4¾–10 inches) long and almost as wide, three-lobed, central lobe larger than the outer lobes, margins serrate, underside of leaves somewhat rusty when young. Flowers yellow-green, appearing after the leaves. Samaras 2–3 cm (¾–1⅛ inches) long, nutlets flat. Native to eastern North America, from Georgia through the Appalachians to Minnesota and Nova Scotia. Described by Carl Linnaeus in 1753. Given the Royal Horticultural Society's Award of Garden Merit in 1993. Widely cultivated, "goosefoot" or "moosewood" is the only American representative of the otherwise Asiatic section *Macrantha* and is a snakebark maple. It has brilliant golden fall color. Zone 4 (Europe 5)

Acer pensylvanicum 'Erythrocladum'. October

Acer pensylvanicum 'Erythrocladum'

A rather narrowly growing shrub up to 6 m (20 feet); bark coral to salmon-red in winter with conspicuous white stripes, turning dark yellow in summer. Leaves three-lobed, lighter green than characteristic of the species; fall color a glowing yellow. Flowers rarely seen. Introduced by Späth Nurseries, Germany, in 1904. Given the Royal Horticultural Society's Award of Merit in 1976 and First Class Certificate in 1977. It is a strikingly beautiful and well-known cultivar but is nevertheless rare in cultivation due to difficulties in propagating. Grafting is difficult, even on *A. pensylvanicum*. 'Erythrocladum' deserves more attention. *Acer ×conspicuum* 'Phoenix' is similar and a little less difficult to cultivate. Zone 6 (Europe 7)

Acer pentaphyllum

Section *Pentaphylla*, series *Pentaphylla*. A slender, elegant tree possibly up to 10 m (33 feet) but usually smaller; bark somewhat roughened, brown. Leaves 8 cm (3⅛ inches) wide, distinctly five-lobed, divided to the base with narrow lobes, color fresh green, turning yellow in fall. Flowers yellow, rarely seen. Samaras 2 cm (¾ inch) long, in cultivation rarely seen and not viable. Native to the Yalong Valley in southern Sichuan Province in China, very rare if not extinct. Discovered by George Forrest in 1926 and described by Friedrich Ludwig Emil Diels in 1931. The oldest tree and the one from which others in cultivation have been derived grows in the Strybing Arboretum, San Francisco, California. This rare maple is dif-

Acer pentaphyllum. June

Acer pentapomicum. July

icult to propagate and has to be grafted nto understocks that are in fact not closely elated to the species. It is also rather tender and must be grown in sheltered gardens. Nevertheless, it is a "must" for maple collectors. Zone 7 (Europe 8)

Acer pentapomicum

Section *Pubescentia*. A slowly growing shrub up to 3 to 4 m (10–13 feet) in cultivation, in its habitat sometimes a small tree. Leaves 3–10 cm (1⅛–4 inches) wide, variable on the same plant, shallowly three- or five-lobed, of thick texture but not evergreen; no fall color. Flowers yellowish. Samaras 2.5 cm (1 inch) long, rarely seen and usually not viable. Native to low mountains and in dry situations in river valleys in Pakistan, Afghanistan, Turkistan, and Kashmir in India. Described by J. L. Stewart and Dietrich Brandis in 1874. Not a great beauty, it is a collector's item and is very rare in cultivation. Zone 4 (Europe 5)

Acer pictum. October

Acer pictum

Section *Platanoidea*. Synonym, *A. mono*. A tree up to 15 m (50 feet), usually broader than high; bark and branchlets gray, not fissured. Leaves variable in size and shape, sometimes similar to *A. cappadocicum* or *A. truncatum*, five- or seven-lobed, dark green, margins sometimes reddish; fall color yellow to orange. Flowers in umbels, yellow-green. Samaras often imperfectly formed, nutlets flat. Native to Mongolia, Manchuria in China, Korea, the Japanese

Acer pictum. May, Savill Gardens

island of Hokkaidō, and eastern Siberia and Sakhalin Island, Russia. Described by Carl Peter Thunberg and Johan Andreas Murray in 1784. Painted maple is variable. It is present in most collections but rare in public parks and gardens. Zone 5 (Europe 6)

Acer pictum 'Tokiwa nishiki'. July

Acer pictum 'Tokiwa nishiki'

A shrub up to 6 to 8 m (20–26 feet); bark gray. Leaves with parts of the blade white or leaves entirely white. Origin Japanese. Frequently cultivated in Japan, it is rare in Europe and the United States. Branches with green leaves must be removed to restore full variegation. *Acer pictum* 'Hana no arashi' is similar. Zone 6 (Europe 7)

Acer pictum 'Hoshi yadori'. June

Acer pictum 'Hoshi yadori'

A shrubby tree up to 6 m (20 feet) and about as wide; bark gray, smooth. Leaves five- or seven-lobed, margins entire, leaf blade dotted and speckled with yellow. Origin Japanese. It is present in several maple collections but is nevertheless rare in cultivation. Branchlets bearing fully green leaves appear frequently and these reverted branches must be removed by heavy pruning to restore fully variegated foliage. *Acer pictum* 'Naguri nishiki' is similar except the leaves are dotted with white rather than lemon-yellow. Zone 5 (Europe 6)

Acer pictum 'Usugumo'

A slowly growing shrub up to 2 m (6½ feet), densely branched. Leaves five- or seven-lobed, pinkish salmon to whitish, apt to some sunburn but otherwise very nice especially when unfolding. Origin Japanese. More common in Japan than in Western gardens, it is a gem but difficult to propagate and grow. Zone 6 (Europe 7)

Acer pictum 'Usugumo'. April

Acer pilosum var. *stenolobum*. October

Acer pilosum var. *stenolobum*

Section *Pubescentia*. Synonym, *A. stenolo-bum*. A shrubby tree up to 6 m (20 feet) and about as wide; branches reddish brown. Leaves 4–8 cm (1½–3⅛ inches) long and 3–4 cm (1⅛–1½ inches) wide, somewhat leathery, three-lobed, outer lobes short and oblong, margins wavy or toothed. Flowers yellow green. Samaras 1 cm (⅜ inch) long. Native to central China in Gansu, Jiangxi, and Shaanxi Provinces. Originally described as a separate species by Alfred Rehder in 1922. One of the rarest maples in cultivation, specimens are derived from plants at the Arnold Arboretum, Massachusetts, grown from seed from China. Varieties *megalophyllum* (larger in most characteristics) and *pilosum* (lateral lobes not as short) are not in cultivation. Zone 5 (Europe 6)

Acer platanoides

Section *Platanoidea*. A tree sometimes up to 30 m (100 feet), usually not more than 20 m (66 feet) tall and about as wide; bark hardly fissured, dark brown. Leaves 8–25 cm (3⅛–10 inches) wide, five-lobed, lobes caudate, dentate, or slightly serrate, color shiny green turning golden yellow in fall. Flowers more or less erect, golden yellow, appearing before the leaves and spectacular in spring. Samaras 4–7 cm (1½–2¾ inches) long, nutlets flat and produced in abundance. Native to Scandinavia and central Europe (but not in the British Isles or coastal countries of the North Sea) east to Crimea and the Caucasus. Described by Carl Linnaeus in 1753. A common tree in

Acer platanoides. April, a street in Amsterdam, Netherlands

Acer platanoides. September, Hof ter Saksen

Acer platanoides. April

Acer platanoides 'Almira'. November, Von Gimborn Arboretum

cultivation, Norway maple is used as a street tree and is present in large gardens and parks. Many selections have been made and propagated vegetatively. In addition to the illustrated cultivars, listed alphabetically below, some more cultivars are listed at the end of the entries for *A. platanoides*. Zone 4 (Europe 5)

Acer platanoides 'Almira'

A compactly growing tree up to 6 to 7 m (20–23 feet) and 4–5 m (13–16 feet) wide. Fall color yellow. Flowers less profusely than the species. Raised and introduced by E. H. Scanlon, Ohio, in 1955. This useful plant grows somewhat faster than the well-known 'Globosum' and has a more egg-shaped habit. It is suitable for public areas. Zone 4 (Europe 5)

Acer platanoides 'Charles Joly'. April

Acer platanoides 'Charles Joly'

A tree up to 10 m (33 feet) or more with an irregular, almost pendulous crown. Leaves deeply incised, purplish when young and dark green later. Origin unknown, before 1985. It is an interesting tree for parks and is suitable as a solitary tree on lawns but it needs a large amount of space for the best effect. Zone 4 (Europe 5)

Acer platanoides 'Cleveland'. October

Acer platanoides 'Cleveland'

A tree up to 15 m (50 feet) with an oval crown. Leaves marbled with red when young. Raised and introduced by E. H. Scanlon, Ohio, in 1948. It is a good tree for narrower streets and small parks, planted more in the United States than in Europe. Zone 4 (Europe 5)

Acer platanoides 'Columnarbroad'. July

Acer platanoides 'Columnarbroad'

Synonym, *A. platanoides* Parkway (trademark name). A tree up to 15 m (50 feet) with an oval to pyramidal crown, rather densely branched. Raised and introduced by J. Frank Schmidt & Son, Oregon, before 1970. It is an excellent street tree. Zone 4 (Europe 5)

Acer platanoides 'Columnare'

A tree up to 15 m (50 feet) or occasionally more, of broadly conical habit, not truly fastigiate. Leaves somewhat smaller than those of the species. Flowers profusely. Fruits usually few. Originally described as a botanical form by Elie Abel Carrière in 1878. Suitable for smaller gardens, public areas, and also as a tree for narrow streets, this cultivar has declined in popularity compared to newer introductions from E. H. Scanlon, Ohio. Zone 4 (Europe 5)

Acer platanoides 'Columnare'. September, Hof ter Saksen

Acer platanoides 'Crimson King'. October, Research Station for Nursery Stock

Acer platanoides 'Crimson King'

A tree up to 20 m (66 feet) or occasionally more, crown about as high as wide. Leaves dark purple-red; fall color usually absent. Flowers in profusion, purplish with yellow, spectacular because appearing before the leaves. Fruits not very abundant. Raised by Tips Brothers, Belgium, and introduced by Barbier & Company, France, in 1937. Given the Royal Horticultural Society's Award of Garden Merit in 1984. In very dry conditions it loses some color toward the end of summer. Vigorously growing plants may be attacked by mildew. It is commonly planted in parks and public gardens and is also used as a street tree. It is difficult to distinguish from the similar 'Royal Red' in maritime climates. Similar cultivars include *A. platanoides* 'Goldsworth Purple', with brown-purple leaves, less dark than those of 'Royal Red' or 'Crimson King', and 'Royal Crimson', a sport of 'Crimson King' or 'Goldsworth Purple' and with crimson-purple leaves. Zone 4 (Europe 5)

Acer platanoides 'Crimson Sentry'. July

Acer platanoides 'Crimson Sentry'

A compactly growing treelike shrub up to 6 to 8 m (20–26 feet), densely branched, sometimes growing as a tree with a straight trunk. Leaves smaller than those of the species, dark purple-red, hardly fading. Raised and introduced by A. McGill & Son, Oregon, in 1974. It is gaining in popularity but be aware of the possibility of mildew during a cool, moist summer. Zone 4 (Europe 5)

Acer platanoides 'Cucullatum'

A medium-sized tree of the same habit as the species but smaller. Leaves with lobes heavily crimped, overlapping, color dark green with a purplish hue. Originally described as a botanical entity by Elie Abel Carrière in 1866. Too massive for small gardens, it is found in some botanical gardens and public parks. It is interesting but peculiar rather than beautiful. Zone 4 (Europe 5)

Acer platanoides 'Cucullatum'. May, Westonbirt Arboretum

Acer platanoides 'Deborah'

A tree up to 15 m (50 feet) and as wide. Leaves bright purple-red when unfolding, later turning green, becoming orange in fall. Raised from a seedling of 'Schwedleri' and introduced by Connor Nurseries, Canada, in 1975. It is a good tree for planting along wide streets, or as a solitary tree in parks. Zone 4 (Europe 5)

Acer platanoides 'Dieckii'

Synonym, *A.* ×*dieckii*. A tree up to 20 m (66 feet) and as wide. Leaves similar to those of the species but irregularly lobed or almost without lobes. Originally described as a variety of *A. lobelii* (a synonym of *A. cappadocicum* subsp. *lobelii*) by Ferdinand Albin Pax in 1886. Once thought to be a hybrid, *A. platanoides* × *A. cappadocicum* subsp. *lobelii*, 'Dieckii' is encountered in older parks but is now almost forgotten. Zone 4 (Europe 5)

Acer platanoides 'Deborah'. July, van den Bijl

Acer platanoides 'Dieckii'. October, Royal Botanic Gardens, Kew

Acer platanoides 'Drummondii'. June, Fratelli Gilardelli

Acer platanoides 'Drummondii'. June, Fratelli Gilardelli

Acer platanoides 'Drummondii'

A tree sometimes up to 14 to 15 m (46–50 feet). Leaves with creamy white variegated margins. Raised by Drummond Brothers, Scotland, and described by Fritz Graf von Schwerin in 1910. Given the Royal Horticultural Society's Award of Merit in 1956 and Award of Garden Merit in 1993. Rather commonly planted in parks and gardens, this beautiful tree tends to revert to green foliage and those branchlets must be removed. Zone 4 (Europe 5)

Acer platanoides 'Emerald Queen'. October

Acer platanoides 'Emerald Queen'

A strongly growing tree up to 15 m (50 feet) or more and about as wide, crown densely branched. Introduced by A. McGill & Son, Oregon, in 1963. One of the best street trees, with good yellow fall color, it is less

Acer platanoides 'Emerald Queen'. May

commonly planted in gardens. Similar cultivars include *A. platanoides* 'Eurostar' (large dark green leaves, yellow in the fall), 'Peterse's Grüne', and 'Scanlon Gold' (very good fall color). Zone 4 (Europe 5)

Acer platanoides 'Globosum'. June, Arboretum Belmonte

Acer platanoides 'Globosum'

A modestly growing tree with a flat-topped crown, densely branched. Leaves slightly smaller than those of the species, coloring well in fall. Fruits hardly ever formed. Raised and introduced by Louis Van Houtte, Belgium, in 1873. It is a common and useful tree for public areas, patios, and smaller gardens but is less useful as a street tree because the crown becomes too large. Most specimens are grafted onto *A. platanoides* understocks 2–2.4 m (6½–7¾ feet) high. It is not possible to form trees if grafting is done at the base. More recently, this cultivar has been grafted onto fast-growing cultivars such as *A. platanoides* 'Farlake's Green' or 'Peterse's Grüne' in order to obtain identical specimens. Zone 4 (Europe 5)

Acer platanoides 'Golden Globe'. June, Arboretum Thiensen, courtesy of J. R. P. van Hoey Smith

Acer platanoides 'Golden Globe'

A tree of the same habit as 'Globosum'. Leaves with good yellow color, not burning in full sun. Found as a sport of 'Globosum' about 1990, named and introduced by G. Hartung, Germany, in 1995. Zone 4 (Europe 5)

Acer platanoides 'Maculatum'. June

Acer platanoides 'Maculatum'

A tree usually not more than 7 to 8 m (23–26 feet) high, rather densely branched. Leaves slightly smaller than those of the species, spotted with cream and yellow. Introduced by George Nicholson in 1873. At its best when leafing out in the spring, it is interesting but does not excel in beauty. It is rare even in maple collections. Zone 4 (Europe 5)

Acer platanoides 'Laciniatum'. May, Arboretum Trompenburg

Acer platanoides 'Laciniatum'

A tree up to 10 m (33 feet) and as wide. Leaves peculiarly shaped, lobes convex and incised with the shape of the talons of a bird. Introduced by James Sutherland, Scotland, as early as 1683. It is interesting but rare, a collector's item. Zone 4 (Europe 5)

Acer platanoides 'Meyering'. October, Hillier Gardens and Arboretum

Acer platanoides 'Meyering'

A tree up to 15 m (50 feet) or occasionally more. Leaves brown-red when unfolding, later turning olive-green. Raised by J. Meyering and introduced by Herman J. Grootendorst, Netherlands, in 1969. Potentially a good street tree, it is intermediate between the green- and purple-leaved cultivars, similar to *A. platanoides* 'Schwedleri' and with better attributes than 'Reitenbachii'. Zone 4 (Europe 5)

Acer platanoides 'Palmatifidum'. May, Savill Gardens

Acer platanoides 'Palmatifidum'

Synonym, *A. platanoides* 'Lorbergii'. A densely branched tree up to 12 m (39 feet) and with a crown at least as wide. Leaves with lobes dissected to the base and somewhat overlapping each other, color dark green, turning brilliant yellow in fall. Flowers profusely. Fruits rarely set. Originally described as a botanical entity by Ignaz Friedrich Tausch in 1829. It is eye-catching, a good solitary tree in parks. *Acer platanoides* 'Greenlace' and 'Oregon Pride' are similar. Zone 4 (Europe 5)

Acer platanoides 'Olmsted'. June, Research Station for Nursery Stock

Acer platanoides 'Olmsted'

A broadly pyramidal tree up to 15 to 18 m (50–59 feet) and about as wide. Leaves slightly smaller than those of the species. Raised and introduced by E. H. Scanlon, Ohio, in 1955. It is considered one of the best of the more or less pyramidal cultivars and is quite common in parks and is also used as a street tree. *Acer platanoides* 'Cavalier' and 'Superform', the latter up to 25 m (82) feet, are similar. Zone 4 (Europe 5)

Acer platanoides 'Pyramidale Nanum'. April

Acer platanoides 'Pyramidale Nanum'. August, Arboretum Trompenburg

Acer platanoides 'Reitenbachii'. July

Acer platanoides **'Pyramidale Nanum'**

A very densely branched, almost columnar tree up to 8 to 10 m (26–33 feet); internodes usually very short and when longer branches sometimes appear, very small branchlets again produced. Leaves smaller than those of the species, fresh green, turning yellow in fall. Flowers in profusion, yellow. Fruits not produced. Raised and introduced by Louis Van Houtte, Belgium, in 1877. This attractive small tree is only rarely available in the nursery trade and it deserves more attention. Zone 4 (Europe 5)

Acer platanoides **'Reitenbachii'**

A tree up to 15 to 20 m (50–66 feet). Leaves reddish brown when unfolding, later turning dull green. Flowers pinkish yellow. Originated at the nursery of J. Reitenbach, Russia at the time, now Poland, named by Johann Xaver Robert Caspary, and introduced by Louis Van Houtte, Belgium, in 1874. As better cultivars have been introduced, for example, 'Schwedleri', 'Reitenbachii' has become rare. Zone 4 (Europe 5)

Acer platanoides 'Royal Red'. June, Von Gimborn Arboretum

Acer platanoides 'Royal Red'

A tree up to 15 to 20 m (50–66 feet) and about as wide. Leaves dark purple-red, usually not fading to a lighter color. Flowers orange-reddish yellow instead of clear yellow. Fruits not abundant, samaras somewhat purplish. Raised and introduced by Pacific Coast Nursery, Oregon, in 1963. The most commonly planted red-leaved Norway maple, 'Royal Red' cannot be distinguished from 'Crimson King' in countries with a maritime climate such as those of western Europe. *Acer platanoides* 'Faassen's Black', with leaves dark purple, is similar. Zone 4 (Europe 5)

Acer platanoides 'Schwedleri'. May, Westonbirt Arboretum

Acer platanoides 'Schwedleri'

A tree up to 15 to 20 m (50–66 feet) and usually as wide. Leaves dark purple when unfolding, turning dull brown in the summer; fall color can be dramatic orange-yellow. Flowers orange-yellow. Fruits not abundant. Named by Karl Koch in 1869. Given the Royal Horticultural Society's Award of Garden Merit in 1993. Surpassed by more recently introduced cultivars with darker leaves, 'Schwedleri' is becoming rare. It can still be found in older parks and along avenues, especially in southern and central Europe. Zone 4 (Europe 5)

Acer platanoides 'Summershade'

A fast-growing tree up to 20 m (66 feet). Leaves somewhat leathery and heat resistant, dark green turning to yellow. Raised and introduced by Princeton Nurseries, New Jersey, in 1958. It is an undemanding tree, good for landscaping and as a street tree, well known in the United States. *Acer platanoides* 'Chas. F. Irish', 'Cleveland', and 'Jade Glen' (with a more open crown) are similar. Zone 4 (Europe 5)

Acer platanoides 'Summershade'. April

Acer platanoides 'Tharandt'. August, Tharandt, courtesy of J. R. P. van Hoey Smith

Acer platanoides 'Tharandt'

A tree of moderate size. Leaves almost round and only slightly lobed if at all, unusual for the species. The tree was discovered at Tharandt, at the university in Dresden, Germany, where it had been growing unnoticed for a long time. It is now in cultivation in the Netherlands. Zone 4 (Europe 5)

Acer platanoides 'Walderseei'. June, Fratelli Gilardelli

Acer platanoides 'Walderseei'

A tree up to 10 m (33 feet), densely branched. Leaves somewhat smaller than those of most of the cultivars of the species, handsomely dotted and speckled with white. Raised and introduced by Späth Nurseries, Germany, in 1904. A "forgotten" cultivar, this handsome tree deserves more attention. Zone 5 (Europe 6)

Acer platanoides 'Walderseei'. June, Romberg Park

Other Cultivars of *Acer platanoides*

In addition to those illustrated or discussed, we mention the following:

'Cindy Lou'. An extreme dwarf with very small leaves. It grows slowly and remains erect.

'Farlake's Green'. A very strong-growing tree, the whips of which are used as understock on which to graft more slowly growing cultivars.

'Jakobsen's Micropot'. An extreme dwarf, probably not more than 1 m (3¼ feet) tall, with tiny leaves.

'Standfast'. An exceptionally small plant, growing 80 cm (31 inches) in 25 years.

Acer pseudoplatanus. May, Valley Gardens

Acer pseudoplatanus

Section *Acer*, series *Acer*. A tree up to 30 m (100 feet) or more, usually as wide though habit is variable; bark and branches rough. Leaves 8–15 cm (3⅛–6 inches) wide, five-lobed, lobes rounded and of different shape, colors varying, dark to light green, purple or not underneath; fall color often not very conspicuous. Flowers in long, hanging trusses. Fruits many per truss, samaras 2–4 cm (¾–1½ inches) long, nutlets rounded. Native to many European countries except the British Isles, the low countries and adjacent areas, and Scandinavia. Described by Carl Linnaeus in 1753. The type species of the genus *Acer*, the sycamore maple is one of the most commonly encountered trees in Europe, sometimes almost weedy along with alder (*Alnus*), ash (*Fraxinus*), and willow (*Salix*). It is also used for many purposes, planted along streets and in parks and gardens, and its wood is useful, for example, in making tools and various musical instruments. In addition to the illustrated cultivars, listed alphabetically below, some more cultivars are listed at the end of the entries for *A. pseudoplatanus*. Zone 3 (Europe 4)

Acer pseudoplatanus. May, Rivierenhof

Acer pseudoplatanus 'Atropurpureum'. May, Arboretum Belmonte

Acer pseudoplatanus 'Atropurpureum'

Synonym, *A. pseudoplatanus* 'Spaethii'. A large tree, in size and habit as for the species. Leaves with undersides remarkably reddish violet. Described by J. Groinland in 1862. Given the Royal Horticultural Society's Award of Garden Merit. Sometimes regarded as a naturally occurring variety, such individuals are always found mixed in populations with more typical leaf coloration. It is used as a street tree and a particularly good form is now handled as a clone propagated by grafting for uniformity. Zone 4 (Europe 5)

Acer pseudoplatanus 'Brilliantissimum'

A small, slowly growing tree, the crown eventually reaching several meters (yards) in diameter. Leaves brilliantly colored with golden yellow, salmon-pink, some green spots when unfolding, color mix slowly disappearing and turning greenish yellow, becoming light green in summer; leaf underside green. Described by J. Clark in 1905 but probably older. Given the Royal Horticultural Society's Award of Merit in 1925 and Award of Garden Merit in 1993. Suitable for even the smallest gardens, when grafted at ground level it forms a bushy shrub. It may be confused with *A. pseudoplatanus* 'Prinz Handjéry' but the leaves of that cultivar are purplish underneath. Zone 4 (Europe 5)

Acer pseudoplatanus 'Brilliantissimum'. May

Acer pseudoplatanus 'Brilliantissimum'. July

Acer pseudoplatanus 'Corstorphinense'. April

Acer pseudoplatanus 'Corstorphinense'

A tree up to 15 m (50 feet), narrower than characteristic of the species. Leaves clear yellow when unfolding, turning light green in summer. Flowers profusely. Fruits rarely produced. Described by James Sutherland, Scotland, in 1683. Unfortunately, this beautiful tree is uncommon in parks. Yellow-leaved trees in spring usually are *A. pseudoplatanus* 'Worley', the leaves of which are also later greenish. 'Worley' was given the Royal Horticultural Society's Award of Garden Merit in 1993. Zone 4 (Europe 5)

Acer pseudoplatanus 'Leat's Cottage'

A small tree, crown grafted onto *A. pseudoplatanus*, up to 2 m (6½ feet) in diameter. Leaves similar to those of 'Brilliantissimum' but less brilliantly colored. Introducer unknown, possibly a chance seedling. It is rare in cultivation, known to us only at Savill Gardens, England. Zone 4 (Europe 5)

Acer pseudoplatanus 'Erythrocarpum'. September, Arboretum Trompenburg, courtesy of J. R. P. van Hoey Smith

Acer pseudoplatanus 'Erythrocarpum'

A large tree of the same habit as the species. Flowers profusely. Fruits many, samaras conspicuously red. Known since 1727, introduced by S. Vaillant, France, later described botanically by Elie Abel Carrière and Ferdinand Albin Pax. Trees of this form are found mixed in populations trees with more common fruit coloration, so it is treated as a cultivar. It is not uncommon but when it is found in collections it is not usually labeled as distinct. Zone 4 (Europe 5)

Acer pseudoplatanus 'Leat's Cottage'. May, Savill Gardens

Acer pseudoplatanus 'Leopoldii'. July

Acer pseudoplatanus 'Leopoldii'. July, Rivierenhof

Acer pseudoplatanus 'Leopoldii'

Synonym, *A. pseudoplatanus* 'Variegatum', in part. A up to 20 m (66 feet) or more. Leaves more or less heavily speckled and spotted with yellow. Flowers, fruits abundant. Introduced by Vervaene Nursery, Belgium, in 1864. Given the Royal Horticultural Society's First Class Certificate in 1865 and Award of Garden Merit in 1993. It is common in parks and large gardens. Seedlings are also usually variegated but are not to be confused with the true, vegetatively propagated cultivar. The plant shown in the photograph with the trunk is probably the first grafted specimen. Zone 4 (Europe 5)

Acer pseudoplatanus 'Negenia'

A tree up to 30 m (100 feet) high and 20 m (66 feet) wide. Introduced by the Nederlandse Algemene Keuringsdienst voor Boomkwekerijgewassen (NAKB), the Dutch Selection Service for Horticulture, in 1948. Tolerant of windy conditions, it is much planted in Europe as a street tree. Zone 4 (Europe 5)

Acer pseudoplatanus 'Negenia'. July, van den Bijl

Acer pseudoplatanus 'Nizetii'

A tree up to 12 to 15 m (39–50 feet). Leaves like those of 'Leopoldii', more or less heavily speckled and spotted with yellow but even more heavily variegated and purplish underneath. Introduced by Makoy Nurseries, France, in 1887. It is much rarer than 'Leopoldii' and the nicely variegated 'Nizetii' deserves more attention. Zone 4 (Europe 5)

Acer pseudoplatanus 'Prince Camille de Rohan'

A tree with a crown 8–10 m (26–33 feet) wide, sometimes grafted onto whips of the species. Leaves dark green and sturdy, heavily pink and white variegated, purple underneath. Introduced by P. T. P. Bijhouwer, Netherlands, in 1927. Becoming too large for most gardens, it is rarely planted. It differs from other variegated cultivars mainly in the pink flecks on the leaves. Zone 4 (Europe 5)

Acer pseudoplatanus 'Prinz Handjéry'

A tree with a crown 4–5 m (13–16 feet) wide, usually grafted onto whips of the species. Leaves similar to those of 'Brilliantissimum', salmon-yellow when unfolding, fading to greenish yellow and light green, purple rather than green underneath. Introduced by Späth Nurseries, Germany, in 1883. It is a commonly planted small tree but is often confused with 'Brilliantissimum.' When grafted at the base 'Prinz Handjéry' becomes a dense shrub. Zone 4 (Europe 5)

Acer pseudoplatanus 'Nizetii'. August, Bömer

Acer pseudoplatanus 'Prince Camille de Rohan'. July

Acer pseudoplatanus 'Prinz Handjéry'. May, Westonbirt Arboretum

Acer pseudoplatanus 'Prinz Handjéry'. May

Acer pseudoplatanus 'Rotterdam'. August, van den Bijl

Acer pseudoplatanus 'Rotterdam'

A tree up to 20 to 25 m (66–82 feet). Raised and introduced by H. W. Vink, Netherlands, in 1944. It is suitable as a street tree along large avenues and roads. It remains one of the best trees for general planting in poor situations and is common in western Europe. Zone 4 (Europe 5)

Acer pseudoplatanus 'Spring Gold'. July

Acer pseudoplatanus 'Simon Louis Frères'. May, Arboretum Belmonte

Acer pseudoplatanus 'Simon Louis Frères'

A rather slowly growing tree up to 8 to 10 m (26–33 feet), sometimes a shrub. Leaves three-lobed, pale pink when unfolding, turning white variegated with only a few wholly green leaves. Raised and introduced by F. Deegen, Simon Louis Frères Nurseries, France, in 1881. Only occasionally available in the nursery trade, it is a rare but appealing plant worthy of more attention. Zone 4 (Europe 5)

Acer pseudoplatanus 'Spring Gold'. April

Acer pseudoplatanus 'Spring Gold'

A tree up to 3 to 4 m (10–13 feet), usually grafted onto whips of the species. Leaves like those of 'Brilliantissimum', brilliantly colored with golden yellow, salmon-pink, some green spots when unfolding, color mix slowly disappearing and turning greensh yellow sooner than in 'Brilliantissimum', ecoming light green in summer; leaf underide green. Found as a sport of 'Brilliantissinum', raised, and introduced by K. W. Veroom, Netherlands, in 1991. It grows more uickly than 'Brilliantissimum' and will ikely replace 'Prinz Handjéry' because it as a better habit and color. It remains hrubby when grafted at the base. Zone 4 Europe 5)

Acer pseudosieboldianum subsp. *pseudosieboldianum*. May, Herkenrode Gardens

cultivation and now sunk into synonymy. Some have been recognized as cultivars. Zone 6 (Europe 7)

Other Cultivars of *Acer pseudo-platanus*

In addition to those illustrated or discussed, we mention the following:

'Amry'. A large tree for wide streets, able to withstand wind.

'Bruchem'. A large tree for wide streets, able to withstand wind.

'Constant P.' A large tree for wide streets, able to withstand wind.

'Erectum'. A narrowly columnar tree.

'Puget Pink'. Foliage pink.

Acer pseudosieboldianum

Section *Palmata,* series *Palmata.* Originally described (as *A. parvifolium*) by A. F. Budishchev in 1864. Two subspecies are cultivated, *pseudosieboldianum* and *takesimense.*

Acer pseudosieboldianum subsp. pseudosieboldianum

An openly branched shrub, rarely a tree up to 8 to 10 m (26–33 feet) and as wide; ranches gray and slightly striped. Leaves 0–15 cm (4–6 inches) wide, nine- or leven-lobed, margins doubly serrate, green, urning orange-yellow in fall. Flowers terninal, reddish purple, appearing before the eaves. Samaras variable in size. Native to Korea and along the Ussuri River in Manhuria in China. Although present in most naple collections, Korean maple is othervise rare in cultivation. The variably sized amaras have given rise to the description f a number of varieties, such as variety nacrocarpum, and segregate species by Takenoshin Nakai, most of them not in

Acer pseudosieboldianum subsp. *takesimense.* May, Herkenrode Gardens

Acer pseudosieboldianum subsp. takesimense

A shrubby tree, more densely branched than subspecies *pseudosieboldianum;* branches and twigs reddish green, similar to those of *A. palmatum.* Leaves 5–10 cm (2–4 inches) wide, nine- or eleven-lobed, pubescent when young, glabrous when mature, margins serrate; fall color yellow. Flowers reddish, appearing before the leaves. Fruits small, samaras parallel. Native to Ullung Do, an island east of the Korean mainland. Originally described as a separate species by Takenoshin Nakai in 1918 and introduced into Europe about 1985 by J. G. S. Harris, Mallet Court Nursery, England. It is rare in cultivation. Zone 7 (Europe 8)

Acer pubipalmatum. May, Herkenrode Gardens

Acer pycnanthum. May, Westonbirt Arboretum

Acer pubipalmatum

Section *Palmata*, series *Palmata*. An openly branched shrub probably up to 4 to 5 m (13–16 feet) in cultivation but taller in its habitat. Leaves 6–9 cm (2⅜–3½ inches) wide, five- or seven-lobed, almost split to the base, margins doubly serrate, color fresh green, veins densely gray-white pubescent below; fall color yellow. Flowers with purple sepals, cream petals. Samaras 2–3 cm (¾–1⅛ inches) long, pubescent. Native to Zhejiang Province in China, 700–1000 m (2300–3300 feet). Described by Fang Wen-pei in 1932. The first scions came to Europe from China via Japan courtesy of Masato Yokoi. Young grafted plants survived the cold winters of 1995 and 1996. It is a maple rare in cultivation. Zone 6 (Europe 7)

Acer pycnanthum

Section *Rubra*. A tree up to 15 m (50 feet) in its habitat, smaller in cultivation; similar in appearance to *A. rubrum*. Leaves 4–8 cm (1½–3⅛ inches) wide, ovate, shallowly three-lobed, fresh green, glaucous underneath; fall color yellow to orange-red. Flowers red. Samaras 3 cm (1⅛ inches) long, erect, ripening in June and losing viability very soon afterward. Native to wet places on Honshū Island, Japan. Described by Karl Koch in 1864. Rare in cultivation, it is a collector's item. It is the Japanese counterpart of the closely related *A. rubrum* from North America. When seed is not available grafting onto *A. rubrum* provides a good alternative for propagation. *Acer pycnanthum* 'Asayake nishiki' has leaves with pink and yellow dots, and 'Kihin nishiki' has yellow speckled leaves. Zone 6 (Europe 7)

Acer ×rotundilobum

Synonym, *A. barbatum* in the sense of Schwerin, not A. Michaux. A garden hybrid, *A. monspessulanum × A. opalus* subsp. *obtusatum*, both parents belonging to section *Acer*, series *Monspessulana*. A small or medium-sized tree with a dense crown; young branches reddish. Leaves 5–7 cm (2–2¾ inches) wide, almost round, somewhat thinner than those of either parent and smoother. Described by Fritz Graf von Schwerin in 1894. The original tree grew in the Muskau Arboretum, now in Poland. An old tree grows in the Arboretum des Barres, France. Zone 5 (Europe 6)

Acer ×rotundilobum. May, Hillier Gardens and Arboretum, courtesy of J. R. P. van Hoey Smith

Acer rubescens. June

Acer rubescens

Section *Macrantha*. Synonym, *A. morriso-
ense* in the sense of Hui-lin Li, not Hayata. A tree up to 20 m (66 feet) in its habitat,
much smaller in cultivation, 6–8 m (20–26
feet) at most; bark striped with green, reddish when young. Leaves 7–15 cm (2¾–6
inches) wide, pointed, three- or five-lobed,
petioles reddish, young leaves somewhat
pubescent, becoming glabrous when mature; fall color clear yellow. Flowers terminal, yellow. Samaras 2–3 cm (¾–1⅛ inches)
long, nutlets flattened. Native to mountain
forests, 2000 m (6500 feet), on Taiwan. Described by Bunzō Hayata in 1911. Rare in
cultivation, it flourishes only in sheltered
locations. A mighty tree may be admired at
Trewithen, England. Zone 8 (Europe 9)

Acer rubescens 'Summer Surprise'

A shrub approximately 4–5 m (13–16 feet)
high and wide when mature; branches and
twigs striped with green, often not very
conspicuously. Leaves 5–10 cm (2–4 inches)
wide, three-lobed, green with abundant
white and pink variegation, in summer
somewhat crinkled and apt to revert to
green. Raised and introduced by R. Cave,
New Zealand, in 1987. 'Summer Surprise'
is similar to a few other forms in cultivation, all of which are somewhat tender and
not easy to grow in harsher climates. These
include *A. rubescens* 'Kofuji nishiki' (leaves
strongly variegated, even whiter than those
of 'Summer Surprise'), 'Kongō nishiki' (alternatively, 'Kongoh nishiki'; leaves with yellow dots), 'Tickled Pink' (erroneously labeled
as "*A. ukurunduense*" when imported from

Acer rubescens 'Summer Snow'. June

Acer rubescens 'Summer Snow'

A shrub, occasionally a small tree, openly
branched, possibly up to 3 to 4 m (10–13
feet); bark striped with green, often not very
conspicuously. Leaves 5–8 cm (2–3⅛
inches) wide, three-lobed, somewhat crinkled, heavily white and pink variegated. Received from the nursery of Hirose-noen
Ltd., Japan, as "*Acer insulare variegatum*,"
an illegitimate name, and renamed by Firma C. Esveld, Netherlands, in 1993. Zone 8
(Europe 9)

Acer rubescens 'Summer Surprise'. June

Acer rubrum. September, Von Gimborn Arboretum

Acer rubrum. October, Arboretum Belmonte

Japan and renamed by Firma C. Esveld, Netherlands, in 1995), 'Wakisaka nishiki' (young leaves coral-salmon, later variegated), and 'Yakushima nishiki' (yellow leaves beautiful when unfolding and later white and yellow variegated). Zone 8 (Europe 9)

Acer rubrum. May, Arboretum Belmonte

Acer rubrum

Section *Rubra.* A tree up to 25 m (82 feet) and almost as wide, especially in continental climates, often much smaller in maritime conditions; bark smooth, dark gray. Leaves 6–10 cm (2⅜–4 inches) wide, sometimes longer than wide, three- or five-lobed, lobes triangular or ovate, color gray underneath, sometimes light green; fall color spectacular red, orange, and yellow. Flowers in profusion, fiery red, appearing before the leaves. Samaras connivent, 2.5 cm (1 inch) long, ripening early, often by June; seeds must be harvested and sown immediately as they lose viability soon after ripening. Native to eastern North America, west to central Canada and the Dakotas, south to Florida, Texas, and New Mexico, growing in acid soil in moist situations. Described by Carl Linnaeus in 1753. Perhaps the most common maple in North America, red maple or scarlet maple is also frequently planted in Europe. It is a magnificent maple that has provided a range of cultivars, including those used as street trees. In addition to the illustrated cultivars, listed alphabetically below, a couple of other cultivars are listed at the end of the entries for *A. rubrum.* Zone 3 (Europe 4)

Acer rubrum 'Bowhall'

A columnar tree up to 25 m (82 feet) or occasionally more. Found in Olmsted, Ohio, named by E. H. Scanlon in 1951. It is a good tree for narrower roads and is also suitable as a solitary tree in smaller gardens. It may be compared with *A. rubrum* 'Excelsior', 'Karpick', and 'Scanlon', the latter even more columnar than 'Bowhall'. Zone 4 (Europe 5)

Acer rubrum 'Columnare'. October, Washington Park Arboretum, courtesy of J. R. P. van Hoey Smith

Acer rubrum 'Columnare'

A columnar tree of somewhat irregular habit up to 15 to 20 m (50–66 feet). Originally described as a botanical entity by Alfred Rehder in 1900. Although its fall color is very good this tree has gone into retirement; more recently introduced cultivars tend to be more regular and shapely. Zone 4 (Europe 5)

Acer rubrum 'Bowhall'. July, Arboretum Belmonte

Acer rubrum 'Morgan'. October

Acer rubrum 'Red King'. April

Acer rubrum 'Red King'

Synonym, *A. rubrum* 'Effegi'. An upright-growing tree up to 20 m (66 feet) and perhaps 10 m (33 feet) wide. Leaves five-lobed, lobes rounded; fall color spectacular crimson to orange-red even in maritime climates. Flowers in profusion, crimson-red. Raised and introduced by Fratelli Gilardelli, Italy, in 1988. Zone 4 (Europe 5)

Acer rubrum 'Morgan'

Synonym, *A. ×freemanii* 'Morgan'. A large tree with a more regular habit than that of the species. Leaves with brilliant scarlet fall color. Introduced by the Sheridan Arboretum, Canada, in 1972. A good street tree deserving of more attention, it is more frequently planted in North America than in Europe. *Acer rubrum* 'Armstrong' (synonym, *A. ×freemanii* 'Armstrong'), a strongly growing tree with good fall color, and 'Tilford', a large tree with a round crown, are similar. Zone 3 (Europe 4)

Acer rubrum 'Red Sunset'. October, a street in Alphen, Netherlands

Acer rubrum 'Red Sunset'

A tree up to 15 to 18 m (50–59 feet) with a broadly pyramidal crown. Leaves slightly larger than usual for cultivars of the species; fall color orange-red to crimson even on young trees. Selected by J. Frank Schmidt & Son, Oregon, and introduced by Amfac Cole Nurseries in 1966. Suitable for somewhat smaller gardens and streets, it is more common in the United States than in Europe. *Acer rubrum* 'Autumn Glory', a tall tree with a rounded crown, is similar. *Acer rubrum* 'October Glory', also similar, may be the best of all cultivars of this species; it was given the Royal Horticultural Society's Award of Merit in 1988 and Award of Garden Merit in 1993. Zone 3 (Europe 4)

Acer rubrum 'Red Sunset'. September, Herkenrode Gardens

Acer rubrum 'Scanlon'. October, Von Gimborn Arboretum

Acer rubrum 'Scanlon'

A narrowly columnar tree up to 15 m (50 feet). Leaves with good fall color, golden yellow to orange-red to orange, speckled with crimson. Flowers few. Raised and introduced by E. H. Scanlon, Ohio, in 1956. Given the Royal Horticultural Society's Award of Garden Merit in 1993. Although commonly planted this beautiful tree tends to lose its leaves too soon in humid conditions, such as those prevailing in areas with maritime climates. *Acer rubrum* 'Doric' is even narrower than 'Scanlon', and 'Gerling', also with a columnar habit, has very good fall color. Zone 3 (Europe 4)

Acer rubrum 'Scanlon'. October, Scott Arboretum, courtesy of J. R. P. van Hoey Smith

Acer rubrum 'Schlesingeri'. October, Hillier Gardens and Arboretum

Acer rubrum 'Schlesingeri'

Leaves with margins more wavy and serrate than usual for cultivars of the species; fall color dark wine-red. Selected by Charles Sprague Sargent of the Arnold Arboretum, Massachusetts, in 1896, described by Fritz Graf von Schwerin, and introduced by Späth Nurseries, Germany. Given the Royal Horticultural Society's Award of Merit in 1976. Common in earlier years, it is now less popular. Zone 3 (Europe 4)

Other Cultivars of *Acer rubrum*

In addition to those illustrated or discussed, we mention the following:

'Ablaze'. With rounded crown and a tree for large streets.

'Autumn Flame' (synonym, *A. ×freemanii* 'Autumn Flame'). With very good fall color.

'Embers'. A vigorously growing tree with a narrow habit and bright red fall color.

'Northwood'. A tree with a broadly oval crown and variable fall color, not always very good.

'Scarsen' (synonyms, Red Sentinel, Scarlet Sentinel, trademark names; *A. ×freemanii* 'Scarsen'). A tree with a strong upright habit; fall colors red, orange, and yellow.

Acer rubrum 'Schlesingeri'. September, Von Gimborn Arboretum

Acer rufinerve. July, Research Station for Nursery Stock

Acer rufinerve. October, Westonbirt Arboretum

Acer rufinerve

Section *Macrantha.* A multistemmed shrubby tree up to 10 m (33 feet) or occasionally more; bark green, white striped, young growth often bluish. Leaves 6–15 cm (2⅜–6 inches) wide, three- or five-lobed, the undersides showing small tufts of rusty hair when young, becoming glabrous when mature. Flowers pale green. Samaras 2 cm (¾ inch) long, nutlets rounded, not flat. Native to mountain forests of Japan, most islands except Hokkaidō. Described by Philipp Franz von Siebold and Joseph Gerhard Zuccarini in 1845. Given the Royal Horticultural Society's Award of Garden Merit in 1993. It is the most commonly planted snakebark maple. Easily propagated from seed, this maple is generally available in the nursery trade and when offered as the species does not display much variation. Zone 5 (Europe 6)

Acer rufinerve 'Albolimbatum'. May, Westonbirt Arboretum

Acer rufinerve 'Albolimbatum'

Synonym, *A. rufinerve* 'Hatsuyuki kaede', perhaps. A multistemmed shrubby tree. Leaves three- or five-lobed, white variegated, some leaves more so than others; leaves tending to revert to green. Originally described as a botanical entity by Joseph D. Hooker in 1869. Seedlings of this cultivar sometimes have variegated leaves but usually revert to green quickly. Zone 5 (Europe 6)

Acer rufinerve 'Erythrocladum'. October

Acer rufinerve 'Erythrocladum'. October

Acer rufinerve 'Erythrocladum'

A slowly growing shrub; bark salmon-yellow with white stripes in winter, in summer inconspicuously yellow-green. Leaves lighter green than those of the species, becoming creamy yellow in fall. Described by R. Marshall, Brimfield Gardens Nursery, Connecticut, in 1953. Not be confused with *A. pensylvanicum* 'Erythrocladum', which has coral-red bark, this beautiful plant is difficult to propagate and is rare in collections. Zone 6 (Europe 7)

Acer saccharinum

Section *Rubra*. A tree up to 25 m (82 feet) in cultivation, in its habitat sometimes up to 40 m (130 feet); bark smooth, dark gray, branches often pendulous and the thinner ones brittle. Leaves 8–15 cm (3⅛–6 inches) wide, deeply five-lobed, sometimes divided to the base, fresh green, whitish underneath; fall color usually yellow. Flowers greenish to white. Samaras almost horizontal, 3–4 cm (1⅛–1½ inches) long, ripening in June and soon losing their viability. Native to eastern North America, Quebec to Florida and west to Minnesota, Kansas, and

Acer saccharinum. September, Hillier Gardens and Arboretum

Oklahoma. Described by Carl Linnaeus in 1753. Silver maple is a common tree in larger parks and gardens. Although planted as a street tree for many years the wood is too brittle and falling branches cause too many problems for that use. Zone 3 (Europe 4)

Acer saccharinum 'Beebe's Cutleaf Weeping'. July

Acer saccharinum. July, Von Gimborn Arboretum

Acer saccharinum 'Laciniatum Wieri'. July, Von Gimborn Arboretum

Acer saccharinum 'Beebe's Cutleaf Weeping'

A tree up to 15 m (50 feet) with horizontal to pendulous branches. Leaves more deeply incised than those of the species. Raised and introduced by the Cole Nursery, Ohio, in 1953. Similar to *A. saccharinum* 'Laciniatum Wieri', 'Beebe's Cutleaf Weeping' is seen less often because it takes much space in the garden and has a rather untidy character. Zone 3 (Europe 4)

Acer saccharinum 'Laciniatum Wieri'

Synonym, *A. saccharinum* 'Wieri'. Leaves more deeply cut than those of the species and more variable in size and form. Found in 1873 by D. B. Wier, Belgium, and introduced by the firm of Ellwanger & Barry, New York. Common in older parks and gardens, also used as a street tree, it is planted less frequently now because it needs much space and its wood is brittle. *Acer saccharinum* 'Silver Queen', with a more regular habit, is also a monumental tree for large parks. Zone 3 (Europe 4)

Acer saccharinum 'Lutescens'. July

Acer saccharinum 'Lutescens'

A tree of smaller stature than the species. Leaves clear yellow in spring, turning light green in summer; fall color yellow. Raised and introduced by Späth Nurseries, Germany, in 1883. Although not uncommon in collections it deserves more attention, in medium-sized parks, for example, because it is beautiful in spring, providing a nice splash of color. It does require space, however. Zone 4 (Europe 5)

Acer saccharinum 'Pyramidale'. July, Von Gimborn Arboretum

Acer saccharinum 'Pyramidale'

A more or less pyramidal tree up to 20 m (66 feet), much narrower than characteristic of the species; branches brittle. Leaf shape variable and lobes more deeply cleft than characteristic of the species; leaf underside gray, fall color usually yellow. Introduced by Späth Nurseries, Germany, in 1885. Common in parks and large public gardens, it is also in use as a street tree. Zone 4 (Europe 5)

Acer saccharum

Section *Acer*, series *Saccharodendron*. Described by Humphry Marshall in 1785. The classification of sugar maple is complex with subspecies *(floridanum, grandidentatum, leucoderme, nigrum,* and *saccharum)*, varieties *(schneckii)*, and forms *(glaucum)* recognized. Those listed in parentheses are cultivated and are illustrated in addition to the cultivars. All of these are listed alphabetically below. Also, a few more notable cultivars are listed at the end of the entries for *A. saccharum*.

Acer saccharum 'Brocade'. October

Acer saccharum 'Brocade'

A medium-sized tree with more or less erect branching. Leaves about 10 cm (4 inches) wide, very deeply cleft, almost to the base; fall color orange-yellow. Named by T. J. Delendick, U.S.A., in 1984. Not to be confused with *A. palmatum* 'Brocade', it is a beautiful plant that deserves more attention. Zone 4 (Europe 5)

Acer saccharum subsp. *floridanum*. October

Acer saccharum f. *glaucum*. October, Royal Botanic Gardens, Kew

Acer saccharum f. glaucum

Leaves bluish underneath. Originally described as a variety by Friedrich S. Schmidt in 1885. Apart from the difference in leaf color, the tree's characteristics are the same as those of *A. saccharum*. Zone 4 (Europe 5)

Acer saccharum subsp. floridanum

Synonyms, *A. barbatum* of various authors, not A. Michaux, *A. floridanum*. A tree up to about 12 m (39 feet) in its habitat high, smaller in cultivation. Leaves 10–15 cm (4–6 inches) wide, five-lobed, lobes obtuse; fall color yellow to orange. Native to the southeastern United States, Florida, Texas, and south to Mexico. Originally described as a variety by Alvan Wentworth Chapman in 1860. It is a rare tree in cultivation, found in maple collections or botanical gardens. Zone 5 (Europe 6)

Acer saccharum 'Goldspire'. May, Princeton Nurseries, courtesy of J. R. P. van Hoey Smith

Acer saccharum 'Goldspire'

A narrow, columnar tree up to 12 to 15 m (39–50 feet) and about 3 m (10 feet) wide. Leaves turning golden yellow in fall. Raised and introduced by Princeton Nurseries, New Jersey, in 1973. It is more frequently planted in the United States than in Europe. *Acer saccharum* 'Cary' is similar. Zone 4 (Europe 5)

Acer saccharum subsp. *grandidentatum*

Synonym, *A. grandidentatum*. A small tree or a shrubby tree with more than one stem up to 10 to 12 m (33–39 feet) and almost as wide; bark dark gray. Leaves 5–10 cm (2–4 inches) wide, distinctly five-lobed, margins entire; fall color usually in the yellow range, quite spectacular. Flowers yellow. Nutlets slightly smaller than those of subspecies *saccharum*. Native to the Rocky Mountains from Montana south to northern Mexico, west to Utah and Arizona. Originally described as a separate species by John Torrey and Asa Gray in 1838. Big-tooth maple, also called canyon maple, is more commonly cultivated in the United States than in Europe. Zone 4 (Europe 5)

Acer saccharum subsp. *grandidentatum*. May, Herkenrode Gardens

Acer saccharum subsp. *leucoderme*

Synonym, *A. leucoderme*. A tree or a shrub up to 8 m (26 feet) or occasionally more, densely branched with a flat-topped crown. Leaves 5–8 cm (2–3⅛ inches) wide, sometimes larger on vigorous branches, three- or five-lobed, lobes almost triangular, color bluish underneath; fall color usually yellow-orange. Flowers whitish yellow, usually abundant. Samaras 2–3 cm (¾–1⅛ inches) long, hairy when young. Native to the southern United States, North Carolina to Florida, west to Louisiana and Arkansas. Originally described as a separate species by John Kunkel Small in 1895. Chalk maple is rare in cultivation. The bluish color underneath the leaves is not always seen. For example, the trees at Westonbirt Arboretum, England, do not display much of this phenomenon. Zone 4 (Europe 5)

Acer saccharum subsp. *leucoderme*. April

Acer saccharum 'Louisa Lad'

A slender tree up to 12 m (39 feet), much taller than wide. Leaves with intense fall color. Named and introduced by J. J. W. M. van den Oever, Netherlands, in 1984. Rare in cultivation, its excellent fall color is developed well even in a maritime climate. *Acer saccharum* 'Green Mountain', broadly pyramidal and a tree for planting along wide avenues, is similar in several respects. Zone 4 (Europe 5)

Acer saccharum 'Louisa Lad'. October

Acer saccharum 'Newton Sentry'. August, Morris
Arboretum, courtesy of J. R. P. van Hoey Smith

Acer saccharum subsp. *nigrum.* October

Acer saccharum 'Newton Sentry'

An extremely narrow tree up to 10 m (33 feet) or more. Leaves slightly smaller than usual for cultivars of the species and more leathery. The original tree grows in Newton Cemetery, Massachusetts. It is almost a broomstick with some minor side branches. Not a great beauty, this cultivar can be useful in places with very limited space. Zone 4 (Europe 5)

Acer saccharum subsp. *nigrum*

Synonym, *A. nigrum.* A tall tree, in its habitat up to 40 m (130 feet), considerably smaller in cultivation in other parts of the world. Leaves 10–15 cm (4–6 inches) wide, three- or five-lobed, usually with small stipules on the petioles; fall color yellow-orange. Native to eastern North America, southern Quebec and Ontario south to Kentucky, west to Kansas, often on calcareous soils. Originally described as a separate species by François André Michaux in 1812. Outside the United States black maple is rarely planted, except in maple collections and arboretums, but this splendid tree deserves more attention. It is useful in dry situations. The stipules are sometimes almost leafy but may also be absent. *Acer saccharum* subsp. *nigrum* 'Greencolumn' is a columnar form. Zone 4 (Europe 5)

Acer saccharum subsp. *saccharum*. June, Herkenrode Gardens

Acer saccharum subsp. *saccharum*. October, Hillier Gardens and Arboretum

Acer saccharum subsp. *saccharum*

A tree up to 40 m (130 feet) in its habitat, in cultivation usually not more than 25 m (82 feet) high and in maritime climates even smaller; bark smooth, dark gray. Leaves 5–8 cm (2–3⅛ inches) wide, distinctly five-lobed or three-lobed with less conspicuous outer lobes, color dark green with a whitish felt underneath. Flowers abundant, yellow, appearing before the leaves unfold; fall color usually clear yellow to orange. Samaras 2–4 cm (¾–1½ inches) long, profusely borne on wild trees, less so in cultivation. Native to eastern North America from Canada to Mexico and Guatemala. Commonly planted, sugar maple is also used as a street tree and a stylized version of its leaf is the national symbol of Canada. Zone 4 (Europe 5)

Acer saccharum var. *schneckii*. June, Arboretum Belmonte, courtesy of J. R. P. van Hoey Smith

Acer saccharum var. *schneckii*

A tree up to 20 m (66 feet). Leaves five-lobed, the veins softly pubescent underneath and petioles villous. Native to the midwestern United States, Indiana, Illinois, and Missouri. Described by Alfred Rehder in 1913. Only slightly different from subspecies *saccharum*, this tree is rarely seen in cultivation. Zone 4 (Europe 5)

Acer saccharum 'Sweet Shadow Cutleaf'

A tree with ascending branches up to 15 m (50 feet) and almost as wide. Leaves 8–12 cm (3⅛–4¾ inches) wide, deeply incised, the lobes again dissected and slightly overlapping, color dark green, turning orange-yellow in fall. Named and introduced by

Acer saccharum 'Sweet Shadow Cutleaf'. October, Arboretum Trompenburg

Powell Valley Nursery, Oregon, in 1962. Its leaves are similar to those of 'Brocade' but more dissected. Zone 4 (Europe 5)

Acer saccharum 'Sweet Shadow Cutleaf'. October, Washington Park Arboretum, courtesy of J. R. P. van Hoey Smith

Other Cultivars of *Acer saccharum*

In addition to those illustrated or discussed, we mention the following:

'Commemoration'. A vigorously growing tree with a large crown.

'Fairview'. A strongly growing tree with a large crown.

'Legacy'. A strongly growing tree with a spreading habit.

'Moraine'. A fast-growing tree with a spreading habit.

Acer saccharum 'Temple's Upright'. October, Hillier Gardens and Arboretum

Acer saccharum 'Temple's Upright'

A slender, almost fastigiate but not columnar tree up to 15 to 20 m (50–66 feet) usually with a strong leader. Leaves larger than those characteristic of the species and somewhat leathery; fall color can be very beautiful depending on weather. Preferring a marked continental climate in which fall coloring is particularly well developed, it is more commonly planted in the United States than in Europe. Zone 4 (Europe 5)

Acer sempervirens. October, Royal Botanic Gardens, Kew

Acer sempervirens

Section *Acer*, series *Monspessulana*. Synonyms, *A. creticum* of various authors, not P. Miller, not Linnaeus, *A. orientale* of various authors, not Linnaeus. A densely branched shrub up to 5 to 7 m (16–23 feet) or occasionally a small tree up to 10 m (33 feet). Leaves half-evergreen, in cold winters the plants losing all leaves except those in the center, leaves unlobed or three-lobed (lobes often underdeveloped), leathery, margins entire, color shiny green, sometimes whitish underneath. Flowers greenish. Samaras 1.5 cm (⅝ inch) long, brown. Native to Crete, especially central Crete on Mount Ida, and coastal areas of Turkey and Lebanon. Described by Carl Linnaeus in 1767. Cretan maple is rare in cultivation. The name *sempervirens* is misleading as plants rarely are truly evergreen; a well-known tree in the Jardin des Plantes, Paris, is evergreen. Zone 7 (Europe 8)

Acer sempervirens. October, Royal Botanic Gardens, Kew

Acer shirasawanum 'Aureum'. October

Acer shirasawanum 'Aureum'. May

Acer shirasawanum

Section *Palmata*, series *Palmata*. Described by Gen'ichi Koidzumi in 1911. Two varieties are recognized, *shirasawanum* and *tenuifolium*, in addition to the cultivars, all listed alphabetically.

Acer shirasawanum 'Aureum'

Synonyms, *A. japonicum* 'Aureum', 'Kinka-kure'. A rounded, shrubby tree sometimes up to 5 to 6 m (16–20 feet) and as wide; specimens with only one or two stems sometimes seen. Leaves 7–12 cm (2¾–4¾ inches) wide, almost round, nine- to thirteen-lobed, golden yellow when unfolding, turning light greenish yellow; in fall the foliage may turn orange but leaves often shrivel and do not show much color. Flowers in erect corymbs, dotted among the leaves and developing with them. Fruits in small erect corymbs above the leaves; samaras often reddish. Described by J. A. Siesmayer, Germany, in 1888 but introduced into Europe about 1860 by Philipp Franz von Siebold and later also by Louis Van Houtte, Belgium. Given the Royal Horticultural Society's First Class Certificate in 1884 and Award of Garden Merit in 1993. A frequently planted cultivar in many kinds of gardens, the oldest and largest specimen is in the Esveld Aceretum, Netherlands, measuring about 7 to 8 m (23–26 feet) high and 8 to 10 m (26–33 feet) in diameter. *Acer shirasawanum* 'Autumn Moon', with pale yellow leaves, is similar. *Acer shirasawanum* 'Kakure gasa' (also seen labeled as a cultivar of *A. japonicum*) is generally considered to be synonymous with 'Aureum' but its leaves might be somewhat lighter yellow. Zone 6 (Europe 7)

Acer shirasawanum 'Aureum'. May

Acer shirasawanum 'Aureum'. October

Acer shirasawanum 'Diana'. July, Von Gimborn Arboretum

Acer shirasawanum 'Diana'

A multistemmed tree or large shrub up to 5 to 6 m (16–20 feet) and almost as wide. Leaves 10–15 cm (4–6 inches) wide, round, eleven- or thirteen-lobed, fresh green, turning yellow in fall. Named and introduced by the Von Gimborn Arboretum and Firma C.

Acer shirasawanum 'Gloria'. October, Von Gimborn Arboretum

Esveld, Netherlands, in 1995. The original plant grows at the Von Gimborn Arboretum. Zone 6 (Europe 7)

Acer shirasawanum 'Ezo no o momiji'. August

Acer shirasawanum 'Ezo no o momiji'

Synonym, *A. japonicum* 'Ezo no o momiji'. A large shrub up to 6 to 8 m (20–26 feet) and as wide. Leaves 8–12 cm (3⅛–4¾ inches) wide, nine- or eleven-lobed, dark green, turning yellow in fall. A plant rare in collections, it deserves more attention. Zone 6 (Europe 7)

Acer shirasawanum 'Gloria'. June, Von Gimborn Arboretum

Acer shirasawanum 'Gloria'

A slender and upright-growing shrubby tree up to 8 m (26 feet) or sometimes more. Leaves 8–12 cm (3⅛–4¾ inches) wide, seven- to eleven-lobed, deeply incised, dark brown-red, turning lighter in fall. Samaras purplish. Found as a chance seedling in the

Esveld Aceretum, Netherlands, and planted in the Von Gimborn Arboretum; named by Firma C. Esveld in 1995. Arising, perhaps, from cross-pollination of *A. shirasawanum* 'Palmatifolium' from a nearby *A. palmatum* 'Bloodgood', the flowers and fruits show strong affinity with *A. shirasawanum* and 'Gloria' is treated as a cultivar of that species. Similar to *A. shirasawanum* 'Yasemin', the leaves of 'Gloria' are less shiny and more brown. Zone 6 (Europe 7)

Acer shirasawanum 'Jūni hito e'. May, Westonbirt Arboretum

Acer shirasawanum 'Microphyllum'. October

Acer shirasawanum 'Microphyllum'

Synonym, *A. japonicum* 'Microphyllum'. A shrub up to 8 to 10 m (26–33 feet) and almost as wide. Leaves 6–10 cm (2⅜–4 inches) wide, smaller than those of the species, usually nine- or eleven-lobed; fall color yellow. Named by J. A. Siesmayer, Germany, in 1888 and sometimes treated as a botanical form, for example, by T. J. Delendick. Rare in collections, it seems to us there is no reason to try to distinguish 'Microphyllum' from 'Jūni hito e'. *Acer shirasawanum* 'Helena' is similar to 'Microphyllum'. Zone 6 (Europe 7)

Acer shirasawanum 'Palmatifolium'

A shrub, usually multistemmed, up to 10 m (33 feet) and almost as wide. Leaves eleven-lobed, deeply divided, fresh green; fall color yellow but the leaves dry quickly. The cultivar name was used by J. D. Vertrees, Oregon, but its origin has not been traced in the literature. It may be attributable to Gen'ichi Koidzumi. A worthwhile plant but

Acer shirasawanum 'Jūni hito e'

Alternatively, *A. shirasawanum* 'Juhni hito e'. A shrub up to 8 to 9 m (26–30 feet) and almost as wide. Leaves 6–8 cm (2⅜–3⅛ inches) wide, smaller than those of the species and nearly identical to those of *A. shirasawanum* 'Microphyllum', nine- to thirteen-lobed, yellowish green, turning yellow in fall. The cultivar name has been used by various authors for different plants. Its current expression seems to us to be identical with 'Microphyllum'. Zone 6 (Europe 7)

Acer shirasawanum 'Palmatifolium'. October

Acer shirasawanum 'Palmatifolium'. October

Acer shirasawanum var. *shirasawanum*. October, Von Gimborn Arboretum

Acer shirasawanum 'Susanne'. July

not often seen, there are large specimens in the Esveld Aceretum, Netherlands; Arboretum Kalmthout, Belgium; and Hergest Croft Gardens, England. Zone 5 (Europe 6)

Acer shirasawanum var. *shirasawanum*. September, Herkenrode Gardens

Acer shirasawanum var. *shirasawanum*

A small tree in its habitat, up to 15 m (50 feet), in cultivation a large shrub sometimes up to 10 m (33 feet) or more and about as wide. Leaves 6–12 cm (2⅜–4¾ inches) wide, almost round, nine- to thirteen-lobed, margins finely or more roughly serrate, color fresh green, turning yellow in fall. Flowers in erect corymbs. Fruits in erect trusses, standing above the leaves, nutlets round. Native to Honshū and Shikoku Islands of Japan. Less rare in cultivation than originally thought, several misidentified specimens in collections were not recognized as *A. shirasawanum*. It is a beautiful plant but the cultivar 'Aureum' is more common. Zone 6 (Europe 7)

Acer shirasawanum 'Susanne'

A shrub possibly up to 5 to 6 m (16–20 feet), rather densely branched. Leaves lemon-yellow when unfolding, turning soft green in the summer. Found in the Arboretum Thiensen and raised by H. J. Drath, Germany, and named by Firma C. Esveld, Netherlands, in 1992. The cultivar was named for the daughter of H. D. Warda, director of the Arboretum Thiensen. Its appearance is in between that of 'Aureum' and 'Microphyllum', filling a gap. Zone 5 (Europe 6)

Acer shirasawanum var. *tenuifolium*

A tree or large shrub up to 10 m (33 feet) in its habitat, usually smaller in cultivation. Leaves 5–8 cm (2–3⅛ inches) wide, seven- or nine-lobed, deeply divided, almost to the base, light green, turning orange-yellow in fall. Native to southern Hokkaidō Island and Honshū and Shikoku Islands of Japan. Described by Gen'ichi Koidzumi in 1911. Sometimes wrongly labeled in collections, this rather inconspicuous plant is interesting because it is so rare. Zone 6 (Europe 7)

Acer shirasawanum 'Yasemin'. August

Acer shirasawanum 'Yasemin'

Synonym, *A. palmatum* 'Yasemin'. A slender, shrubby tree up to 10 m (33 feet) and 3–4 m (10–13 feet) wide. Leaves nine- or eleven-lobed, margins finely dissected, leaf blade slightly convex, color shiny dark purple. Flowers, fruits in erect bundles. Named for Mirte Yasemin van Gelderen, daughter and granddaughter of the authors of the present book. Raised and introduced by Firma C. Esveld, Netherlands, in 1995. Given an Award of Merit by the Royal Boskoop Horticultural Society in 1995. Arising as a chance seedling in the Esveld Aceretum under a large plant of *A. shirsawanum* 'Palmatifolium', it is possible that 'Yasemin', like *A. shirasawanum* 'Gloria', is the result of cross-pollination from a nearby *A. palmatum* 'Bloodgood'. Zone 6 (Europe 7)

Acer shirasawanum var. *tenuifolium*. June, Herkenrode Gardens

Acer sieboldianum. July, Hof ter Saksen

Acer sieboldianum 'Kinugasa yama'. May, Herkenrode Gardens

Acer sieboldianum 'Mi yama nishiki'. July

Acer sieboldianum

Section *Palmata*, series *Palmata*. A slender upright-growing shrub up to 8 to 9 m (26–30 feet) and 3 to 4 m (10–13 feet) wide; branches somewhat downy. Leaves 5–8 cm (2–3⅛ inches) wide, seven- (or nine-) lobed, dark green, veins underneath slightly tomentose, a feature useful in distinguishing it from *A. palmatum.* Flowers, fruits small, greenish yellow and gray-white pubescent. Native to Japan, rather common in mountain forests of Honshū, Shikoku, and Kyūshū Islands. Described by Friedrich Anton Wilhelm Miquel in 1865, honoring Philipp Franz von Siebold. The species is not as rare as it may seem in cultivation because specimens are often wrongly labeled. 'Kunpu nishiki' is similar to the species but has some creamy yellow spots on the leaves. Zone 5 (Europe 6)

Acer sieboldianum 'Kinugasa yama'

A shrub up to 6 m (20 feet) and as wide. Leaves seven- or nine-lobed, green with silky hairs underneath; fall color yellow-orange. Flowers and fruits inconspicuous as in the species. Origin Japanese, before 1960. A beautiful shrub, it has unfortunately been neglected and is present only in a few collections. Zone 5 (Europe 6)

Acer sieboldianum 'Mi yama nishiki'

A shrub up to 8 to 10 m (26–33 feet), well-branched; bark of young slender shoots reddish brown. Leaves five-lobed, somewhat tomentose underneath, turning yellow in fall. Origin Japanese, before 1970. It is a rare shrub. Zone 6 (Europe 7)

Acer sieboldianum 'Ogura yama'. August

Acer sieboldianum 'Osiris'. July, Von Gimborn Arboretum

Acer sieboldianum 'Ogura yama'

Synonyms, *A. japonicum* 'Ogura yama', *A. shirasawanum* 'Ogura yama', 'Ogure yama'. A shrubby plant with more characteristics of *A. sieboldianum* than of *A. shirasawanum*. Origin Japanese. Size and habit are similar to *A. shirasawanum* but branches and branchlets are tomentose, not glabrous, indicating close affinity to *A. sieboldianum* as noted by J. D. Vertrees in *Japanese Maples*. It is rare in cultivation and sometimes wrongly labeled. Zone 6 (Europe 7)

Acer sieboldianum 'Osiris'

A slender, multistemmed, upright-growing tree up to 10 m (33 feet). Leaves nine-lobed, dark green, distinctly gray-white pubescent underneath; fall color yellow. Flowers greenish yellow. Samaras brown. The original tree has been growing in the Von Gimborn Arboretum, Netherlands, for many years. In accordance with P. C. de Jong, former director of the arboretum, it has been named as a cultivar by Firma C. Esveld. Zone 6 (Europe 7)

Acer sieboldianum 'Sode no uchi'. May, Herkenrode Gardens

Acer sieboldianum 'Sode no uchi'

A dwarf shrub hardly more than 3 m (10 feet) high and about as wide. Leaves 2–5 cm (¾–2 inches) wide, nine-lobed, green with purplish edges; fall color can be attractive. Origin Japanese. Rare in cultivation, it is probably a witches'-broom and like many witches'-brooms it may not be very long lived. Useful as a bonsai, it is also nice for larger rockeries. Zone 6 (Europe 7)

Acer sieboldianum 'Sode no uchi'. May, Savill Gardens

Acer sikkimense subsp. *sikkimense.* June

Acer sikkimense subsp. *sikkimense*

Section *Macrantha.* Synonym, *A. hookeri.* In its habitat a tree up to 12 m (39 feet), in cultivation much smaller, often only a straggling shrub. Leaves 6–15 cm (2⅜–6 inches) long and 5–8 cm (2–3⅛ inches) wide, unlobed, shiny dark green, somewhat leathery; not much fall color because it is half-evergreen. Native to the eastern Himalayas, about 2500 m (8200 feet), in Sikkim and Assam in India, Bhutan, northern Myanmar (Burma), and Yunnan Province in China. Described by Friedrich Anton Wilhelm Miquel in 1867. Hardy in cultivation only in sheltered places, such as in western Scotland or Cornwall, England, it is rare and sometimes grown as a greenhouse plant. Subspecies *metcalfii* is probably not in cultivation. Zone 8 (Europe 9)

Acer sinopurpurascens. May, Arboretum Trompenburg, courtesy of J. R. P. van Hoey Smith

Acer sinopurpurascens

Section *Lithocarpa.* Synonym, *A. diabolicum* subsp. *sinopurpurascens.* A small tree of regular habit up to 8 to 10 m (26–33 feet) and about as wide. Leaves deeply five-lobed, sometimes only three-lobed and with very small basal lobes, leaf-margins sometimes slightly serrate, color dark green, turning yellow in fall, leaf underside glaucous; petioles exuding latex when broken. Flowers greenish yellow, plants dioecious. Samaras large, often parthenocarpic. Native to Zhe-

Acer sinopurpurascens. May, Valley Gardens

iang Province in China. Described by
Cheng Wan-chun in 1931. Very rare in cultivation, there is a male tree in the Arboretum Trompenburg, Netherlands, and a
female tree in Valley Gardens, England.
Vegetative propagation is difficult if not
impossible because there are no closely
related species with latex. Viable seed is
almost never available in the nursery trade.
Zone 5 (Europe 6)

Acer sinopurpurascens. October, Arboretum Trompenburg

Acer spicatum. July

Acer spicatum. May, Westonbirt Arboretum

Acer spicatum

Section *Parviflora*, series *Caudata*. Synonym, *A. parviflorum*. A large shrub, rarely
a tree up to 10 m (33 feet) or more, densely
branched; bark green, striped but often not
very conspicuously. Leaves 6–12 cm (2⅜–
4¾ inches) wide, three- or five-lobed, margins conspicuously serrate, leaf underside
glabrous, never hairy; fall color good yellow-
orange. Flowers greenish, plants usually
dioecious. Samaras small, brown, in long
trusses; fruits on solitary plants usually not
viable. Native to eastern North America,
Newfoundland west to Saskatchewan and
Iowa, south to northern Georgia. Described
by Jean Baptiste Pierre Antoine de Monet
de Lamarck in 1786. A decorative shrub,
mountain maple deserves more attention.
Rare in cultivation, it may be confused with
A. caudatum subsp. *ukurunduense* but that
maple has leaves that are tomentose underneath, not smooth. Zone 4 (Europe 5)

Acer stachyophyllum

Section *Glabra,* series *Arguta.* Described by William P. Hiern in 1875. Two subspecies are recognized, *betulifolium* and *stachyophyllum.*

Acer stachyophyllum subsp. *betulifolium.* July

Acer stachyophyllum subsp. *stachyophyllum.* May, Westonbirt Arboretum

Acer stachyophyllum subsp. *betulifolium*

Synonym, *A. betulifolium.* A multistemmed treelike shrub in habit similar to subspecies *stachyophyllum* but with many suckers from the base of the plant, unusual for maples. Leaves 3–5 cm (1⅛–2 inches) long and 2–3 cm (¾–1⅛ inches) wide, almost unlobed or three-lobed (the lobes often underdeveloped), fresh green, turning yellow in fall. Native to Gansu Province in China. Originally described as a separate species by Karl Johann Maximowicz in 1889. A rare plant, it is present in few collections. There is a large specimen in the Esveld Aceretum, Netherlands, that produces many suckers. That plant originated from a packet of seed and has been propagated vegetatively because plants are dioecious. Zone 6 (Europe 7)

Acer stachyophyllum subsp. *stachyophyllum*

Synonym, *A. tetramerum.* A multistemmed treelike shrub up to 10 m (33 feet) or more with an erect habit, stems usually closely set together; bark striped but often not very conspicuously. Leaves 4–8 cm (1½–3⅛ inches) long and 3–5 cm (1⅛–2 inches) wide, ovate, three-lobed or sometimes unlobed; fall color yellow but plant has tendency to drop leaves early in the season. Flowers yellowish, plants dioecious. Samaras 2–3 cm (¾–1⅛ inches) long, produced when plants of different sex grown together. Native to mountainous forests, 2000–3000 m (6500–9800 feet), Sikkim in India to Hubei and eastern Sichuan Provinces in China. Represented in a few botanical collections, this nice maple may be propagated from softwood cuttings when viable seed is unavailable. Zone 6 (Europe 7)

Acer sterculiaceum

Section *Lithocarpa,* series *Lithocarpa.* Described by Nathaniel Wallich in 1830 and introduced into Great Britain by Joseph D. Hooker in 1835. Three subspecies are recognized, *franchetii, sterculiaceum,* and *thomsonii.*

Acer sterculiaceum subsp. *sterculiaceum.* May, Westonbirt Arboretum

Acer sterculiaceum subsp. *franchetii.* October, Westonbirt Arboretum

Acer sterculiaceum subsp. *franchetii*

Synonyms, *A. franchetii, A. schoenermarkiae.* Usually a shrub or multistemmed tree up to 6 to 8 m (20–26 feet), in cultivation usually much smaller. Leaves similar to those of subspecies *sterculiaceum* but almost always three-lobed although five-lobed leaves may be present on the same plant. Flowers, fruits like those of subspecies *sterculiaceum* but female plants producing viable seeds occasionally. Native to Tibet and Guangxi Autonomous Region and Guizhou, Hubei, western Sichuan, and northern Yunnan Provinces in China, farther north than subspecies *sterculiaceum.* Originally described as a separate species by Ferdinand Albin Pax in 1889, honoring Adrien René Franchet. Rarer in cultivation than even subspecies *sterculiaceum,* there is little experience in growing it. Zone 6 (Europe 7)

Acer sterculiaceum subsp. *sterculiaceum*

Synonym, *A. villosum* in the sense of Wallich, not J. Presl & K. Presl. A tree up to 20 m (66 feet) with a spreading crown that can reach 15 m (50 feet) in diameter; bark dark brown and fissured, branches stout and villous when young. Leaves 15–25 cm (6–10 inches) wide, three- or five-lobed, texture firm, especially on younger trees. Flowers, fruits in long panicles, plants dioecious. Samaras to 6 cm (2⅜ inches) long, solitary female trees forming fruits that are not viable. Native to the Himalayas, Kashmir and Sikkim in India, and Nepal. Present in several collections, some especially good trees are present in Westonbirt Arboretum, England. It is an interesting tree but difficult to grow in western Europe. Young plants tend to leaf out early in spring and have a tendency to die back suddenly or drop foliage early, in August. Zone 6 (Europe 7)

Acer sterculiaceum subsp. *thomsonii*. May

Acer sterculiaceum subsp. *thomsonii*

Synonym, *A. thomsonii*. A tree up to 15 m (50 feet), in shape and color like subspecies *sterculiaceum*. Leaves to 30 cm (12 inches) wide, three- or five-lobed, margins slightly serrate, color dark green, texture firm; young leaves may have purplish color, disappearing in summer. Native to the Himalayas, Assam and Sikkim in India, Bhutan, and Nepal, the same area as subspecies *sterculiaceum*. Originally described as a separate species by Friedrich Anton Wilhelm Miquel in 1867. With very few trees in cultivation, experience with material is restricted. There is a small tree in the Royal Botanic Gardens, Kew, and a young typical specimen in the Esveld Aceretum, Netherlands. Grafting onto subspecies *sterculiaceum* is the only means of propagation as seeds seem never to be available in the nursery trade. Zone 6 (Europe 7)

Acer tataricum

Section *Ginnala*. Described by Carl Linnaeus in 1753. Four subspecies are recognized, *aidzuense*, *ginnala*, *semenovii*, and *tataricum*.

Acer tataricum subsp. *aidzuense*

A densely branched shrub or small tree up to 8 to 10 m (26–33 feet), in habit much like subspecies *tataricum*. Leaves variable on the same plant, unlobed or three-lobed, juvenile leaves sharply three-lobed, color with hint of salmon-green; fall color not spectacular. Flowers whitish green. Samaras small, brown. Native to Hokkaidō, Honshū, Kyūshū, and Shikoku Islands of Japan. Originally described as a variety by Adrien René Franchet in 1879. Seldom seen in collections and then often wrongly labeled. Horticulturally, it can hardly be separated from subspecies *tataricum*. *Acer tataricum* subsp. *aidzuense* 'Awayuki' has leaves covered with white dots, 'Tenshan no nishiki' has leaves white variegated and speckled with white dots, and 'Yūzuki nishiki' (alternatively, 'Yuhzuki nishiki') has leaves with yellow dots. Zone 4 (Europe 5)

Acer tataricum subsp. *aidzuense*. May, Zuiderpark

Acer tataricum subsp. *ginnala*

Synonym, *A. ginnala.* A shrub or multi-stemmed tree, rarely a single-stemmed tree up to 10 to 15 m (33–50 feet), densely branched, branches rather thin. Leaves 4–8 cm (1½–3⅛ inches) long and 2–4 cm (¾–1½ inches) wide, three-lobed with an elongated apex, fresh green with variegation on some leaves; fall color can be spectacular. Flowers yellowish. Fruits abundant. Native to Manchuria in China, Siberia in Russia, northern Korea, and Honshū, Kyūshū, and Shikoku Islands in Japan. Originally described as a separate species by Karl Johann Maximowicz in 1857. Given the Royal Horticultural Society's Award of Garden Merit in 1993. Amur maple is one of the most common maples in cultivation. It can also be used for extensive plantings in larger parks and public gardens. Zone 4 (Europe 5)

Acer tataricum subsp. *ginnala* 'Durand Dwarf'

A compact shrub up to 1.5 m (5 feet), very densely branched, being a witches'-broom. Leaves quite small, three-lobed, dark green, turning glowing red and orange in fall. Flowers, fruits not produced, as usual for witches'-brooms. Raised and introduced by Bernard E. Harkness, New York, in 1955. It is prone to sudden dieback. Zone 4 (Europe 5)

Acer tataricum subsp. *ginnala* 'Fire'

A large bushy shrub, densely branched with long, cascading branches when mature. Leaves distantly lobed, dark green and keeping green color well, turning brilliant orange-red shades in fall. Received from Canada and introduced by Firma C. Esveld, Netherlands, in 1982. Zone 4 (Europe 5)

Acer tataricum subsp. *ginnala.* October, Sortimentstuin Zundert

Acer tataricum subsp. *ginnala* 'Durand Dwarf'. August, van der Maat

Acer tataricum subsp. *ginnala* 'Fire'. June

Acer tataricum subsp. *ginnala* 'Flame'. June

Acer tataricum subsp. *tataricum*. May, Arboretum Belmonte

Acer tataricum subsp. *tataricum*. May, Arboretum Belmonte

Acer tataricum subsp. *ginnala* 'Flame'

A shrubby tree growing fast and developing long, arching branches, reaching 7–8 m (23–26 feet) in height and even wider. Leaves without any variegation; fall color often spectacular, usually better than the average plant of subspecies *ginnala*. Received from Canada and introduced by Firma C. Esveld, Netherlands, in 1982. Zone 4 (Europe 5)

Acer tataricum subsp. *semenovii*. August

Acer tataricum subsp. *semenovii*

Synonym, *A. semenovii*. A dense shrub up to 4 m (13 feet) and wider in cultivation. Leaves 2–5 cm (3/4–2 inches) long and 2–3 cm (3/4–1 1/8 inches) wide, unlobed to three-lobed with slight serration, light green; fall color not spectacular. Native to dry and sunny places in Afghanistan, Turkistan, and the Tian Shan mountainous area. Originally described as a separate species by Eduard August von Regel and Ferdinand Gottfried Maximilian Theobald von Herder in 1866. The only maple that could be used successfully as a ground cover, it is, however, hardly used in cultivation. Zone 5 (Europe 6)

Acer tataricum subsp. *tataricum*

A shrub or tree with crowded branches up to 10 m (33 feet), rarely more; bark dark reddish brown. Leaves 5–8 cm (2–3 1/8 inches) long and 3–4 cm (1 1/8–1 1/2 inches) wide, un-lobed, lobed leaves appearing only on juvenile shoots; leaves usually dropped early, little or no fall color. Flowers in erect terminal panicles, almost white, quite decorative. Fruits ripening early, samaras 2 cm (3/4 inch) long, dark brown. Native to eastern Europe, Austria, Hungary, Serbia, Romania, Ukraine, to the Caucasus, and Turkey. Tatarian maple is quite common in cultivation, often mixed with subspecies *ginnala*. Zone 4 (Europe 5)

Acer tegmentosum

Section *Macrantha*. A tree or multistemmed shrub up to 10 m (33 feet) and as wide; bark green and white striped, young shoots having a bluish color, later turning green. Leaves to 20 cm (8 inches) wide on juvenile shoots, usually smaller on adult branches, three- or five-lobed, foliage also bluish; fall color golden yellow. Flowers in pendulous terminal racemes. Samaras 3 cm (1⅛ inches) long, brown. Native to wet areas in eastern Siberia in Russia, the Amur and Ussuri River regions, and mountainous areas of northern Korea and Manchuria in China. Described by Karl Johann Maximowicz in 1857. It is closely related to the North American *A. pensylvanicum*. Zone 5 (Europe 6)

Acer tegmentosum.

Acer tenellum. June

Acer tonkinense subsp. *kwangsiense.* May

Acer tonkinense subsp. **kwangsiense**

Section *Palmata*, series *Sinensia*. In its habitat a tree or shrub up to 10 m (33 feet) and as wide, in cultivation much smaller; branches green. Leaves 10–15 cm (4–6 inches) wide, shallowly three-lobed or tridentate, margins serrate, especially on juvenile shoots. Native to the Guangxi Autonomous Region of China. Originally described as a separate species by Fang

Acer tenellum

Section *Platanoidea*. A tree or merely a shrub, especially in cultivation, up to 7 to 8 m (23–26 feet) and about as wide; young branches yellow-green and thin. Leaves 4–8 cm (1½–3⅛ inches) wide, three-lobed, side lobes sometimes only small or absent, shiny green, of thin texture; leaves trembling in a breeze somewhat like those of quaking aspen, *Populus tremula*. Samaras reported to be small. Native to Jiangxi, Sichuan, and Yunnan Provinces in China. Described by Ferdinand Albin Pax in 1889. It is difficult to propagate and is rare in cultivation, being primarily of botanical interest only. Zone 6 (Europe 7)

Acer triflorum. May, Herkenrode Gardens

Wen-pei and his son in 1966. This very rare maple was introduced into Europe through the courtesy of Wang Dajun, former curator of the Long Wu Lu Botanic Gardens, Shanghai. Subspecies *tonkinense*, which has leaves with entire margins, is not in cultivation. Zone 8 (Europe 9)

Acer triflorum

Section *Trifoliata*, series *Grisea*. In its habitat a tree up to 10 to 12 m (33–39 feet), in cultivation usually much smaller or even a shrub; bark yellowish brown, peeling in woolly scales, not papery as in *A. griseum*. Leaves 3–7 cm (1⅛–2¾ inches) long and 2–3.5 cm (¾–1⅜ inches) wide, trifoliolate, glaucous underneath; fall color orange to scarlet. Flowers yellow in small umbels of three flowers each. Samaras 4–5 cm (1½–2 inches) long, nutlets woody, hairy. Native to hills of northern China and Korea, abundant but not forming forests. Described by Vladimir L. Komarov in 1901. Although fairly common in maple collections, three-flowered maple is otherwise not much used in horticulture. Propagation is similar to that required for *A. griseum*; the percentage of viable seed is usually very low. Zone 5 (Europe 6)

Acer triflorum. October, Royal Botanic Gardens, Kew

Acer triflorum. October, Wisley Garden

Acer truncatum

Section *Platanoidea*. A densely branched tree or shrub up to 10 to 12 m (33–39 feet) and about as wide; bark roughly fissured unlike that of the closely related *A. pictum*. Leaves 7–10 cm (2¾–4 inches) wide, five- or seven-lobed, somewhat wavy, young leaves greenish purple, turning green and with good yellow or reddish fall color; petioles exuding milky sap when broken. Flowers yellow. Samaras 3–4 cm (1⅛–1½ inches) long. Native to forests of northern China and Korea and the Amur region of Siberia in Russia, also present on Sakhalin Island, Russia, and Hokkaidō Island, Japan. Described by Aleksandr A. von Bunge in 1833. Frequently used as a street tree in northern China, purpleblow maple or Shantung maple is otherwise not much used in horticulture. Zone 5 (Europe 6)

Acer truncatum. May, Westonbirt Arboretum

Acer truncatum 'Akikaze nishiki'

Synonym, *A. truncatum* 'Shūhū nishiki'. A shrub up to 5 to 6 m (16–20 feet), densely branched. Leaves smaller than those of the species, three- or five-lobed, light green and white speckled and variegated. Origin Japanese, before 1960, introduced by J. D. Vertrees, Oregon. A nicely ornamental plant, it also has a tendency to revert to fully green leaves and branches bearing such leaves should be removed. *Acer truncatum* 'Akaji nishiki' is a yellow variegated cultivar that also reverts readily. Zone 6 (Europe 7)

Acer truncatum 'Akikaze nishiki'. June

Acer tschonoskii subsp. *tschonoskii*

Section *Macrantha*. A tree or shrub in its habitat up to 10 to 12 m (33–39 feet), smaller in cultivation; branches green with stripes that are not always very conspicuous. Leaves 5–10 cm (2–4 inches) long and 4–7 cm (1½–2¾ inches) wide, five- or seven-lobed, margins incised, base cordate, apex elongated; fall color orange to red. Flowers in terminal trusses. Samaras obtuse, 2–3 cm (¾–1⅛ inches) long, set only occasionally. Native to northern Japan, Hokkaidō and Honshū Islands. Described by Karl Johann Maximowicz in 1886. It is rare in cultivation in the Western world, as is subspecies *koreanum* (originally described under the synonym, variety *rubripes*, by Vladimir L. Komarov in 1904), which has reddish branches. Zone 5 (Europe 6)

Acer tschonoskii subsp. *tschonoskii*. May

Acer tutcheri. July

Acer tutcheri

Section *Palmata,* series *Sinensia.* In its habitat a tree or shrub up to 10 m (33 feet); branches olive-green to purplish brown. Leaves about 15 cm (6 inches) long and 10 cm (4 inches) wide, three-lobed with an elongated central lobe, dark olive-green, juvenile leaves with serrate margins, adult leaves less serrated. Native to southeastern China, Hong Kong, Guangxi Autonomous Region, and Guandong and Yunnan Provinces, and Taiwan. Described by John Firminger Duthie in 1908. We received seeds of this species from China incorrectly identified as "*A. metcalfii*" (a synonym of *A. sikkimense* subsp. *metcalfii*) and it has proven to be hardier than expected. Zone 7 (Europe 8)

Acer velutinum

Section *Acer,* series *Acer.* Synonym, *A. insigne* of Boissier & Buhse, not Nicholson. Described by Pierre Edmond Boissier in 1846. Three varieties are tentatively recognized, *glabrescens, vanvolxemii,* and *velutinum.* Seedlings of varieties *glabrescens* and *vanvolxemii* display a range of variation that overlaps with variety *velutinum* and the two atypical "varieties" might well be treated as cultivars and propagated vegetatively.

Acer velutinum var. *glabrescens.* May

Acer velutinum var. *glabrescens*

Leaves glabrous but seedlings display leaves of varying hairiness. Originally described (as *A. insigne*) by Pierre Edmond Boissier and Friedrich Alexander Buhse in 1860. Zone 5 (Europe 6)

Acer velutinum var. *vanvolxemii*

Leaves larger than those of variety *velutinum* but seedlings show all sizes of leaves. G. van Volxem brought seeds from the Caucasus to the Royal Botanic Gardens, Kew; originally described as a separate species by Maxwell Tylden Masters in 1877. Zone 5 (Europe 6)

Acer velutinum var. *velutinum*

A tree up to 25 m (82 feet) or more and even as wide; branches glabrous, rather stout, brown to gray. Leaves 20–25 cm (8–10 inches) wide, five-lobed, dark green, leaf underside glaucous and tomentose, margins coarsely lobulate, petioles long; fall color yellow. Flowers in terminal erect corymbs, yellowish white. Samaras to 6 cm (2⅜ inches) long, erect. Native to the Caucasus and northern provinces of Iran. Easily propagated by seed and often used as a street tree in Russia, it becomes too large for many gardens and is limited to maple collections and public parks. It would be interesting to see how it performs as a street tree in Europe and North America. Zone 5 (Europe 6)

Acer 'White Tigress'

A multistemmed tree or shrub up to 10 m (33 feet); bark green with conspicuous white stripes. Leaves 12–16 cm (4¾–6¼ inches) wide, five-lobed, dark green, turning yellow in fall. Possibly a hybrid between *A. tegmentosum* and another, unknown parent. Introduced by Mark and Jolly Krautmann of Heritage Seedlings, Salem, Oregon, before 1992. Zone 5 (Europe 6)

Acer velutinum var. *vanvolxemii*. May, Westonbirt Arboretum

Acer velutinum var. *velutinum*. May, Westonbirt Arboretum

Acer 'White Tigress'. May, Valley Gardens

Acer ×zoeschense 'Annae'. May, Westonbirt Arboretum

Acer ×zoeschense 'Annae'. May, Westonbirt Arboretum

Acer ×zoeschense 'Annae'

Synonym, *A. neglectum* 'Annae'. *Acer ×zoeschense* a garden hybrid, *A. campestre* × *A. cappadocicum* subsp. *lobelii*, both parents belonging to section *Platanoidea*. Described by Ferdinand Albin Pax in 1886. 'Annae' a tree up to 20 m (66 feet) or more and almost as wide. Leaves five-lobed, shiny dark green with purplish edges, petioles producing milky sap when broken. Flowers in terminal umbels. Fruits none, a sterile hybrid. Raised by Zoeschen Nurseries, Germany, described by Fritz Graf von Schwerin in 1908. 'Annae' is a forgotten, old-fashioned tree waiting for a revival. It is a valuable street tree and good for large parks. *Acer ×zoeschense* 'Kinka' is of Japanese origin and has pale variegated foliage. Zone 5 (Europe 6)

Where to See Maples

Listed below are selected arboretums, gardens, and parks, open to the public unless mentioned otherwise, where at least several species and cultivars of *Acer* may be seen and studied. Some additional localities, where maples were photographed for this book, are listed in the chapter "The Maples," under the heading "Photographic Locations."

Belgium
Arboretum Kalmthout, Heuvel 2, 2920 Kalmthout

Bokrijk Arboretum, Domein Bokrijk, 3600 Genk

Groenendaal, public park, Hoeilaart near Brussels

Herkenrode Gardens (owned by Philippe de Spoelberch, by appointment only), Bosveld 26, 3150 Wespelaar

Hof ter Saksen, public park, Beveren

Jardin Botanique National de Belgique, Domein de Bouchout, 1860 Meise

Mariemont Public Park, Morlanwelz, La Louvière

Plantentuin der Rijksuniversiteit, K. L. Ledeganckstraat 35, 9000 Ghent

Rivierenhof, public park, Antwerp

Tervuren Arboretum and Public Park, Vlaktedreef, Brussels

Czech Republic
Research Institute of Ornamental and Landscape Architecture, 252 43 Pruhonice

Denmark
Botanisk Have, University of Aarhus, 8250 Aarhus

Hørsholm Arboretum, Sören Öduns, 2970 Hørsholm

Københavns Universitets Botaniske Have, Øster Farimagsgade 2b, 2000 Copenhagen

France
Arborea de Gondremer (Michel Madre, curator), 88700 Autrey

Arboretum des Barres et Fruticetum Vilmorinianum, 45290 Nogent-sur-Vernisson, Loiret

Jardin Botanique de l'Université Louis Pasteur, 28 Rue Goethe, 87073 Strasbourg

Jardin Botanique de la Ville et de l'Université, 5 Place Blot, 14000 Caen

Jardin des Plantes, 43 Rue Bouffon, 75005 Paris

Service Espaces Verts et Jardin Botanique, Ville de Nantes, 44000 Nantes

Ville de Bourges, Chemin de Cortiot, 48000 Bourges

Germany
Arboretum Thiensen, Thiensen 17, 25373 Ellerhoop

Berggarten, Herrenhäuser Strasse, 30419 Hanover

Botanischer Garten, Grimmerstrasse 88, 17485 Greifswald

Botanischer Garten der Justus-Liebig Universität, Senckenbergstrasse 6, 35390 Giessen

Botanischer Garten der Universität, Hesten 10, 22609 Hamburg

Botanischer Garten der Universität Bonn, Meckenheimer-Allee 171, 53115 Bonn

Botanischer Garten Rombergpark, 44225 Dortmund-Brünninghausen

Botanischer Garten und Botanisches Museum Berlin-Dahlem, Königin-Luise-Strasse 6–8, 14195 Berlin

Florapark, near the zoo, Cologne

Forstbotanischer Garten, Schillingroter Strasse, 50996 Rodenkirchen

Forstbotanischer Garten und Arboretum, Universität Göttingen, Benfeyweg 2, 37075 Göttingen

Kurpark, Staatliche Bäderverwaltung, Kaiserstrasse 5, 79410 Badenweiler

Nymphenburg, Menzingerstrasse 61, 80992 Munich

Palmengarten, Siesmayerstrasse 72, 60275 Frankfurt on the Main

Tharandt, Forstbotanischer Garten der Universität, 01737 Dresden, Germany Wilhelmshöhe, public park, Kassel

Ireland and Northern Ireland
Birr Castle Demense, Birr, County Offaly

Castlewellan National Arboretum, Castlewellan BT31 9BU, County Down

Dunloe Castle, Beaufort, County Kerry

John F. Kennedy Arboretum, New Ross, County Wexford

Mount Congreve, Waterford, County Waterford

Mount Usher Gardens, Ashford, County Wicklow

National Botanic Gardens, Glasnevin, Dublin 9

Rowallane Garden, Saintfield, Ballynahinch BT24 7LH, County Down

Talbot Botanic Garden, Malahide Castle, County Dublin

Italy
Ente Giardini di Villa Taranto, Intra Pallanza, Lago Maggiore

Netherlands

Arboretum Belmonte, Botanical Gardens of the Wageningen Agricultural University, Generaal Foulkesweg 37, 6700 ED Wageningen

Blijdorp, Stichting Rotterdamse Diergaarde, Van Aerssenlaan 49, 3039 KE Rotterdam

Botanische Tuinen der Rijksuniversiteit Utrecht, Fort Hoofddijk, Boedapestlaan 2, De Uithof, Harvardlaan 2, 3508 TD Utrecht

Cultuurtuin voor Technische Gewassen, Technische Universiteit Delft, Julianalaan 67, 2600 GB Delft

Esveld Aceretum (owned by Firma C. Esveld, keeper of the Dutch Acer Collection), Rijneveld 72, 2771 XS Boskoop

Hortus Haren, Kerklaan 34, 9751 NN Haren

Dr. H. J. Oterdoom (by appointment only), Groningerstraat 103, 9493 TC De Punt

Stichting Arboretum Trompenburg, Honingerdijk 86, 3062 NX Rotterdam

Stichting Botanische Tuin Kerkrade, St. Hubertuslaan 74, 6467 CK Kerkrade

Von Gimborn Arboretum, Vossesteinsesteeg, Doorn; Rijksuniversiteit Utrecht, Harvardlaan 2, 3508 TD Utrecht

Zuiderpark, public park, Melis Stokelaan, The Hague

Norway

Milde Arboretum, Mildeveien 240, 5067 Store Milde, Bergen

Poland

Kórnik Arboretum, Kórnik near Poznan

Rogow Arboretum, Szkola Glowna, Rogow

Sweden

Göteborg Botanical Garden, Carl Skottbergs Gata 22, 413 19 Göteborg

University of Uppsala Botanic Garden, Villavägen 8, 750 07 Uppsala

Switzerland

Arboretum du Vallon de l'Aubonne, 1185 Aubonne VD

Arboretum und Botanischer Garten, Im Eichholz, 8627 Grüningen ZH

Botanischer Garten, Universität Zürich, Zollikerstrasse 107, 8008 Zürich

Botanischer Garten St. Gallen, Stephanshornstrasse 4, 9000 St. Gallen SG

Brüglingen, Botanischer Garten der Universität Basel, St. Alban Vorstadt 5, 4000 Basel

Centre d'Horticole, Lullier, 1254 Jussy GE

Conservatoire et Jardin Botaniques de la Ville de Genève, Rue de Lausanne, 1200 Geneva

Kannenbergpark, 4000 Basel

United Kingdom

Blagdon (owned by Viscount Ridley), Seaton Burn, Newcastle upon Tyne, Tyne and Wear NE13 6DD, England

Bodnant Gardens (owned by Lord Aberconway), Tal-y-Cafn, Colwyn Bay, Clywd LL28 5RE, Wales

Borde Hill Gardens, Hayward Heath, West Sussex RH16 1XP, England

Caerhays Castle, near Gorran, south of St. Austell, Cornwall FA1 7DE, England

Castle Howard, near York, North Yorkshire YO7 7DA, England

Chyverton Garden, Zelan, Truro, Cornwall, England

Dawyck Gardens (owned by the Royal Botanic Garden, Edinburgh), Stobo, Peebles EH45 5JU, Scotland

Hergest Croft Gardens, Ridgebourne, Kington, Hereford and Worcester HR5 3EG, England

High Beeches, Handcross, West Sussex RH17 6HQ, England

Sir Harold Hillier Gardens and Arboretum, Jermyns Lane, Ampfield, near Romsey, Hampshire SO51 0PA, England

Keir Garden, Dunblane, Perthshire, Scotland

Knightshayes Court, Bolham, Tiverton, Devonshire EX16 7RQ, England

Mallet Court Nursery, Curry Mallet, near Taunton, Somerset TA3 6SY, England

Nymans Garden, Handcross, near Haywards Heath, West Sussex RH17 6EB, England

Rosemoor Garden (owned by the Royal Horticultural Society), Great Torrington, Devonshire EX38 8PH, England

Royal Botanic Garden, Inverleith Row, Edinburgh EH3 5LR, Scotland

Royal Botanic Gardens, Kew, Richmond, Surrey TW9 3AB, England

Saling Hall (Hugh Johnson), Great Saling, near Braintree, Essex CM7 5DT, England

Savill and Valley Gardens, The Great Park, Windsor, Surrey SL4 2HT, England

Stourhead, Stourton, Warminster, Wiltshire BA12 6QH, England

Talbot Manor, Fincham, Ling's Lynn, Norfolk PE33 9AB, England

Trewithen, Grampound Road near Truro, Cornwall TR2 4DD, England

Wakehurst Place Garden (owned by the Royal Botanic Gardens, Kew), near Ardingly, Haywards Heath, West Sussex RH17 6TN, England

Westonbirt Arboretum, Westonbirt, near Tetbury, Gloucestershire GL8 8QS, England

Winkworth Arboretum, Hascombe Road, Godalming, Surrey GU8 4AD, England

Wisley Garden (owned by the Royal Horticultural Society), near Ripley, Woking, Surrey GU23 6QB, England

United States of America

Arnold Arboretum of Harvard University, 125 Arborway, Jamaica Plain, Massachusetts 02130

Brooklyn Botanic Garden, 1000 Washington Avenue, Brooklyn, New York 11225

County of Monroe Department of Parks, 375 Westfall Road, Rochester, New York 14620

Longwood Gardens, Kennett Square, Pennsylvania 19348

Morris Arboretum of the University of Pennsylvania, 9414 Meadowbrook Ave, Philadelphia, Pennsylvania 19118

New York Botanical Garden, 200th Street and Southern Boulevard, Bronx, New York 10458

Planting Fields Arboretum, Planting Fields Road, Oyster Bay, New York 11771

Strybing Arboretum and Botanical Gardens, Golden Gate Park, 9th Avenue and Lincoln Way, San Francisco, California 94122

U.S. National Arboretum, 3501 New York Avenue, N.E., Washington, D.C. 20002

Washington Park Arboretum, University of Washington, 2300 Arboretum Drive East, Seattle, Washington 98195

Willowwood Arboretum, 300 Longview Road, Far Hills, New Jersey 07931 (mailing address: Willowwood Arboretum, Morris County Park Commission, P.O. Box 1295, Morristown, New Jersey 07962)

APPENDIX 2

Maples for Particular Purposes

Large Trees for Parks and Streets

Acer campestre
  'Elsrijk'
  'Queen Elizabeth'
  'Zorgvlied'
Acer cappadocicum 'Rubrum'
Acer ×freemanii 'Autumn Blaze'
Acer heldreichii
Acer macrophyllum
Acer negundo
  'Baron'
  subsp. *californicum*
  'Sensation'
  'Violaceum'
Acer opalus subsp. *opalus*
Acer pictum
Acer platanoides
  'Almira'
  'Cleveland'
  'Deborah'
  'Farlake's Green'
  'Greenlace'
  'Standfast'
Acer pseudoplatanus
  'Amry'
  'Atropupureum'
  'Bruchem'
  'Constant P.'
  'Erythrocarpum'
  'Negenia'
  'Prince Camille de Rohan'
  'Rotterdam'
Acer rubrum and cultivars
Acer saccharinum
Acer saccharum
  'Commemoration'
  'Fairview'
  'Legacy'
  subsp. *nigrum*
Acer velutinum
Acer zoeschense 'Annae'

Medium-sized Trees for Large Gardens and Smaller Parks

Acer caesium
Acer cappadocicum
  'Aureum'
  subsp. *sinicum*
Acer cissifolium
Acer ×conspicuum 'Silver Vein'
Acer davidii
Acer ×hybridum
Acer hyrcanum
Acer longipes subsp. *amplum*
Acer opalus subsp. *obtusatum*
Acer pectinatum subsp. *taronense*
Acer saccharum
  subsp. *grandidentatum*
  subsp. *leucoderme*
  'Louisa Lad'
  'Moraine'
  'Sweet Shadow Cutleaf'
Acer sterculiaceum
  subsp. *sterculiaceum*
  subsp. *franchetii*
Acer tataricum
Acer truncatum

Multistemmed Trees or Shrubs for Large Gardens

Acer argutum
Acer buergerianum
  subsp. *ningpoense* 'Kōshi miyasama'
  'Subintegrum'
Acer campestre 'Microphyllum'
Acer capillipes
Acer carpinifolium
Acer caudatum
Acer davidii
Acer glabrum
Acer griseum

Acer hyrcanum subsp. *intermedium*
Acer japonicum
  'Aconitifolium'
  'Meigetsu'
  'Ōisami'
  'Taki no gawa'
  'Vitifolium'
Acer maximowiczianum
Acer monspessulanum
Acer opalus subsp. *hispanicum*
Acer pectinatum
  subsp. *forrestii* 'Sparkling'
  subsp. *maximowiczii*
Acer pensylvanicum
Acer platanoides 'Tharandt'
Acer pseudoplatanus 'Leat's Cottage'
Acer rufinerve
Acer shirasawanum
  'Diana'
  'Ezo no o momiji'
  'Jūni hito e'
  'Microphyllum'
  'Palmatifolium'
Acer sieboldianum
  'Mi yama nishiki'
  'Osiris'
Acer spicatum
Acer stachyophyllum
Acer tataricum
  subsp. *aidzuense*
  subsp. *ginnala*
  'Fire'
  'Flame'
  subsp. *tataricum*
Acer tschonoskii

Trees with a Columnar or Fastigiate Habit

Acer acuminatum
Acer cappadocicum subsp. *lobelii*

Acer longipes subsp. *amplum*
Acer mandshuricum
Acer pectinatum subsp. *forrestii* 'Sparkling'
Acer platanoides
  'Columnarbroad'
  'Columnare'
  'Olmsted'
Acer pseudoplatanus 'Erectum'
Acer rubrum
  'Bowhall'
  'Columnare'
  'Scanlon'
Acer saccharinum 'Pyramidale'
Acer saccharum
  'Goldspire'
  'Newton Sentry'
  'Temple's Upright'

Trees with Compact Crowns Suitable for Smaller Gardens or Other Public Places

Acer platanoides
  'Crimson Sentry'
  'Globosum'
  'Golden Globe'
  'Pyramidale Nanum'
Acer pseudoplatanus
  'Brilliantissimum'
  'Prinz Handjéry'
  'Spring Gold'

Trees with a Pendulous Habit

Acer campestre 'Green Weeping'
Acer platanoides 'Charles Joly'
Acer saccharinum
  'Beebe's Cutleaf Weeping'
  'Laciniatum Wieri'

Compact or Spreading Shrubs Suitable for Most Gardens

Acer campestre 'Nanum'
Acer carpinifolium 'Esveld
    Select'
Acer japonicum
    'Green Cascade'
    'Dissectum'
Acer shirasawanum
    'Aureum'
    'Susanne'
Acer sieboldianum
    'Kinugasa yama'
    'Ogura yama'
    'Sode no uchi'
Acer tataricum
    subsp. *ginnala* 'Durand
      Dwarf'
    subsp. *semenovii*

Trees with Purple Leaves During Spring and Early Summer

Acer campestre
    'Red Shine'
    'Royal Ruby'
Acer palmatum, see below
Acer pectinatum subsp. *for-*
    restii 'Sirene'
Acer platanoides
    'Meyering'
    'Reitenbachii'
    'Schwedleri'
Acer shirasawanum 'Gloria'

Trees with Purple Leaves Throughout Summer

Acer palmatum, see below
Acer platanoides
    'Crimson King'
    'Crimson Sentry'
    'Royal Red'
Acer shirasawanum 'Yasemin'

Maples with Yellow Leaves During Spring and Summer

Acer campestre 'Postelense'
Acer cappadocicum 'Aureum'
Acer ×hillieri 'Summergold'
Acer longipes subsp. *amplum*
    'Gold Coin'
Acer negundo
    'Auratum'
    'Kelly's Gold'
Acer palmatum, see below
Acer pseudoplatanus 'Cor-
    storphinense'
Acer saccharinum 'Lutescens'
Acer shirasawanum 'Aureum'

Maples with Variegated Leaves

Acer buergerianum
    'Goshiki kaede'
    'Kifu nishiki'
Acer campestre
    'Carnival'
    'Pulverulentum'
Acer ×conspicuum 'Silver
    Cardinal'
Acer crataegifolium 'Veitchii'
Acer negundo
    'Aureomarginatum'
    'Elegans'
    'Flamingo'
    'Variegatum'
Acer palmatum, see below
Acer pectinatum subsp. *for-*
    restii 'Alice'
Acer pictum
    'Hoshi yadori'
    'Tokiwa nishiki'
Acer platanoides
    'Drummondii'
    'Maculatum'
    'Walderseei'
Acer pseudoplatanus
    'Leopoldii'
    'Nizetii'
    'Simon Louis Frères'
Acer rubescens
    'Summer Snow'
    'Summer Surprise'
Acer rufinerve 'Albolimbatum'

Maples with Exceptional Fall Color

Acer circinatum
Acer ×conspicuum 'Silver
    Vein'
Acer japonicum
    'Aconitifolium'
    'Ō isami'
    'Ōtaki'
    'Vitifolium'
Acer palmatum, see below
Acer pensylvanicum
Acer platanoides
Acer rubrum
    'Bowhall'
    'Morgan'
    'October Glory'
    'Red Sunset'
    'Scanlon'
Acer saccharum, most culti-
    vars
Acer tataricum subsp. *ginnala*
    'Fire'
    'Flame'

Evergreen Maples

Acer cordatum
Acer coriaceifolium
Acer fabri
Acer laevigatum
Acer laurinum
Acer lucidum
Acer oblongum
Acer obtusifolium
Acer paxii
Acer sempervirens

Maples with Unusual Leaves

Acer buergerianum
    'Jōroku aka me'
    'Miyasama yatsubusa'
    'Naruto'
    'Tanchō'
Acer carpinifolium 'Esveld
    Select'
Acer distylum
Acer japonicum 'Attaryi'
Acer negundo 'Heterophyllum'
Acer palmatum, see below
Acer platanoides
    'Cucullatum'
    'Laciniatum'
    'Palmatifidum'
Acer saccharum 'Brocade'

Maples with Attractive Bark

SNAKEBARK MAPLES

Acer capillipes
Acer caudatifolium
Acer ×conspicuum
    'Elephant's Ear'
    'Phoenix'
    'Silver Vein'
Acer crataegifolium
Acer davidii
Acer micranthum 'Candela-
    brum'
Acer pectinatum
Acer pensylvanicum
Acer rufinerve 'Erythrocla-
    dum'
Acer tegmentosum
Acer 'White Tigress'

ROUGH BARK MAPLES

Acer buergerianum 'Mitsu-
    batō kaede'
Acer miyabei
Acer palmatum
    'Amime nishiki'
    'Ara kawa'
    'Ibo nishiki'
    'Issai nishiki kawazu'
    'Nishiki gawa'

PAPERY BARK MAPLES

Acer griseum
Acer triflorum
Acer truncatum

SMOOTH BARK MAPLES

Acer maximowiczianum
Acer pictum
Acer sterculiaceum
Acer velutinum

Maples with Prominent Flowers

Acer cappadocicum subsp.
    sinicum
Acer diabolicum
Acer platanoides
    'Palmatifidum'
    'Royal Red'
Acer rubrum 'Red King'
Acer shirasawanum 'Aureum'

Maples with Ornamental Fruits

Acer cissifolium
Acer davidii 'Madeline Spitta'
Acer griseum
Acer heldreichii subsp. *traut-*
    vetteri
Acer negundo
Acer pseudoplatanus 'Eryth-
    rocarpum'
Acer sterculiaceum

Maples Suitable for Bonsai

Acer buergerianum, most
    cultivars
Acer palmatum, see below
Acer pictum 'Usugumo'

Subtropical Maples

Acer buergerianum subsp.
    ningpoense
Acer calcaratum
Acer campbellii
    subsp. *campbellii*
    subsp. *flabellatum*
    subsp. *sinense*
Acer caudatifolium
Acer cordatum
Acer coriaceifolium
Acer elegantulum
Acer miaoshanicum
Acer olivaceum
Acer oliverianum subsp. *for-*
    mosanum
Acer paxii
Acer pentaphyllum
Acer rubescens
Acer sikkimense
Acer tutcheri

Rare Maples for Connoisseurs
Acer acuminatum
Acer barbinerve
Acer ×*bornmuelleri*
Acer caesium subsp. *giraldii*
Acer calcaratum
Acer cordatum
Acer coriaceifolium
Acer ×*coriaceum*
Acer ×*durettii*
Acer elegantulum
Acer erianthum
Acer fabri
Acer henryi
Acer hyrcanum
 subsp. *keckianum*
 subsp. *reginae-amaliae*
 subsp. *sphaerocarpum*
 subsp. *stevenii*
 subsp. *tauricolum*
Acer laevigatum
Acer laurinum
Acer longipes
 subsp. *amplum* 'Gold Coin'
 subsp. *longipes*
Acer lucidum
Acer mandshuricum
Acer miaoshanicum
Acer morifolium
Acer nipponicum
Acer oblongum
Acer obtusifolium
Acer olivaceum
Acer oliverianum
Acer pauciflorum
Acer paxii
Acer pentaphyllum
Acer pentapomicum
Acer pilosum var. *stenolobum*
Acer pseudosieboldianum
Acer pubipalmatum
Acer pycnanthum
Acer ×*rotundilobum*
Acer rubescens
Acer sempervirens
Acer sikkimense
Acer sinopurpurascens
Acer sterculiaceum subsp.
 thomsonii
Acer tenellum
Acer tonkinense subsp.
 kwangsiense
Acer tutcheri

Acer palmatum
Cultivars of *Acer palmatum* may be divided into groups with similar characteristics. An explanation of the groups is provided just before the

entries for *A. palmatum* in the alphabetical arrangement of maple photographs.

Group 1a
Upright-growing shrubs or small trees, leaves green or green with reddish margins
'Ao yagi'
'Ara kawa'
'Beni kawa'
'Eddisbury'
'Hanami nishiki'
'Ibo nishiki'
'Issai nishiki kawazu'
'Kiyo hime'
'Kogane nishiki'
'Koko'
'Mama'
'Mon zukushi'
'Murasaki kiyo hime'
'Nishiki gawa'
'Okushimo'
'Rising Sun'
'Sango kaku'
'Seiun kaku'
'Sekka yatsubusa'
'Shigarami'
'Shishi gashira'
'Tama hime'
'Tana'
'Tsuchi gumo'
'Volubile'
'Wabito'
'Waka midori'
'Waka momiji'

Aureum Group
Group 1a cultivars, densely branched shrubs, leafing out clear yellow to orange, fading to yellow-green or light green in summer, turning yellow again in fall, not variegated
'Aka ne'
'Aureum'
'Katsura'
'Orange Dream'
'Sode nishiki'
'Ueno homare'

Group 1b
Upright-growing shrubs or small trees, leaves purple, sometimes fading to dark green
'Atropurpureum'
'Attraction'
'Bloodgood'
'Fireglow'
'Koriba'

'Nigrum'
'Nure sagi'
'Purpureum'
'Red Flash'

Corallinum Group
Group 1b cultivars, leaves brilliant scarlet to red when unfolding, later turning bluish green
'Beni maiko'
'Chishio'
'Chishio Improved'
'Corallinum'
'Deshōjō'
'Otome zakura'
'Seigen'
'Shin deshōjō'

Group 1c
Upright-growing shrubs or small trees, leaves variegated
'Beni tsukasa'
'Bonfire'
'Hama otome'
'Higasa yama'
'Kasen nishiki'
'Ko shibori nishiki'
'Nishiki gasane'
'Tennyo no hoshi'
'Tsuma gaki'
'Uki gumo'

Roseomarginatum Group
Group 1c cultivars, leaves with white, pink, or bicolored margins, not speckled
'Ao kanzashi'
'Banda hime'
'Beni shichi henge'
'Butterfly'
'Hohman's Variegated'
'Itami nishiki'
'Kagiri nishiki'
'Kara ori nishiki'
'Matsu ga e'
'Okukuji nishiki'

Versicolor Group
Group 1c cultivars, leaves white and pink speckled all over, some leaves perhaps entirely white or pink
'Asahi zuru'
'Karasu gawa'
'Mai mori'
'Oridono nishiki'
'Waka momiji Variegated'

Group 2a
Upright-growing shrubs or small trees, leaves green
'Elegans'
'Harusame'
'Heptalobum'
'Herbstfeuer'
'Hōgyoku'
'Hondoshi'
'Ide no sato'
'Koreanum'
'Lutescens'
'Matsuyoi'
'Momiji gasa'
'Omato'
'Ōsaka zuki'
'Samidare'
'Saoshika'
'Sa otome'
'Satsuki beni'
'Shūzankō'
'Tatsuta gawa'
'Utsu semi'

Group 2b
Upright-growing shrubs or small trees, leaves purple, sometimes fading to dark green
'Ariake nomura'
'Boskoop Glory'
'Chikumano'
'Fior d'Arancio'
'Heptalobum Rubrum'
'Hessei'
'Lozita'
'Margaret Bee'
'Marjan'
'Masu murasaki'
'Moonfire'
'Nomura'
'Ōkagami'
'Oshio beni'
'Rubrum'
'Shichihenge'
'Shikage ori nishiki'
'Shōjō'
'Shōjō nomura'
'The Bishop'
'Tsukuba ne'
'Tsukushi gata'
'Ume ga e'
'Whitney Red'
'Yezo nishiki'
'Yūba e'

Group 2c
Usually upright-growing shrubs, leaves variegated
'Masu kagami'
'Reticulatum'
'Wakehurst Pink'

Group 3a
Large shrubs with green, deeply divided leaves
'Golden Pond'
'Green Trompenburg'
'Kihachijō'
'Kishūzan'
'Kurabu yama'
'Mirte'
'Mizu kuguri'
'Mure hibari'
'Muro gawa'
'Nicholsonii'
'Omure yama'
'Rufescens'
'Sazanami'
'Semi no hane'
'Shigure bato'
'Shinonome'
'Tsuri nishiki'

Group 3b
Large shrubs with purple, deeply divided leaves, sometimes fading to dark green
'Akegarasu'
'Azuma murasaki'
'Beni kagami'
'Burgundy Lace'
'Chitose yama'
'Iijima sunago'
'Inazuma'
'Kinran'
'Matsukaze'
'Ōgon sarasa'
'Sherwood Flame'
'Sumi nagashi'
'Toshi'
'Trompenburg'
'Yūgure'

Group 3c
Large shrubs with variegated, deeply divided leaves
'Aka shigitatsu sawa'
'Ariadne'
'Kasagi yama'
'Peaches and Cream'
'Rugose Select'
'Shigure zome'
'Taimin nishiki'

Group 4a
Mushroom-shaped shrubs with dissected green leaves
'Ao shidare'
'Dissectum'
'Dissectum Flavescens'
'Dissectum Paucum'
'Dissectum Rubrifolium'
'Ellen'
'Green Globe'
'Green Lace'
'Kiri nishiki'
'Red Autumn Lace'
'Seki mori'
'Suisei'
'Waterfall'

Group 4b
Mushroom-shaped shrubs with dissected purple leaves, sometimes fading to dark green
'Beni shidare'
'Crimson Queen'
'Dissectum Nigrum'
'Garnet'
'Inaba shidare'
'Nomura nishiki'
'Orangeola'
'Ornatum'
'Pendulum Julian'
'Pink Filigree'
'Red Dragon'
'Red Select'
'Shōjō shidare'
'Stella Rossa'
'Tamuke yama'
'Washi no o'

Group 4c
Mushroom-shaped shrubs with dissected variegated leaves
'Dissectum Variegatum'
'Felice'
'Filigree'
'Goshiki shidare'
'To yama nishiki'

Group 5a
Upright-growing shrubs, leaf lobes threadlike, green
'Ao meshime no uchi'
'Kinshi'
'Koto no ito'
'Linearilobum'
'Shinobu ga oka'

Group 5b
Upright-growing shrubs, leaf lobes threadlike, purple or purple-brown
'Aka shime no uchi'
'Angustilobum'
'Atrolineare'
'Beni otaki'
'Enkan'
'Koto ito komachi'
'Purpureum Angustilobum'
'Red Pygmy'
'Villa Taranto'

Group 6a
Dwarf shrubs suitable for bonsai, leaves green
'Ao ba jō'
'Coonara Pygmy'
'Crippsii'
'Eagle's Claw'
'Eimini'
'Hupp's Dwarf'
'Kamagata'
'Kashima'
'Koto hime'
'Koto maru'
'Kōya san'
'Kurui jishi'
'Little Princess'
'Matthew'
'Mikawa yatsubusa'
'Ōjishi'
'Oto hime'
'Ryokū ryū'
'Ryūzu'
'Shaina'
'Sharp's Pygmy'
'Tarō yama'
'Tsukomo'
'Yurihime'

Group 6b
Dwarf shrubs suitable for bonsai, leaves purple or rusty brown
'Akita yatsubusa'
'Ara tama'
'Beni fushigi'
'Beni hime'
'Beni komachi'
'Brandt's Dwarf'
'Garyū'
'Pixie'
'Red Filigree Lace'
'Ruby Stars'
'Skeeter's Broom'

Group 6c
Dwarf shrubs suitable for bonsai, leaves variegated
'Coral Pink'
'Wilson's Pink Dwarf'

Group 7
Upright-growing shrubs with unusual leaf forms or colors
'Hagoromo'
'Hazeroino'
'Jirō shidare'
'Kaba'
'Koshi mino'
'Maiko'
'Nanase gawa'
'Seiryū'

Hardiness Zone Maps

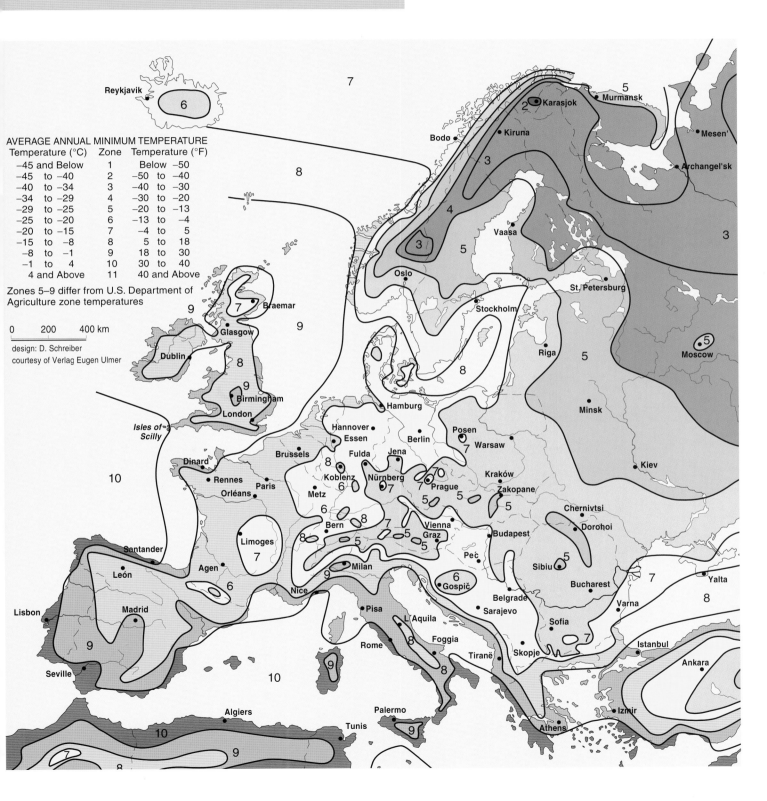

AVERAGE ANNUAL MINIMUM TEMPERATURE

Temperature (°C)	Zone	Temperature (°F)
−45 and Below	1	Below −50
−45 to −40	2	−50 to −40
−40 to −34	3	−40 to −30
−34 to −29	4	−30 to −20
−29 to −25	5	−20 to −13
−25 to −20	6	−13 to −4
−20 to −15	7	−4 to 5
−15 to −8	8	5 to 18
−8 to −1	9	18 to 30
−1 to 4	10	30 to 40
4 and Above	11	40 and Above

Zones 5–9 differ from U.S. Department of
Agriculture zone temperatures

0   200   400 km

design: D. Schreiber
courtesy of Verlag Eugen Ulmer

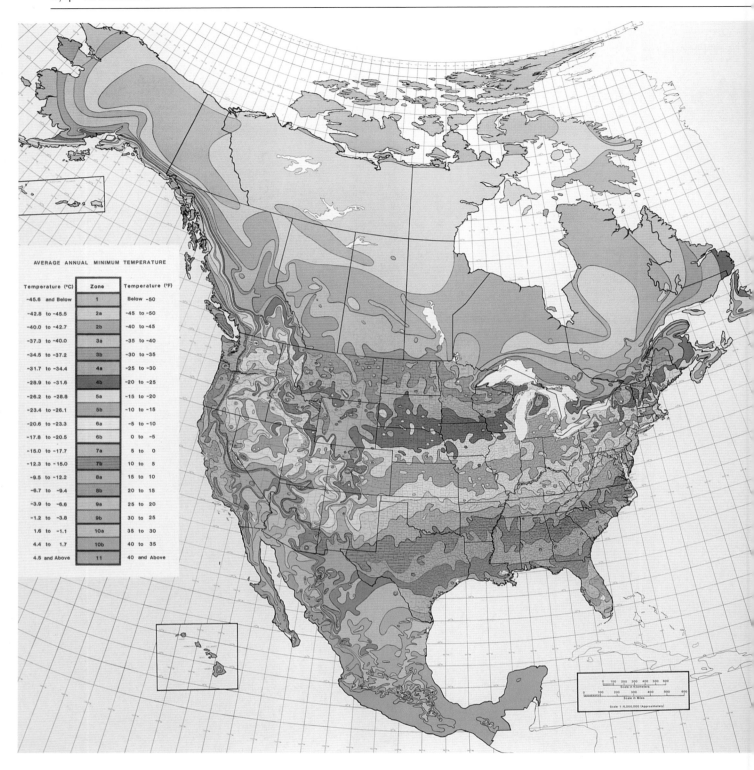

AVERAGE ANNUAL MINIMUM TEMPERATURE

Temperature (°C)	Zone	Temperature (°F)
-45.6 and Below	1	Below -50
-42.8 to -45.5	2a	-45 to -50
-40.0 to -42.7	2b	-40 to -45
-37.3 to -40.0	3a	-35 to -40
-34.5 to -37.2	3b	-30 to -35
-31.7 to -34.4	4a	-25 to -30
-28.9 to -31.6	4b	-20 to -25
-26.2 to -28.8	5a	-15 to -20
-23.4 to -26.1	5b	-10 to -15
-20.6 to -23.3	6a	-5 to -10
-17.8 to -20.5	6b	0 to -5
-15.0 to -17.7	7a	5 to 0
-12.3 to -15.0	7b	10 to 5
-9.5 to -12.2	8a	15 to 10
-6.7 to -9.4	8b	20 to 15
-3.9 to -6.6	9a	25 to 20
-1.2 to -3.8	9b	30 to 25
1.6 to -1.1	10a	35 to 30
4.4 to 1.7	10b	40 to 35
4.5 and Above	11	40 and Above

Scale in Kilometers
0 100 200 300 400 500 600
Scale in Miles
0 100 200 300 400 500 600
Scale 1:8,000,000 (Approximately)

Glossary

ACUMINATE. Tapering to a point

CAUDATE. Tapering gradually into a tailed appendage

CLONE. A group of individual plants that are genetically identical, arising when one plant is propagated vegetatively

CONNIVENT. Converging, perhaps even coming into contact but not fused

CORDATE. Heart-shaped

CORYMB. A flat-topped inflorescence in which the outer flowers open first; compare with umbel

DENTATE. Toothed; compare with serrate and serrulate

DIOECIOUS. When separate male and female flowers are borne on different plants; compare with monoecious

FASTIGIATE. The habit of a plant that is erect and has a narrow crown, with branches that are also erect

FOLIOLATE. Bearing leaflets

GLABROUS. Smooth and without hairs; compare with puberulous, tomentose, and villous

GLAUCOUS. Coated with a fine, waxy covering

GRAFT. See scion and understock

GREX. A group of cultivars resulting from crossing the same two parents even if the crosses are made at different times in different places

INFLORESCENCE. A cluster of flowers

INTERNODE. The portion of a stem between two nodes (the points at which leaves are borne)

LOBULATE. Bearing lobules, that is, small lobes

MONOECIOUS. When separate male and female flowers are borne on the same plant; compare with dioecious

NUTLET. The small one-seeded part of the maple fruit; see samara

PALMATE. With lobes or veins radiating from a common point, like a hand with fingers spread

PANICLE. A branched inflorescence in which the flowers open from the base to the tip; compare with raceme

PARTHENOCARPIC. Bearing fruits without fertilization

PUBERULOUS. Covered with small, soft hairs; compare with glabrous, tomentose, and villous

RACEME. An unbranched inflorescence in which the flowers open from the base to the tip; compare with panicle

ROOTSTOCK. See understock

RUGOSE. Irregularly wrinkled

SAMARA. The winged fruit of the maple, comprising a wing and a nutlet

SCION. The upper part of a graft, the plant grafted onto the understock (also called rootstock) and the part from which the shoots and leaves will grow

SERRATE. Marginal teeth resembling those of a saw; compare with dentate and serrulate

SERRULATE. Marginal teeth sawlike but smaller than those of a serrate leaf; compare with dentate and serrate

STANDARD. An erect understock

STIPULE. A small leafy appendage at the base of a leaf

TOMENTOSE. Densely covered with small stiff hairs; compare with glabrous, puberulous, and villous

UMBEL. A flat-topped inflorescence, like a corymb, but in which all the flower pedicels or stalks arise from the same point

UNDERSTOCK. The lower part of a graft, the plant on which the scion is grafted and the part supplying the root system (also called a rootstock); see also standard

VILLOUS. Covered with shaggy hairs; compare with glabrous, puberulous, and tomentose

For Further Information on Maples

The present book is a companion to D. M. van Gelderen, P. C. de Jong, and H. J. Oterdoom's *Maples of the World* (1994, Portland, Oregon: Timber Press). Since the publication of that book there have been few important changes. One involves *"Acer mono,"* considered here as *A. pictum.* In Appendix 4 of *Maples of the World* Dr. D. O. Wijnands made an argument for the conservation of the name *A. mono.* Sadly, he died before he could defend his argument before the nomenclatural committee, his proposition was rejected, and the name *A. pictum* has had to be restored. Another change involves the transliteration of Japanese cultivar names as explained in the chapter "Classification of Maples," under the heading "Cultivars." The status of a number of the cultivar names cited as synonyms in *Maples of the World* has been reconsidered and a number of them are considered sufficiently different to be recognized. Finally, new cultivars of maples continue to be introduced.

Maples of the World contains an extensive bibliography on maples. Nevertheless, it is useful here to list a few of the most important additional sources of information:

Bean, W. J. 1970–1988. *Trees and Shrubs Hardy in the British Isles, Eighth Edition,* Volumes 1–4 and Supplement. London: John Murray

Griffiths, Mark (editor). 1992. *The New Royal Horticultural Society Dictionary of Gardening,* Volumes 1–4. London: Macmillan. Information from the *Dictionary* is incorporated into a single volume: Mark Griffiths (editor). 1994. *Index of Garden Plants.* Portland, Oregon: Timber Press

Krüssmann, Gerd. 1984–1986. *Manual of Cultivated Broad-leaved Trees and Shrubs,* Volumes 1–3. Portland, Oregon: Timber Press (translated from the German, *Handbuch der Laubgehölze.* 1976–1978. Berlin: Paul Parey)

Pirc, Helmut. 1994. *Ahorne.* Stuttgart: Ulmer (in German)

Vertrees, J. D. 1987. *Japanese Maples, Second Edition* (first edition: 1978). Portland, Oregon: Timber Press (translated into German, *Japanische Ahorne.* 1993. Stuttgart: Ulmer)

The Maple Society, founded in 1990, publishes a newsletter four times a year. Information on membership may be obtained by writing to

Peter A. Gregory
Oakley Hall
Somerford Road
Cirencester
Gloucestershire GL7 1FZ
England

Index of Maples by Scientific Name

Index of Maples
by Common or Cultivar Name